AN · EDUCATED · MAN

Other Books by David Rosenberg

AN

E·D·U·C·A·T·E·D

MAN

∞

A Dual Biography of Moses and Jesus

BY DAVID ROSENBERG

COUNTERPOINT

BERKELEY

Library of Congress Cataloging-in-Publication Data
Rosenberg, David, 1943–
An educated man : a dual biography of Moses and Jesus / by David Rosenberg.
p. cm.
Includes bibliographical references.
ISBN-13: 978-1-58243-552-7
ISBN-10: 1-58243-552-9
1. Moses (Biblical leader). 2. Jesus Christ—Biography.
3. Education. 4. Religion. I. Title.
BS580.M6R59 2010
220.9'2—dc22
2009038083

Cover design by Attebery Design
Interior design by David Bullen Design
Printed in the United States of America

COUNTERPOINT
2117 Fourth Street
Suite D
Berkeley, CA 94710

www.counterpointpress.com

Distributed by Publishers Group West

10   9   8   7   6   5   4   3   2   1

To the memory of Philip Rieff
My colleague in Jerusalem
Who remembered to honor his zaydeh

And to Rhonda
My coauthor in the Everglades
Who remembers where we're going

·CONTENTS·

It takes an educated man
to love the world more than himself

C. N. BIALIK

AN
E·D·U·C·A·T·E·D
MAN

∞

· P R O L O G U E ·

The idiom "an educated man" was usually used, up until recent times, to indicate the college graduate. In contrast, "an educated woman" might have negative connotations, as if she could be too smart. In nineteenth-century North America, the term "an educated man" was especially applied to those studying for the ministry, and in any case the colleges of the day were sponsored by religious denominations. It was inconceivable, for example, that a graduate would be ignorant of the Bible—even in England, and even a hardened scientist like Charles Darwin.

We've lost such inferences today, and even the average professor with a Ph.D. is unversed in the Bible. We don't expect our astronomy professors or law professors to know much about the difference between Isaiah and Matthew. It has become clear to me, however, that what is missing is more than reading experience, historical knowledge, or religious belief. It's time to recognize that what has been lost is the Judeo-Christian cosmic theater, with its penetrating vision of a future, its broader grasp of the limits of human knowledge, its deeper sense of time, and its larger universe that includes unknown as well as unknowable meanings of our existence as a human species.

The Judeo-Christian educated man or woman is an interpreter of texts, skilled in the self-critical art of reading history. At its elemental level, this reading is what we call "reading between the lines," and today, anyone immersed in our media can be sophisticated in seeing through the texts of commercials and the commentary of political or social bias. But this interpreting power does not extend to the classic moral text of the Bible, or to a disciplined understanding of how civilization forms a "classic." It's as if living in a media-driven world absolves us of claiming deeper layers of historical meaning.

Those meanings, as we find them in the Bible, are often poorly described as the pillars of civilization. Who wants pillars, in an age of fluid information and seemingly endless possibility? Judeo-Christian civilization must be defined as a cosmic journey, driven toward negotiating and enacting a sublime Covenant. Whether that's the journey out of slavery in Egypt, toward the Torah; toward Israel and the Torah's elaboration; or into the Jewish Diaspora and the Torah's dual interpretation as Jewish Talmud and Christian New Testament after the first century AD, the mental journey of interpreting the Covenant remains basic to either the restoration of Israel or the spreading of the Gospel.

Taken together, as a civilization, neither the particular history of Judaism nor the universal ambition of Christianity could hold sway, but rather the *tension* between them. It can now be envisioned as a creative tension. Once we become aware of their parallel journeys, we can no longer use one to diminish the other. For those journeys are contained in the singular civilization we call Judeo-Christian, and in the kind of reading and interpreting that is essential to it. Without it, an educated man can be as large as his library and yet, bereft of this essential compass, he is lost in an unknowable cosmos. Moses could not have existed without that compass of the Covenant, and Jesus could not have existed without Moses as his teacher.

The most familiar facts concerning the historical Jesus are scattered among the various books of the New Testament. The same may be said for the life of Moses, its earliest details dispersed among several books of the Torah. For this reason, a chronology is called for, to allow the reader to orient him- or herself at all times. However, many kinds of chronology can suddenly vie for supremacy.

There is the progression of Jewish history in the Hebrew Bible and the Christian Testament, but there is also the outline of history to be gleaned from objective history, which has supplied us with proliferating, up-to-the-minute factoids. Further, there is the chronology of the writers who inscribed the lives of Moses and Jesus in the Bible, and the chronology of *Biblical* canon-making. In the latter process, many additional writings concerning Moses and Jesus were left out or deemed inauthentic. However it happened, most of the details about the early lives and education of these remarkable individuals are missing. In order to form a chronology of their first thirty years, I would have to create it myself, drawing upon fact and inference from all of the possible chronologies I have mentioned.

But even as I did that, there were simply not enough known events throughout their lives to build upon. Nevertheless, I found an inner correspondence between these primary *Biblical* lives hiding in plain sight. I'm not the first to point it out, but in order to experience its significance, and the magnitude of the debt, it's time to dig deeper into a subject usually avoided: the complex educations that each man would have needed if the profound reports of their existence are to be believed. Much more can be known about Moses and Jesus by piecing together their educations.

So I began with the assumption that the various events and recorded dialogue were largely believable, and this is borne out by a study of the culture at the time. The high probability of their having received an intense education was confirmed. And yet the overarching narrative for both of their lives not only covers the fact over, it goes out of its way to create the impression that Moses and Jesus were unexceptional men in their coming to maturity. Humble, ordinary men—even slow-witted in the case of Moses, and unprivileged in the case of Jesus. We can understand why the humility of each man might be accentuated in such an assessment, yet the actual text of the Bible belies it.

Jesus' education in the Hebrew Bible is so extraordinary that he is able to quote a wide variety of texts with ease—and to interpret them with great depth. His knowledge of Moses' Torah in particular is deep-rooted. Indeed, we can say that, poetically, Moses was his teacher. But poetry is only a part of what we are after. When we examine the Jewish society in which Jesus lived, as well as the larger Hellenistic culture, and then apply what we learn to a close reading of the *Biblical* text, the shape of a particular man and mind emerges.

If we are to say the same for Moses, we must return to Egyptian sources, most of which have come to light only in recent times. These are the texts he would have studied within the royal precincts of Egypt. And what we will find is that he absorbed his Egyptian education in a surprisingly Jewish way, but then later interpreted and transformed it into the core of what are known as the five *Biblical* books of Moses.

When I was well along in this research for the Egyptian education available to Moses among the ruling classes, I visited the Metropolitan Museum of Art in New York. I wanted to review their collection of mummy coffins, which had been recently reorganized to display greater detail, including the texts inscribed on the insides and lids of the cases. At the same time, there was a special exhibit of an Egyptian medical scroll, and I hoped to leave myself a few minutes to scan it, since I didn't expect the Egyptian palace education of Moses to have much to do with setting broken bones. I was wrong, and I was recently reminded of it while rereading Martin Buber's religious and philosophical study, *Moses* (1944), where I came upon this sentence: "Here [in ancient Egypt] religion was in practice little more than regulated magic."

Buber too was wrong, though it hardly mattered, for his concern was to describe how, "in the revelation at the Burning Bush, religion is demagicized." Egyptian magic was just a foil for his argument. But what I was forced to face in examining the long medical scroll (two volumes in the Met reprint) was the immense sophistication of Egyptian writing. It was written not in hieroglyphics but in the swift hieratic script of intellectuals of the day, several centuries before Moses was born. It was precisely for the graphic beauty of the writing, along with stunningly precise descriptions of various diseases and surgeries, that this scroll was borrowed from the library of the New York Academy of Medicine and displayed in an art museum. Suddenly, one could imagine Moses not only writing his own comment but also reading a wide body of knowledge in such texts, where religion and science, theology and anti-demonic spells, bumped up against each other. Sure enough, I found the conception of Moses' broad study in an accompanying text to the Met's exhibition:

The prolonged stay of the Hebrews in Egypt during the late second millennium BCE left its mark not only on their daily way of life and their vocabulary but also on their medicine. There are many points of similarity between the five Mosaic books of the Pentateuch and the pharaonic medical papyri, particularly with regard to obstetric techniques, circumcision, and the prevention of epidemics. (Halioua and Ziskind, Medicine in the Days of the Pharaohs [2005])

So when Moses first questioned a Creator's motive for singling him out, at a burning bush sighted from a wilderness pasture, he began a drama of negotiation with the supernatural that did not come out of nowhere. His Egyptian education had prepared him for questioning natural phenomena as well as for questioning gods. And up until that moment, Moses continued to identify as an Egyptian, a foreman in the house of an esteemed Midianite priest, Jethro, whose daughters describe Moses as foremost "an Egyptian man." I had to face not only Moses' Egyptian education but the process through which the core of Moses' books, the Torah, was built upon a partially Egyptian foundation. The Egyptian dream of life journeying after death was transformed into the history of the Israelites' journey through an earthly wilderness and earthbound time. Nevertheless, it was as full of perils as the mummy's journey was subject to demonic forces in the Egyptian "Book of the Dead."

In order to read the books of Moses properly, we must become believers in the supernatural—that is, while we read. We should be prepared to see ourselves as God or an angel does: two-legged creatures who must die. Is there any power that humans can muster to equal, let alone surpass, eternal life? There remains the imaginative power of the Egyptian scribe who records the words of the supernatural king and renders them immortal by writing them in a papyrus scroll.

Such a scribe, Amenhotep in the fourteenth century BCE, was himself rendered sacred by his Pharaoh in the century before Moses would have studied in the royal schools. I learned of it during one of my visits to the mummies at the Met, coming upon a life-sized seated statue of Amenhotep, with a papyrus scroll spread over his knees. At the base of the sculpture is written: "Come to me and I shall relay your words to Amun [Creator god] . . . for I am the spokesman appointed by the king."

Prior to the Bible being written in Jerusalem, ancient myth and even the Mesopotamian Epic of Gilgamesh presented a quest for eternal life—missions that must end in failure. But the Bible presents something new: coming face to face with eternal life and bringing back a written record. In it, we find more than gods and angels; we encounter the presiding presence of eternity, a Creator whose connection to human form and time can be dramatized in a Covenant—both in the making of it and the ongoing interpreting of it.

So Moses and the Israelites left Egypt for the Covenant-making at Mount Sinai and for a new land; Jesus, however, did not leave Israel, nor did most Jewish Christians for centuries. The mature life of Jesus of Nazareth was formed through an education in Jewish culture, and he instructed his disciples: "Go not into the way of the Gentiles . . . but go rather to the lost sheep of the house of Israel" (Matthew 10:5–6).

Further, Jesus had clarified his Jewishness and devotion to the Covenant, as Matthew dutifully recorded:

Do not imagine that I have come to abolish the Law or the Prophets. I have come not to abolish but to complete them. I tell you solemnly, till heaven and earth disappear, not one dot, not one little stroke, shall disappear from the Law. (Matthew 5:17–19)

· · ·

The "dot" and "stroke" refer specifically to Moses' Torah text and remind us of the initial hand that wrote it.

And yet, in other places, the Gospel of Matthew pioneers an adversarial reading of Jesus in relation to Moses—as if the latter's "Law" (a later Greek translation of "Torah") is to be discounted. It will be more than a hundred years from Matthew's writing that the New Testament is thought by some to supersede the "Old," but the seeds are there in his Gospel, even as he proclaims Jesus' devotion to Moses' Torah. Until today, a polemic has raged about how the living Jesus considered himself superior to Moses. But the argument has always been a denial of historical truth; the facts now available to us, in studies of the Jewish culture and religion of Jesus' era, support Matthew's alternate depiction of Jesus as devoted to the written Torah of Moses.

Still, any tension between Jesus and Moses as Jewish historical figures can be resolved when we've understood that each man engaged the supernatural in the imagined form of negotiating the Covenant. A crucial concept to the history of Judaism and Christianity, the Covenant will receive detailed consideration in the chapters ahead. If any doubt remains that Jesus identified with Moses, it is dispelled by the rigor of their similarly complex educations in the envisioning of the Covenant.

Jesus is already the fruit of the Covenant as a Jewish citizen in the land of Israel. When he reads and studies the Torah, as if written by Moses, he is also witness to the writers who helped create Hebraic culture in the centuries after Moses. This culture produced all sorts of artful books that are lost in time, but also those books that elaborated the Covenant into the full Hebrew Bible as we have it, down through the centuries. It is within Hebraic culture that Jesus can conceive of himself as "creating additional text" to parallel Moses—when engaged in interpreting the Covenant.

Almost two thousand years later, at the time of Passover, 2008, Pope Benedict XVI visited New York City and while there became the first pope to enter a synagogue in America. In his brief speech to the congregation, he invoked the Jewish education of the historical Jesus:

I find it moving to recall that Jesus, as a young boy, heard the words of Scripture and prayed in a place such as this.

Simple as this sounds, it is groundbreaking in its identification with the biography of Jesus as a Jew. This most obvious engagement with history is rarely the first thought in popular commentary. Instead, speculation starts with the more unlikely theories: a Dutch publisher, for example, has announced the future publication of a reputable study that suggests Jesus was the illegitimate son of a Roman soldier and that his mother, Mary, was a runaway. Yet the more probable truth is the least researched: Jesus had a Jewish family and education. It began within a traditional household where *Biblical* stories of Prophets and Messiahs, and even of miraculous births, were commonplace. It should not take Pope Benedict to remind us that Jesus had grandfathers and ancestors, all Jewishly educated, and all of them readers of Moses' Torah.

The Bible was not an anonymous text, divine or otherwise, even to its audiences down through the centuries; once the authors from the early Israelite kingdoms were forgotten through wars, exiles, and other upheavals, the awareness of an ancestral author, Moses, grew stronger. We knew Moses' life because it was recorded in his own conception of history-writing that grew into the Torah. Since it's natural we would want to know more about him, there are many legends apart from the Bible that have survived in Jewish commentary. Yet now we have access to additional sources, in ancient cultures and history, which help situate Moses. These sources, in Egypt and Canaan, have been missing for centuries and millenniums.

A similar concern for the authorship of Jesus led me to Guy Stroumsa, Founding Director of the Center for the Study of Christianity, Hebrew University of Jerusalem. As we sat on a terrace overlooking Jerusalem's Old City walls and facing the Temple Mount where Jesus directed his thoughts and commentary—when the Temple still stood—there was still so much to know about Jewish culture in that era. Guy pointed out some fledgling sociological studies, but he was clearly impatient with the focus of interest. "For the most part, it's politically and religiously driven. It's possible to imagine that Jesus was a politician or theologian, but we still know hardly anything about what that would mean among his Jewish compatriots. Did the thinkers among them live and breathe politics and theological speculation? Or were they inured to it? These questions have barely been asked. We are just at the beginning."

I thought of how little we value such inquiry. We no longer think of the past as holding great authority. We don't look back with sadness—as Ben Sira did, in the second century BCE, lamenting the loss of greatness in his book, *The Wisdom of Ben Sira*. Joshua was his given name, as it was for Joshua Ben Joseph of Nazareth—but Jesus, the Greek translation of Joshua, was preferred when the Christian Bible was canonized much later and when Ben Sira's book was renamed *Ecclesiasticus*. Had he been a Hellenized Jew, Jesus Ben Sira would have lamented the loss of Plato's greatness in philosophy and Aeschylus's in drama, but as a religious Jew he longed instead for the breadth of Moses and the depth of Isaiah.

It was no different for Joshua Ben Joseph of Nazareth, as Jesus was known in his lifetime. And just as the original Joshua, Moses' successor, reminded us of the greatness of Moses, we shall see how the newest Jesus reminds us of it. The authority of the past was strong enough in him and in his time that he could embody a figure such as Moses. And not only would Jesus of Nazareth have known Jesus Ben Sira's book well, but it is apparent he paraphrased it, invoking the language of Wisdom—as it will be reinvoked later, in the idiom of the Christian Eucharist. Two hundred years earlier, Ben Sira imagined God offering his Creation—as if his body—for nourishment:

Then the creator of all things instructed me . . .
"Approach me, you who desire me,

and take your fill of my fruits,
for memories of me are sweeter than honey,
inheriting me is sweeter than the honeycomb.
They who eat me will hunger for more,
They who drink me will thirst for more,
Whoever listens to me will never have to blush,
Whoever acts as I dictate will never sin."
All this is no other than the book of the covenant of the Most High God,
the Law that Moses enjoined on us.

Here the Covenant, as Moses wrote and elaborated it into "Law," was also imagined as the divine body to be thirsted after. And as we shall see, it is also Jesus of Nazareth's words, among his disciples at the Last Supper, which provide the bodily sustenance he speaks of.

I encountered our diminishment of the past in another form when visiting the Oriental Institute Museum at the University of Chicago, which houses a prized collection of ancient Sumerian cuneiform (written) texts. I had long made use of the museum, online and through books, but I was unprepared for the little historical descriptions affixed to each of the myriad glass cases, "helping" one to understand what one is seeing. These contemporary wordings often remythologized the artifacts; thousands of years later we're guided to read the texts literally—as unmediated myths—rather than as the classical works of art the Sumerians cherished: their own historical artifacts.

Here is how it was done: each description begins by explaining that this is what "the Sumerians believed." It's not just that we don't really know what the Sumerians believed; we also know that it was more complicated than the literal words in their works of art. It is just as likely they might have believed the opposite of what was written there.

For example, if someone a thousand years from now—after our civilization has passed—were to dig up an artifact from the year 2006, a book or film called *The Da Vinci Code*, they would be mistaken if they then concluded that it was indicative of what people believed in 2006. We know that we were intended to believe the premises of the film as we watched it, yet after we left the theater we understood it was artful, albeit cheap entertainment.

On a much higher level, the ancient Sumerians and Greeks understood their classics as legend turned into a form of sacred art. But the contemporary curators of Sumerian texts displayed in Chicago are not dissimilar to some Germanic scholars in the nineteenth century who characterized writers of the Hebrew Bible in terms of "they believed this, they believed that."

By the time the Sumerians invented writing more than five thousand years ago, they were using it to record the myths they had heard from thousands of years *before*—retelling them, but somewhat differently. They recorded them as historical, so that they could be newly opened to interpretation and transformation, most famously in new versions of the Epic of Gilgamesh.

We often take for granted the opposition between history and belief. But the real opposition to history, revelation, is not something to believe in but rather an overwhelming drama where we may suspend *disbelief*. The feeling intellect, as Philip Rieff has called it, requires that we read as if we are there. That is, revelation animates the unknowable—what a limited species such as Homo sapiens cannot know—and apprehends eternity as a supernatural realm. We dramatize it with beings and forces that are not limited by death as we are, nor by space and time. And these forces help us to deduce truths about our human situation. In the case of the revelation at Mount Sinai, however, it is not primarily the "event" in which we must believe but rather what flows from it: the negotiation of the Covenant, which probes deeply into what we can know of human nature.

First and foremost, the author Moses was a historian: he tells us what happened, how it happened, and what he has recorded of the commandments of the Covenant. And until more than a century after Jesus' death, Jews and Christians were still reading the Bible in the same way, largely midrashic, a term suggestive of the interpretations found in ancient rabbinic sermons and dialogues.

Yet the rabbis of interpretation were also authors of a kind, writers in creative intimacy with the Torah, as Jesus had been.

According to all the facts we can gather today from many different disciplines, it is clear that both Moses and Jesus were strong readers and interpreters. If they had been modern men, we would assume they were writers. Tradition does in fact credit Moses with being the original writer of the Torah, his five books. In addition, the sayings of Jesus have the skillful quality of profound writing, and it's hard to imagine his Sermon on the Mount not having been written down beforehand. But I have gone a step further in the analogy of a writer; I've found that if we consider their education to be one of an author, a new level of association between Moses and Jesus comes into view.

"All thy deeds are written in a book," wrote Rabbi Judah the Prince about the nature of a human life. It had long been traditional among Jews to think of God himself as an author. This particular quotation comes from "Sayings of the Fathers," a tractate of the Mishnah and Talmud that has roots in the time of Jesus. New kinds of books and ways of writing were prevalent in Hellenistic culture during this age, but the ways of thinking about authorship among Jews were already a venerable tradition. Just as each human life could be envisioned as a text, written on many levels—in deeds and aspirations and errors—one's life could also be valued as reader and interpreter, present in the historical audience of Moses' Torah.

Finally, a historical relationship between Moses and Jesus of Nazareth, informed by thoughtful feeling and audacious research, can form the basis for a redefinition of Judeo-Christianity. But in order to arrive at such a revealing perspective, we must start at the beginning: I began by crafting a brief biography of each man. And then, I started to write about both lives in close connection, moving from one life to the other, forming a dual biography.

·WORDS·

Everyone has a definition for such terms as "Old Testament" and "Covenant" in their heads, in most cases superficial or even unconsciously patronizing. They're just words, but they are the kind that can block empathy. Dictionary or glossary definitions often fail to suggest the reasons for misunderstanding. Instead of pretending we hold these terms in common, I'll address their meanings (and one or two others I've coined), briefly and with any luck succinctly, especially as they concern the lives of Moses and Jesus. We'll then be starting out with a rudimentary compass for passage into ancient history.

Chosen People

Judaism is far from a simple religion, yet it's known to many in the equivalent of sound bites. Let's start with the "Chosen People." As soon as we unpack its meaning—How chosen? Chosen for what? How many people?—we encounter sublime complications. I call them sublime because they lead us to the term's user and his or her state of mind—just as clearly as they lead back to the Jews.

If we want the truth, we must go back to original sources. The concept of "Chosen People" appears during the Israelites' flight from slavery in Egypt, after the arrival at Mount Sinai. There, the Covenant is first written down in detail. It is between a God who represents all that is unknowable to human beings, and Moses, who represents the natural and historical world. It is the same Covenant that was established many centuries earlier by Abraham in Canaan, only now it is to be fully enacted with "the people": all the diverse cultural strands that make up the Israelites.

These people (later denoted as "600,000 souls") are chosen to hear, record, and interpret the words of the supernatural Creator, representing one party to the Covenant. The core of these words, the Ten Commandments, concerns human limitations: the Creator wants Homo sapiens to recognize their human nature and to choose to sublimate their lusting after power. "Thou shalt not murder," for instance, seems simple enough, and yet, because there are exceptional contexts and interpretations of murder that always arise—in war, for one, or in self-defense—even this commandment must be interpreted and reinterpreted, in law and in cultural terms.

"Commandment" is probably not the most accurate translation of the Hebrew. In terms of a covenant between two parties, human and God, these are the Creator's "requirements" of human beings. On his side, the Creator promises to follow and guard the people on their journey through time, toward a promising future in their own land. But the requirement *upon* the Creator is also subject to complex interpretation, for his power too has its limitations in the natural world. If he does not carefully observe the Covenant himself, he is liable to destroy human life. So he has promised: Even if his people appear to trash the Covenant, the punishment that follows will never end the people's life in history or abrogate the Covenant.

But God's requirements are an ideal of civilization that is almost impossible to live up to. Why, then, should any other people resent Israel's being chosen for such a heavy load? The guilt that comes with not being able to maintain the burden of an ideal civilization, as the Covenant requires, is often channeled by the Jews into "modernization." That is, they suffer the consequences by studying harder and reinterpreting; they delve deeper into what it means to aspire to the Covenant. Even when failing in the Covenant, the promise of redemption remains. This desire for greater knowledge, for interpreting and teaching—especially in the quest for the moral dimensions of human nature—can ruffle the feathers of others.

Yet how can redemption (the aspect of being absolved from the guilt of imperfection) be brought about? Education is the answer, which normally means an increased understanding of human nature and how it can be improved. This requirement to know more about how to live challenges us to "walk in his ways"—that is the Creator's hope for us. The Creator too has hope in the Covenant, just as we do; he is equally bound to it. In addition to hope (or "faith"), growth in knowledge of human nature is a requirement, and lack of it is a sin. Education now becomes the bedrock of existence.

It's never enough to "know" the text that Moses has interpreted with the hope of his Creator. After knowing comes reinterpretation for others, starting with children. And not being perfect, we must know our limitations. Even Moses was not perfect, as we shall see. And then, later in history, Jesus of Nazareth suffered the limitations of the human situation, just like the messiah that Hebrew prophets had long envisioned. Yet Jesus' words and his life indicate a complex education in Moses' Torah, the founding document of the Covenant.

One of the Chosen People, Jesus of Nazareth expresses knowledge of the entire Jewish Bible, in Hebrew and in translation; almost all his words in the Gospels quote or interpret it. When he is killed by the Romans, who make fun of him as a "King of the Jews," there is a double irony. As a member of the Chosen People he was burdened with questing after the truth of the human situation— while carrying the Creator's hope of redemption for his chosen people as well as for all creatures.

Cosmic Theater

When the Bible is commonly referred to as the message transmitted to humanity by the Creator, or the Word of God, we have already left the realm of literature and entered into a Cosmic Theater. If we're unaware of it, we will always confuse natural with supernatural, history with myth. A "message transmitted by the Creator" is a supernatural message; the Creator himself is supernatural. But in a cosmic theater, supernatural and natural worlds can meet on a cosmic stage. And that stage, in the Bible, is movable, and denoted as the Covenant: the place not only where a contract between man and God was made and agreed upon in Sinai, but all those further places where it is interpreted and reinterpreted. From Moses to Jesus, the Covenant provides the stage for a cosmic theater.

And as the writing of the Bible becomes a narrative cosmic theater, it spills into the natural landscape of Israel, with the whole world in the wings. It's a known world; even what is unknown stretches out into what can become knowable in the future. Once, the Creator asked Abraham to count the stars, and we are still trying—so far we've counted a hundred billion galaxies but not yet the precise amount of stars in any one galaxy, including our own. Nevertheless, the *unknowable*—what is beyond our limitations as a primate species to know—is something we can still deduce. Homo sapiens have long inferred all that is unknowable in terms of the supernatural. Usually we call it religion.

The prehistoric wall paintings discovered in the Chauvet Cave in southern France less than two decades ago inspire awe. We recognize them as great art, in terms of both aesthetics and inspiration. We're moved by their historical and cultural contexts: these people lived 30,000 years ago, and yet they appear devoted to a natural accuracy when they represent the world of creatures in which they live, both still and in motion. Nevertheless, we sense that the inspiration behind these paintings is driven by a religion, a deep belief in a larger universe. More than sheer beauty and art are at play, and more than natural curiosity. The cave itself—its inner dynamics and outer geographical situation in the landscape—represents a cosmic stage, an earthly connection between heaven and an underworld.

The Bible too is a cosmic narrative that can be described in similar terms. Beyond its great art and historical dynamic, it's an artifact of a cosmic theater in which the world beyond our senses is invoked. But the cosmos is represented and played out almost entirely within the reality of nature and humanity.

The later Homo sapiens in the Bible who conceived that God existed found themselves interacting with the unknowable realm of their Creator—and wrestling with it, in the form of the Covenant.

Religion became a drama of journey through time and toward moral progress, a journey that is ongoing, with our mortality anchored in the human history of Moses and Jesus. Since it's been written down for us in the Bible, we too can imagine ourselves there, among the original audience. The Hebraic cosmic theater is overarching, so that we witness the Bible as it comes into existence and is written through the centuries; even the New Testament takes place within the drama of Israel's real history.

The cosmic stage, however, has been used through the millenniums of Hebraic culture and religion to counter such reductionism. The distinction between natural and supernatural, knowable and unknowable, is clarified by the Covenant. It's a contract that is never-ending in its written details, whether those of moral law or those of human history. Humanity is on one side, God on the other; but when human beings conceive of themselves as alone and without peer, the law and commentary that flow from the Covenant is there to bring clarity. And when people dismiss the Covenant altogether, it is then that the Hebraic prophets make their voices heard. They quote and interpret Moses, just as Jesus will quote and interpret *them*.

Consider how a contemporary Catholic scholar, Michael Novak, describes the cosmic theater: "Judaism taught the world the *mysterium* and *tremendum*. This perception lies at the heart of the law and the prophets. In our secular world, most educated people seem to have lost the sense of mystery and all sense of *tremendum*." In other words, we have lost the experience of entering the cosmic theater.

Even "The Bible as Literature" courses fail to separate legend from history, as if we are reading the enchantments of Homer's *Odyssey* when we read the Bible. Thus the Covenant shrinks into a metaphor for blind faith, rather than expanding into a dynamic theater. So if you're not a "believer"—or at least fail to become a new kind of "believing reader"—the whole realm of what is unknowable to human creatures seems irrelevant. Why bother with it? Ignore the Covenant and there is no pushing at the boundary between known and *unknowable*, no suspension of disbelief in the great cosmic theater of the Hebrew Bible. The Covenant is precisely that boundary of human limits, and it's represented as a stage where the unknowable yet concerned Creator comes as close to human creatures as he can without destroying them. It's a boundary to be clarified and reinterpreted in every age; and in our own day, by literary interpretation especially, since the Covenant is embedded in a narrative cosmic theater.

In order to enter this theater and experience its power, I suspend disbelief, just as I do when Hamlet's father returns from the dead to speak with him. If I said to myself, when reading Shakespeare, "I don't believe in the supernatural," I'd lose the power of Shakespeare. Yet as I leave the theater or close the book, my scientific or secular disbelief may return. As long as I believe *while* I read, however, I can enter the Judeo-Christian cosmic theater. I'd call such a "believing reader" a cosmic reader.

There is nothing especially modern in this, or post-Biblical. In the ancient Sumerian cosmic theater of Temple life, some two millenniums before the Bible, you would leave behind a small statue of yourself to continue witnessing the perpetual theater of gods and humans, as their statues interacted on the Temple stage. You yourself, however, could return to a secular life in the innovative cities of Sumer—including Ur, the one in which the first Jew, Abraham, would eventually be born.

Similarly, we can leave a synagogue or church today and find ourselves in a completely secular culture. Yet we can also bring the Covenant home with us: with the crucial books of commentary that build on the Hebraic sources, we can read our way back into the cosmic theater. Behind these books stands the Jewish writer, represented most dramatically by Moses and Jesus, who reminds us of the complex balance between known and unknowable.

When Jesus speaks the biblical words of Isaiah—who came many centuries after Moses and many centuries before Jesus—as if they were his own, he lends a numinous persona to the original Jewish Isaiah. In the context of the Hebraic cosmic theater, "numinous" means that one reads the biblical text as if in the presence of the supernatural. As many Jewish sages did also, Jesus turns the numinous narrative of the Hebrew Bible into a real-time interpretive theater. Jesus' divinity, however, was still to be worked out with the completion of the New Testament, where the Covenant is reinterpreted.

In the same way, the divine words once spoken to Moses were part of a process that continued with the smashing of the first-draft tablets. Those first "Ten Commandments" would turn into a much lengthier reinterpretation of the Covenant, with the writing starting after Moses returned to the mountain. It was then he drafted the basis of the Hebrew Bible—and it would be the same Bible that would provide the earthly education of Jesus.

But instead of entering the cosmic theater, as the Bible did with its biographies of Moses and Jesus, secular scholars today tend to explain away the drama as "natural phenomena" in the time of the Exodus, for instance; or, as the social phenomena of cave-burial tactics in the time of Jesus. But let's step back for a larger synthesis of what Judeo-Christianity means, beyond rationalizations and ecumenical movements. We can hardly read the newspaper today without needing to reinterpret the Covenant, if we don't want genocide and extinction to become normal threats. Is it possible that the Ten Commandments can still stand up to suicide or mass murder or both? For answers, we need to dig into the complex thinking that allowed figures like Moses and Jesus to become indelible.

Covenant

Prior to the Covenant, myth was the classic realm where natural and supernatural worlds intermingled. Today, myth still has an exotic cachet for the secular-minded, while the Covenant is consigned merely to "religion." Why? The Covenant throws cold water on our wish for transcendence, making us aware that the origin of this wish is still subject to study. As we continue to probe the boundary of human knowledge, the drama of what lies beyond human limits is what we represent in supernatural terms. This boundary, negotiated down through history by Abraham, Moses, and Jesus, is a drama of coming face to face with what is ultimately unknowable to our species—but which becomes represented in the Covenant as creation itself, in the form of our supernatural Creator, Deity, King, and Father.

And so we're inspired to negotiate our admission of creaturely limits. The negotiation takes different forms in Judaism and Christianity, but myth does no such thing; it is quite content to admit the supernatural into human knowledge without negotiation. The Biblical Covenant, however, *uses* myth for illustration but disavows it at the same time, and this ambivalence is at the heart of Judeo-Christianity and of how Jesus modeled his life upon Moses. It's a complexity that is distressing to enthusiasts of myth, since it requires the hard work of disciplined interpretation.

But when I was a literature major at university, myth was the accessible gold standard. In order to read Homer or James Joyce, we first studied Greek mythology. Even if we had to read snippets from the Bible, the Covenant was a myth never encountered— precisely because it was more than myth. The Covenant calls for more than cultural interpretation, and it also requires a numinous interpretation. Instead, I was privy to the rendezvous of our first great modernist poet, W. B. Yeats, with the poetry of pagan myth.

"I am convinced that the natural and supernatural are knit together . . . Europeans may find something attractive in a Christ posed against a background not of Judaism but of Druidism, not shut off in dead history." And thus Yeats, in an essay on his own work, disposes of Judeo-Christianity by recommending a modernist immersion in myth, in which the boundary between natural and supernatural is blurred and joyfully confused. Judaism and the Judeo-Christian cosmic theater of the Covenant are logically derided as "dead history." Probably Yeats is not to blame for his lack of knowledge of the historical Jesus, which did not become widely known until the early 1960s. Since then, the history of Jesus as a Jew of Nazareth has come strikingly alive, as have the thousands of years of Jewish history in Israel—with the help of archaeologists, biblical scholars, and cultural historians.

But all this required a study of history to which modern writers were averse. Even Freud's *Moses and Monotheism* went unassimilated among creative writers. History, like civilization itself, was suspect, because it did not predict twentieth-century Europe's disastrous and repeated collapse into wars. Yet these consequences can be seen to follow from losing the cosmic theater of Judeo-Christianity and its root in the complex détente between natural and supernatural, characterized by the Covenant. Without knowledge of its parental Judaism, Christianity seemed "dead history" to writers like Yeats, often leading to a tolerance for anti-Semitism.

Myth is dreamlike, but in the Covenant the border between natural and supernatural must be diligently probed, as when the Hebrew prophets question the value of prayer and sacrifice. Meanwhile, scientific knowledge must be asked the supernatural question it can't answer, "Why?" Religious knowledge too must ask a natural question it can't answer by itself: "How do we know?" Thus a clear boundary between science and religion is critical to elaborating the Covenant between natural man and supernatural God. Not a defensive border but rather a meeting place—where each can probe the other in fresh cultural terms. And when Moses and Jesus took up the Covenant in their times, they represented such probing, educated men.

I have already called that place of meeting a "cosmic stage," rooted in civilization by the Bible. For Moses, the stage at the mountain was a place of writing, while Jesus used the landscape of Israel as a stage for his interpretive commentary. On both of these Biblical stages, God and man met, and each had his own distinctive style of speech and act. But in the writing, the contrasting styles are more exciting than either one by itself. The sayings of Jesus, for instance, would lose much without the contrasting biblical narrative of his life. In fact, many styles of writing and speech are brought together in the Bible, into what we may call our civilization's grand collage.

The negotiation of the Covenant can be seen to take place at the border of science and religion. It is a complex cosmic theater where God and man can converse, but rarely has it been described this way, in fresh cultural terms. I first began translating from the Hebrew Bible in my twenties, when I assumed the Biblical dialogue between man and God was *mythopoeia*. Such narrow definitions were all I knew from my Humanities courses. But I came to see on my own that the boundary between natural and supernatural was clear in the Bible, not mixed up as in myths. And although the roles of God and man were not written to be performed in a literal theater, they became visualized in a Hebrew narrative that could be read out loud from a liturgical stage, in Temple or synagogue.

Even the prophetic "Kingdom of Heaven" is always on earth, so the audience is witness to signs of it. Charismatic individuals, uncanny acts, improbable miracles, but most important, writings turn time-bound and context-bound oracles into timeless dramas of the interacting between natural and supernatural representatives, man and God. After centuries of usage by the Hebrew prophets, it has come to represent a perfected society at the time of Jesus, but he reverts to the older prophetic usage, referring to the Kingdom of Heaven within us, inside each individual soul. Thus the cosmic theater is represented within as well: we step out of the audience as witnesses and enter into the drama onstage.

And on that stage, as Jesus defines it, we are each the numinous Son of Man. That is, from witnesses we become actors representing the presence of God: the supernatural and natural interact on the stage of our life's journey. And yet this internalizing of the cosmic theater was already present in the writings of Moses, as the law focuses upon the rights of the individual as God-given. Most crucially, the biblical text itself becomes numinous, so that reading it places one in a *narrative* cosmic theater.

But is not the entire drama of Moses speaking to God an imagined writing rather than a historical witness? This is a legitimate question, of course. Yet the original Hebraic authors, in particular the dominant original, designated in scholarship as J, were devoted

historians and interpreted their sources accordingly. The attention to time and place, to character and incident, almost always
takes precedent over elaboration of the Covenant, which is usually portrayed as high drama—at Mount Sinai, for example—or
even as if in a dream. As well, the Bible presents a historical side
to the Covenant, in terms of how it is developed over time and
subject to historical interpretation, and also in the delineation of
religious ritual and law. The legal side of the Torah is rooted in historical understanding that is theatrically inspired as well, with the
dramatic scene of its writing, by Moses, during the journey in the
wilderness.

Most critically, on the other side of the Covenant contract stands
the representative of the unknowable, God. We humans represent
all that is knowable, even the as-yet-unknown—but we also possess the faculty of inspiration, or inspired thought, that has allowed
us to dramatize the unknowable by deduction from what is known
and what we are constantly learning. It is the same for the deductive
method in science that allows us to "see" exosolar planets that are
far beyond the range of telescopes: we deduce their presence from
a calculation of their effect on something we *can* see—their sun-
star, for instance. But the Covenant has been the focus of interpretation during the thousands of years in which our civilization has
developed. It remains a key to the meaning of our intrepid journey
toward the stars as well.

Torah

In Israel, in late biblical times when the nation was a province of the
Greco-Roman empire known as Judah (Judea in Latin), the first
five books of the Hebrew Bible were called the Torah. The Torah
scroll is still kept in the ark of synagogues today, and brought out
to read from during services. It is the same Torah scroll that Jesus
of Nazareth would have read from during his Bar Mitzvah at age
twelve, and on his own he would have chanted from another section
of the Hebrew Bible, namely Prophets. This latter portion is called

the *Haftarah*; during festivals, a portion from the third section of the Hebrew Bible, Writings, is chanted, known as the Megillah. During Passover, the megillah that Jesus would have chanted was the Book of Ruth.

The term *Torah*, usually without a preceding "the," is also used to loosely designate the entire Hebrew Bible and sometimes the later commentaries as well. During the Greco-Roman days, many Jews lived in other parts all over the empire. After Jerusalem, the largest community of urban Jews was probably located in Alexandria, then a Greek-speaking province of Hellenized Egypt. They read a Greek translation of the Hebrew Bible, in which the Torah was called the Pentateuch, the "five books," after the popular designation, the five "Books of Moses." That is also why the individual in congregations of synagogues today reads from the Chumash, a bound book of the Torah, meaning simply "the five" in Hebrew, Aramaic, and Yiddish. That the Torah was accepted to have been written by Moses underscores its becoming known as the Chumash.

Hebrew Bible

The Hebrew Bible is all writing, but the first two parts, Torah and Prophets, establish the *need* for writing. The revelation of which they tell required interpretive and creative expression. It's a revelation that we all are created creatures, and thus can only come from a higher authority: we're to be inspired by the consequences—historical and ethical—of living as a created creature. YHWH may be ultimately unknowable, but the higher authority of the Creator is something to aspire to and be inspired by—and writing is its embodiment.

How this creation of the Hebrew Bible unfolds is quickly grasped in a Hebrew acronym, by which the text is known. TaNaKh is made up of "T" for Torah, "N" for Neviim (Prophets), and "K" for Ketubim (Writings)—these are the three divisions of *Tanakh*, or Hebrew Bible. Torah for "Telling" (I would call it aspiring to revelation), Prophets for "Seeing" (I'd call it being inspired), and

Writings for "Writing"—implying the necessity for a human audience of readers.

The Hebrew Bible is what scholars of all persuasions used to call the "Old Testament," but that Christian designation is falling away, since Tanakh has always been far more than a testament. It is a honed library of thirty-nine books written in the language of ancient Israel, Hebrew (with the tiny exception of a few late passages in Aramaic). Hebrew, both literary and spoken, went through many changes of idiom and style over several centuries, a creation of a living culture. Even when the lingua franca of the Jews in Israel was brought from exile, whether it was Aramaic or Greek, the Hebrew language continued to evolve and assimilate new influences. So, when referring to the Hebrew language of the Bible, we must locate it in a specific culture, the Hebraic, that includes everything a living culture requires, from artists to carpenters. (It was precisely in order to avoid this necessity of reimagining the original writers that some academics have fabricated what they call biblical "tradition," consisting largely of redactors and scribes, prophets and priests—as if these professions existed outside the parameters of a living civilization.)

The Jewish culture in which Jesus lived and was educated is already different from the earlier one in which the Hebrew Bible was written. It is already two centuries since the canonical books were completed, including one of the last, the Book of Daniel, which Jesus quoted. But the canon was not finalized until many decades after Jesus' death, so while he was alive, Jesus could also read and quote from the later Jewish books, most of them of Hellenistic influence; some of these would be included in the Catholic canon, designated Apocrypha and Pseudepigrapha.

YHWH

The four consonants that make up the earliest name for God in the Bible (the vowels are not included in scrolls, so we can't be sure how it was pronounced) are YHWH. Scholars have adopted the convention of pronouncing it Yahweh, instead of the older, mistaken assumption that it should be pronounced Jehovah. Actually, there are older names for God in the Bible, such as El, or El Shaddai, or El Elyon, but these were probably used as the names for the Creator God among other gods, in a pre-monotheistic and pre-Hebraic pantheon. In whatever way that YHWH was pronounced when Moses requested his name, a new convention was adopted at some point in Jewish history, long before Jesus was living, to hold the name too sacred to pronounce (or more likely, mispronounce). By refusing to pronounce the name, one is also insisting that no magical powers are to be attached to names, as was the case in ancient Egypt and Canaan.

When the Hebrew Bible was translated into Greek, several centuries before Jesus, the name of YHWH was called the Tetragrammaton, referring to the four consonants. Many euphemisms have been employed in its place: the oldest in Hebrew is Elohim and the common ones in translation are Lord and God. Jesus may have addressed him according to the Judeo-Aramaic convention of his day, still employed in Jewish synagogues, as Adonai, which means "My Lord" in Hebrew. But Jesus also used the more familiar euphemisms, such as El-ay, "My God," or those for Almighty and Most High.

The uncanny spelling of YHWH, devoid of vowels, reflects the uncanniness of its meaning. The four capital letters may stand for the original words, rendered in Exodus: "I am that I am."

Midrash

To a large extent, contemporary literary theory is influenced by the way of reading, or hermeneutics, of Jewish midrash. Yet midrash is ancient, almost as old as the Bible itself. Even the Hebrew Bible, written over more than eight centuries, consists of books that are in essence midrashic: later works, such as the books of Prophets, retell, comment upon, and react to older books, especially the Torah. However, until modern times, when it was conventional to assume the Hebrew Bible was one great homogeneous book, there was little sense of how it unfolded over many centuries. Only now, when historical scholarship has come to the forefront, have the literary influences, both within and without, begun to be explored.

Midrash is a word that means "interpretation," but it is a certain kind of interpretation. Today it can be called hermeneutics, which is a science of reading, based in interpreting the Bible. Yet where hermeneutics can be dry and pedantic, midrash is creative and free of jargon. It is intended to stir the soul, not calm it. When "The Midrash" is referred to, in capitals, a large, semi-canonical library of interpretive books about the Hebrew Bible is meant. These books were composed after the Talmud, from about 400 to 1400 AD, but they comprise scrolls and other texts that were written in much earlier times, going back to the Maccabean era in Judea, to 200 BCE. In many cases, they were delivered as sermons or commentary on portions of the Bible, and then later transcribed. Even then, however, older texts—teachings and lectures—were quoted, and these may date back to the initial Babylonian Exile of the sixth century BCE.

Meanwhile, the term *midrash* became popular in the late twentieth century to describe any sort of Bible interpretation: even your aunt Ida or Uncle Mort could write one. And even children can have "midrash workshops," where they tell a story about a biblical character, for instance—one who is most likely their uncle Isaac. Furthermore, Christian Bible readers too may write midrash; thus, although the term *midrash* has been watered down to mere "interpretation," an echo from the Jewish world in the day of Jesus has returned. As we shall see, much of Jesus' teachings either come from the same sources as The Midrash or are a type of midrash in themselves (as was much Jewish literature of the period, such as "Ecclesiasticus," reflecting upon the biblical book of Ecclesiastes). The "Sermon on the Mount" by Jesus, quoted in the Gospels, is an example of classical midrash, which is built upon older Jewish texts, as well as the Torah of Moses.

Talmud

The core of the Talmud, called the Mishnah, was edited in the second century AD, but it was already part of the education of rabbis
in Jesus' day. The Mishnah was based on legal opinions, as well as
moral laws and codes, derived from the Torah, that interpret all
aspects of life and death on earth. It is said to be a transcribing of
the "Oral Law," though it dates to earlier written scrolls; it is also
said to have originated with Moses, at the same time as the Torah,
during the forty years of Israelite wandering in Sinai. As we shall
see, most of the Torah was written in later centuries, in Jerusalem;
in the same way, much of the Mishnah was written in various compilations in the Second Temple period. But after the Temple was
destroyed by the Roman army and the nation killed and dispersed,
and at roughly the time the Jewish disciples of Jesus composed the
early Gospels, the main body of surviving Jewish scholars met at the
small town of Yavneh, in order to complete and codify the Mishnah,
as well as to render final the canon of the Hebrew Bible. Their discussions and commentary on both Mishnah and Bible take up the
Gemara, the larger part of the Talmud; these commentaries and
discussions, in later academies that include Babylonia, continue
until the fifth and sixth centuries AD. At that point the entire sixty-
three volumes, called tractates, are complete, and they now include
a wealth of legendary and historical literature.

Some of this additional literature of the Gemara, which also
dates back to the Second Temple period and earlier, would also
have been known to Jesus. There are echoes of what we find in the
Talmud in his sayings, and these texts would have been familiar to
Jesus by the term "Law of Moses"—using "law" in its loosest sense,
as a designation of all canonical Jewish literature to that day, including commentary.

· T H E · L I F E · O F · M O S E S ·

Before we can tell Moses' story, we must state succinctly what we know and how we know it. What we know about the life of Moses begins in the Hebrew Bible and moves out through ever-widening circles of historical context. The first circle was ancient Egypt; it expanded further just a century ago, with our deciphering of hiero- glyphics initially, and then the demotic script of everyday texts. From these writings we learned a wealth of Egypt's history and cul- tural knowledge: how medicine was taught, for example, through papyrus scrolls, and what the afterlife of mummies entailed, inferred from texts written inside the lids of coffins.

We will not find Moses in particular, yet the details of his educa- tion in the royal palace (what we might see today as a large cam- pus) can be filled in: it is where he grew up, adopted by an Egyptian princess. We learn that such adoptions from among slave peoples were not uncommon; men and women who served in palace life were often the highly educated children of servants, who went to the palace schools.

Of course, the parents of Moses were not in royal service, but his sister, Miriam, was hired by the princess to nurse and perhaps nanny the child found in a basket by the Nile, Moses. This is part of the Bible story, though not Moses' growing up and early adulthood. Yet why should it be unusual that palace life is glossed over? A life of John Fitzgerald Kennedy, when written today, takes it for granted we have a good enough idea of American custom in the twentieth century. We don't need the details (though they may be used to inflate the story) of his sailing and piano lessons, or what goes on in the Ivy League. Similarly, the first five books of the Hebrew Bible, the Torah, take on the appearance of being written in Moses' later years, so at that time in history who would need details of Egyptian

life that was just left behind? And even if much of the Torah was
written centuries later, as scholarship now shows, in Jerusalem and
Samaria (the capital of the northern kingdom of Israel), life had
hardly changed in Egypt by that time.

Our knowledge of the early kingdoms of Judah and Israel is still
expanding; archaeologists continue to unearth ancient libraries,
and linguists reach new depths of understanding. Today, the life of
Moses can be situated in its day and age. For the first time in modern
history, we can account for his missing youth and maturity. We may
never have his bones, but we do possess the remarkably preserved
mummies of the actual Pharaohs he would have known and spoken
with in the thirteenth century BCE. We also have the history of the
Jewish people in Egypt and their escape from slavery; the historical
details of the biblical books are mixed with—but outweigh—their
mythic elements. We are still learning the depth of biblical accuracy
as we consider the actual writer's point of view.

It has become trendy of late among some academics to assert that
the Hebrew Bible is largely fiction. An Israelite kingdom needed
a heroic past and set its court writers to work—six centuries after
the fact. Not only was Moses made up from legend, but also Kings
David and Solomon. Even Jesus and his disciples have been considered from a fictional point of view. I consider these views deluded—
not because we must hold the text sacred, but because they argue
that the Bible writers had a political agenda. If the ancient authors
had an agenda, it was most likely cultural and religious. We can't
know exactly who wrote the New Testament Gospels, for instance,
but we can place the texts in the historical context of their authorship, their genres, and among other works in different languages.
Following upon many decades of inquiry into the historical Jesus,
we are now beginning to generate similar insights into the writers
of the Hebrew Bible.

So although it is still often stated by scholars that the lives of
Moses and Jesus were based on mythic story elements—the birth
story, the wandering, the teaching, and the mythic deaths—a writer
has a different point of view. A mythic way of telling a story may be

employed as a structural element; take the life of Abraham Lincoln, for example, which is often structured as a heroic tale from humble beginnings to the redeemer of a nation. Yet the life of Lincoln bursts through the rudiments of structure, as do the lives of Moses and Jesus in the Bible.

More than four centuries before Moses, Israelites had emigrated to Egypt, prospered, and become enslaved. In the beginning, famine drove them down to fertile Egypt, but then they'd returned to Canaan (as Israel was first known). The history of Abraham and Sarah, the first Jews, as recorded in Genesis, the Torah's first book, contains an episode in which they go down to Egypt during famine and barely survive the Pharaoh's sexual interest in Sarah. Much later, after they had died, their grandson Jacob, now grown old, doted upon the youngest of his twelve sons, Joseph.

But the brothers of Joseph were jealous and pretty much left Joseph for dead in a pit. He was rescued by caravan traders and sold into Egyptian bondage. In the end, Joseph's intelligence was responsible for setting him free and allowing him to rise in social status, so that he ultimately came to the attention of the new Pharaoh and became a renowned governor of Egypt.

Many years later, Joseph's brothers were driven down to Egypt during a famine, seeking provisions to take back home to their father Jacob. They did not recognize Joseph, and the story plays out poignantly. Long after—four hundred years later—the Torah restarts the history:

"A new Pharaoh arose over Egypt who did not know Joseph." In other words, Joseph's Hebrew provenance had long been forgotten, and his people were now confined to a slave province called Goshen.

One day, in an effort to save their son from a royal decree that male Hebrew infants were to be killed (preferably by drowning), Moses' family set him in a watertight basket in the reedy shallows of the Nile, in the hope he would become a foundling. In itself, this is not unusual. Mythic kings of Greece and Rome were also left to the elements in infancy, only to be found by shepherds and raised as peasant sons—until their royal birth could be exposed. Uniquely, Moses was born to slaves, not kings, and he was raised in a palace, not a shepherd's hut.

Yet the writers of this history had no interest in their subject becoming royalty; in fact, their story was meant to stand mythic forms on their head. They made Moses himself the author of his own history, as we shall see, and they attributed to him a princely provenance not known before: the birth of a *writer*—not simply a ruler—and one whose words would create a nation, yet whose sovereign would be the Creator.

Meanwhile, Yochevet, the mother of Moses, was hired to nurse the baby—on the recommendation of Miriam, who watched from seclusion as the princess retrieved the infant. So Moses grew up as a prince, along with all that such an educated life entails. Royalty in itself holds no meaning in this history—unless Moses was to rule, as Joseph had, four centuries earlier. Yet Moses' education would prepare him to rule in a new and revolutionary way; his Egyptian knowledge prepares him to deal with Pharaoh in freeing the Jews, on the one hand, but also in becoming the core writer-figure of the Torah.

As a prince in Egypt, Moses was the prototype of the unassimilable Jew. He could not be satisfied by ruling, or teaching what he knew; he needed to explore further. There had already been an upheaval of knowledge in Egyptian history, and some of Moses' own teachers had been privy to it. It was the religious revolution of Akhenaten, the previous Pharaoh known as Amenhotep before he changed name and religion.

Akhenaten ruled with his talented wife, the queen Nefertiti, for a generation—just long enough to change the religion of Egypt by defacing the old capital and building a new one devoted to a single Creator of the universe. The Creator was represented by the life-giving energy of the sun. It may have seemed a monotheism, with all other gods effaced, but the sole mediator of this new cosmic theater, the king and his heirs, had neither time nor inclination to found a new culture in which the religion could be replanted. There was a beginning made, with new literature and art, but it did not take root in the country as a whole.

Yet Moses would have been exposed to it, even after Akhenaten had been overthrown and the old order restored, for it happened just a generation before Moses was born. The old creator-god of Egypt, the sun-god, Ra, was now restored. Nevertheless, Ra was still invested with the higher prestige that Akhenaten's revolution had instilled. Moses, in other words, would have been exposed to the fledgling Egyptian monotheism, at least intellectually, and thus open in a new way to encounter the Creator of the universe.

Moses walks out of the Egyptian royal precinct a mature young man. What are we expected to know about him? His education, for sure. Much later, when he flees Egypt with the Israelites, it is apparent he knew how to negotiate both with Pharaohs and Hebrews. Then again, the Israelites journeying with Moses in the wilderness toward the promised land of the Covenant had all come from Egypt. Even those without much education of their own would have known what to expect of an educated Egyptian, including the doctors and lawyers, priests and politicians they had encountered in Egypt. There was no need, therefore, for Moses to describe such an education in his writings.

The core elements of the Torah that Moses would write down were also read out to an assembly of the people, including many who were not literate. No one would be surprised at his erudition, his princely self-confidence, or his ability to reject as well as transform worldly Egyptian knowledge.

Meanwhile, Moses walks out of the palace, explores, and suddenly encounters an Egyptian officer beating a Hebrew slave. His sense of injustice overcomes his princely caste and puts him in a life-threatening situation, an emotional outburst that will repeat itself later. It begins with a prophet's sensitivity to injustice, but it is followed by the worst transgression imaginable: murder. Moses kills the Egyptian and worse yet, he hides the evidence by burying the body in the sand. Though Moses did not know this, he was seen.

In a short time, Moses returns to the same quarter and encounters a fight between two Hebrews. He tries to stop them and, not unnaturally, they turn on him, taunting. By what authority, Egyptian or otherwise, does he intervene? they ask. "Do you mean to kill us as you killed the Egyptian?" Thus Moses learns that he is identified as a murderer—and that it will not be long before word gets back to the palace.

In his instinctive wielding of princely power, Moses has renounced his inheritance of it. Murder of a slave might be explained, but this was an Egyptian officer—and besides, Moses covered it up. He was shown no deference by the Hebrews either, who did not see themselves in him. Moses must now begin his own journey—his calling—by fleeing Egypt, his home and the seat of civilization. He leaves behind his Egyptian family, his as-yet-unknown Hebrew family, and all the privilege he accrued. Yet his Egyptian education was worldly, and he already knew something of the languages of Canaan he was about to encounter.

Moses fled through the Sinai wilderness to the outskirts of the Midianite civilization, of Canaanite origin. At a well, he encountered the daughters of a renowned priest, called Jethro (and sometimes also, Reuel—the "el" referring to the high God). Moses defended these women from an injustice, as was his nature, but this time he was rewarded: although a foreigner, he was recognizably a cultivated Egyptian. He was taken in by the priest, made the overseer of his flocks, and eventually married his daughter, Zipporah.

After many years, and after two sons were born, Gershom and Eliezer, Moses had matured and the pastoral life kept him out of harm's way. But he also grew deeply learned in Canaanite culture, reading and writing its texts as known to his father-in-law, Jethro.

Then one day, educated in such visions, Moses saw a burning bush whose flames did not consume it. As he approached, Moses thought he heard the voice of El, the high God of the nearby mountain, calling to him. But it was the voice of Yahweh, as he was soon to discover. Yahweh required that Moses "redeem" Israel from Egypt, informing him that a new Pharaoh now ruled. The previous one, who had known of Moses and his crime, was gone.

But Moses struggled with this call. He found reasons to be excused from the mission, including his old problem with authority and injustice. He remembers the Hebrews talking of him and he doubts they will respect him now. Besides, he admits to being "slow of speech," which can mean many things, from not having natural command of Hebrew speech (or its Canaanite precursor) to having become accustomed to pastoral life.

Still protesting, Moses asks God his name and how it is to be explained to the Hebrews. "I am that I am" is the answer, a name derived from the acronym of Hebrew consonants spelling Yahweh: YHWH. What does it mean? But it evidently carries an echo for the Hebrews of the original Covenant made with Abraham in Canaan—even Joseph, having risen to power in Egypt long ago, would have recognized its meaning.

Further, YHWH explains to Moses that all his questions will be answered after the Israelites have escaped from Egypt and arrived at this same mountain, to assemble before God. Meanwhile, when facing Pharaoh, YHWH—the Creator who allowed man speech—promises to "teach" Moses what to say.

These words are to ask the Egyptian Pharaoh for the right of the Israelites to worship their God at his mountain. All that was required was a three-day journey into the Sinai wilderness. But Moses knew that no king would allow such freedom to his slaves, especially *en masse*, and no powers of persuasion would change that. And certainly the Israelites would not believe it. Yet YHWH continues, offering Egyptian signs that all would be riveted by: a rod that becomes a snake and then restored to a rod; a hand that becomes leprous and then restored; and water from the Nile, poured on the ground, that becomes blood.

Moses still can't believe in this plan; his Egyptian education is too deep, and of course he is right. But YHWH has a deeper purpose in the plan that Moses cannot know. Apart from the Pharaoh, it's even more crucial that the Israelites reacquire their belief in the Covenant and the God with whom it was made—and thus remember that the "three-days journey" into the wilderness is just a prelude to the nation-building journey toward the Promised Land.

So even though angered by Moses' resistance, YHWH goes further, promising Moses that his older brother, Aaron, whose authority was already established among the Hebrews with whom he lived in Egypt, would be the spokesman. Moses, nonetheless, would be in the lead—a former prince—to interpret and project authority to the Egyptian royal court.

Thus Moses and Aaron, accompanied by the elders of Israel, came to the royal court of Pharaoh. They said the words that YHWH inspired and demonstrated the rod and signs that an Egyptian would understand. The Egyptian magicians, however, discounted it all, and things grew even worse for the Israelite slaves. Moses—and in turn the Israelites—were learning that Pharaoh would not accept reason or diplomacy.

Moses returned to Pharaoh's court again and again, YHWH giving him each time one of a series of ten dreadful plagues to threaten and carry out, each more onerous than the last. And each time, as yet unbeknownst to Moses, YHWH "hardened" Pharaoh's heart—in order that the Israelites experience the dramatic price of resentment. For that's what the hardness of Pharaoh's heart represented: *resentment* of facing the real power in the world, as reflected in the Creator's authority, nature. And what could be more humiliating than that natural power itself—as dramatized in the cause of freeing slaves?

Besides, Pharaoh was the Egyptian creator-god's representative on earth—intensifying his embarrassment. So each time Pharaoh was moved by fear to acquiesce, he was subsequently moved by resentment to revoke his initial agreement. The Israelites were slowly learning that resentment, their worst enemy, was awakening them to their own condition of slavery: they had been the ones badly treated, humiliated, and degraded, not the plague-suffering

Egyptians and the embarrassed Pharaoh. They were the ones grievously shamed—and until then, they had hardly realized how demeaning was their fate and how awesome the struggle must be for knowledge of their condition.

So here were the plagues, increasing in severity: blood (polluting the river), frogs (polluting the streets), gnats (attacking the body), swarm of flies (infesting the house), pestilence (infesting the livestock), boils (immobilizing the body), hail (destroying houses), locusts (destroying fields), darkness (bringing everything to a halt), and finally, death of the firstborn, both man and beast. These deaths foreclosed survival into the future—and thus it was the final recognition of human limitations that allowed the Israelites to flee. For a moment, that is; for even this was ignored by the desperation of a king and civilization losing its sense of control (an echo of the failed Akhenaten revolution). The irrational madness at the heart of civilization lay exposed, for Egypt would survive without its Hebrew slaves, and it was not the end of Egypt's existence to let this people go. Only *resentment* could be so great, such hardness of heart that even now they would gather and chase after the Israelites as they crossed the Reed Sea.

Let's consider again the final plague. It entailed the death of Pharaoh's son and heir (and thus his future), but it echoes the original hardheartedness of Pharaoh—calling for the death of Hebrew sons—when Moses was born. Before this final plague is carried out, the Israelites are forewarned to sacrifice a lamb on their last day in Egypt. It will become the Passover meal, as the blood from that lamb will be used to smear a sign on the door of Israelite houses, protecting them from the death that will pass over. The Hebrew firstborn will be blessed rather than killed, as Moses was.

Then the plague entered the palace and killed the Pharaoh's son. There was panic throughout Egypt, and in the panic the resentment of the Israelites was momentarily lost. Thus Moses and the people were allowed to leave, but it had to be quickly, as Pharaoh's fear for Egypt's survival would soon subside. There would be no time for bread for the journey to be leavened; it was baked quickly—and long remembered as the Passover matzot. And so they fled toward the wilderness of Sinai, carrying a new awareness of Israel's heritage of emancipation from physical and mental slavery.

But Pharaoh and his army soon followed, filled with renewed resentment. WHY? This time, the original magician's rod would become more than a familiar sign to the Egyptians: it would be used by Moses to hold back the tide while the Israelites crossed the narrows. It was not a magician's sign but YHWH's promise of eternal survival. As Pharaoh's pursuing horde reached the middle of the sea, and as the last of the Israelites were on the opposite bank, the tide returned with a legendary lesson, drowning the Egyptian army.

So Moses had left Egypt for the second and last time, this time with a necessity to transform his Egyptian education into a new civilization. He didn't set out with such a grandiose goal but rather the journey gradually revealed it. The mission of Akhenaten, the Pharaoh who instituted a failed religious revolution a generation earlier in Egypt, had attempted to impose a monotheistic culture top-down, and it may have been dictatorial. But Moses had left royalty behind, and each stage of the Israelites' journey entailed the struggle to build a new educational foundation, a Hebraic culture.

The Covenant of Abraham, Isaac, and Jacob was about to become a writing civilization, and the Promised Land was not to be entered until the basis for government and society had been established. It would take three months—not the symbolic three days requested of Pharaoh—for the Israelites to arrive at Mount Sinai, the same mountain where Moses had heard the name of YHWH and resisted, at first, his calling. Moses spent forty days on the mountain, returning with the Decalogue, the core contract of a new Covenant, this time in writing. It was the basis for an ethical monotheism to be more elaborately written as a record of the journey ahead: forty years of culture-building, of errors and wrong turns, of despair and hope revived, of death and a new generation forged in the elemental struggles of a wilderness.

But when Moses came down from the mountain with the Decalogue, he was confronted with cultural rebellion. The people, in their privation and fear of being lost in the desert, had smelted a golden cow to worship, a reminder of the beneficence of Egypt. Seeing it, and his people entranced, Moses smashed his tablets, and the Covenant's very existence was threatened.

Then Moses reapproached YHWH and argued his case as writer to writer: "If Thou will not forgive their sin—blot me out of Thy book which Thou has rewritten." So again Moses ascended the mountain and came down with the Decalogue—but this time YHWH had revealed himself in a vision, writer to writer. And this time Moses, after he returned, established a Tabernacle for God's presence and made a "Tent of Meeting" out of his own dwelling. Moses now had the respect of the people, because YHWH had allowed him to bring the elders of Israel up the mountain to share a covenant meal. They had witnessed a vision of the king of heaven on their own.

Moses' tent sat outside of the Israelite camp, where the memory of idolatry was still present; it was there Moses wrote the core of the Torah, continuing year after year. The journey and the writing were filled with trials and new threats of rebellion and return to Egypt. Even Moses' siblings, Miriam and Aaron, grew critical, judging him for marrying a Midianite wife, Zipporah. There were also battles for survival with implacable desert enemies, and out of these a new generation of warriors was united in awe of YHWH and the Torah of Moses. Joshua, unrelated to Moses, was appointed his successor, a sign of the nation's tribal meritocracy. Jethro, the Midianite priest, was welcomed as an advisor to Moses, helping to set up a new system of justice and to organize diplomatic relations with Canaanite kingdoms.

Miriam and Aaron, like most of their generation, had already died when Moses wrote his final words. In these speeches to the people, he retold the history of the past forty years and summed up the essence of the Covenant in the Torah. Like an ideal writer, he took no credit for the results but only in the journey itself. And though the completion of the journey was denied to Moses, the real closure for him was a view of the Promised Land from the nearby mountain, Pisgah. His death acknowledged that the journey was ongoing, and that his work was ongoing too, embedded in the Hebraic culture that would carry the Covenant forward. Like many a writer, he died in obscurity: no one found any trace of his body.

IV

· T H E · L I F E · O F · J E S U S

Joshua (Jesus in translation) was born in the city of Bethlehem, the same birthplace as King David of Israel, almost a millennium earlier. How this happened is told in several different ways. Joseph and Miriam (Mary in translation), the parents of Jesus, lived with their extended family in and around Nazareth, in the Galilee region. Bethlehem is a long distance away, in the region of Judah—a region governed by a regent of Rome different than Galilee.

It is possible that Joseph and Mary were fleeing the Roman census in their native Galilee region—an onerous process that might even have entailed death of the newborn infant. They may have stayed in Bethlehem (fleeing at one point to Egypt) as long as a year, or even two. Most likely they returned to Nazareth after little more than a month (forty days has been designated, to echo the time of Moses on the mountain). The entire story of Joseph and Mary's flight with Jesus resembles the forty-year wilderness journey of the Israelites, a dangerous rite of passage that gave birth to the moral teaching and Hebraic cosmic narrative of monotheism.

Not many details are given in the Gospels of the youth and maturity of Jesus in Nazareth. We are told that his parents took Jesus to Jerusalem during festival days—probably the Passover festival—prior to his Bar Mitzvah. Then they returned to Nazareth among a large group of extended family, not noticing that Jesus was missing at first. Three frantic days later, after returning to Jerusalem, they found him studying with the rabbis in the Temple, a prodigy.

The firstborn son of the village carpenter (a most esteemed craft) held a privileged position. After studying with the rabbi in the local school and synagogue, Jesus was sent to be educated in the larger city nearby. Just as Moses had been adopted by an Egyptian princess, Jesus would have been taken into the circle of a charismatic rabbi. He stayed on to become a member of another rabbinic circle, possibly against his family's wishes—or even without their knowledge. We know this and more from recent historical studies of Jewish Palestine at the time.

Yet until now, it had been assumed that Jesus lacked a formal education, based upon an assertion that no record was found of his ordination at a rabbinical school. This assertion was misinformed about the historical era in Jesus' day, when the official rabbinical schools were limited to the ruling class, largely in Jerusalem. But in Galilee and elsewhere, Jewish education flourished under the Pharisees, who were often at odds with the Temple officials in Jerusalem. And it is highly likely that Jewish education was already compulsory.

There was even an Essene synagogue not far from Nazareth, and Jesus' education reflects some of their biblical interpretations. The Essenes in Galilee were neither celibate nor as extreme as those near Jerusalem; learning and scholarship were their central passions. The Jewish education of Jesus can no longer be placed in doubt by geography.

Before Jesus left Galilee to study with his cousin, John the Baptist, his father Joseph had died. Jesus may have been expected to become head of the family, even though his years of study in rabbinic circles had kept him away from home. But it's doubtful the family of Jesus expected him to return.

Baptism had been a common Jewish rite for centuries; the Essenes, however, had reinterpreted it to symbolize immersion in a renewed Covenant. John was an Essene rabbi of the same movement that Jesus knew, and he had become renowned for initiating the ordinary Jew into the vision of the Hebrew prophets. The Kingdom of Heaven, according to John, was imminent, as it had been to many ancient Hebrew prophets, and open to all who would study and be prophetically baptized.

After Jesus was baptized by John, he began to travel and speak throughout northern Israel, with a base in Capernaum. His following was amazed by his prophetic style of interpretation: bringing the past into the present and removing its yoke. He spoke to his audience as if they had been slaves recently delivered into the freedom of the Kingdom of Heaven. He spoke, that is, as if Moses was speaking to his people in the wilderness.

And as Moses had emphasized, Jesus focused upon the freedom of the individual to make his own commitment. He worked elaborate signs, a not uncommon manner among rabbis in his day, and he learned from John the Baptist the ways of healing that trace back to prophetic biblical interpretation—and further back to Moses. In Capernaum, Jesus named twelve of his followers as apostles, symbolizing the twelve archaic tribes of Israel.

But during this year of Jesus' travels, the Roman regent of the Jerusalem area imprisoned and eventually executed John the Baptist as a traitor. This regent also wanted to kill Jesus, who was now safely out of his jurisdiction in Galilee. Yet Jesus returned to the area of his own accord, and later to Jerusalem, knowing the danger to his freedom. It was specifically at the Passover festival that Jesus entered Jerusalem, as if he were writing his life history in eternal Jewish history. Uncannily, Jesus' return to Jerusalem and his Passion would signify a redemption, just as Israel had been redeemed during the first Passover in Egypt.

During his final year of travels, speaking and teaching, in public and among his circle, Jesus embodied what rabbis of his time called the "sage." I would define it more precisely as the "writer": without the model of Moses as writer, the life of Jesus is impossible to consider. Most of the great writings of Jesus (sometimes called "Sayings" and sometimes teachings) include speeches that come from this last year, when he was probably twenty-nine years old. Moses' identifiable writing in the Torah also consists largely of his speeches (called teachings) and his poems (called prayers). Certainly they were written down beforehand, or at least copied and rewritten after. The words of Jesus are no less deliberate; his wanderings no less full of struggle, event, and intellectual achievement. They too comprised a writing.

At the time of his last return to Jerusalem, Jesus was well-known

to the Temple officials, mostly Sadducees, for censuring their control of the Temple. The Sadducee priesthood was already despised
by most Jews, including the Pharisees, and thus could not abide
attacks. It was as if Jesus, like Moses before the golden calf, accused
them of idolatry—of supporting Hellenism, just as Aaron, Moses'
brother, had sanctioned the Egyptian idol in the Sinai wilderness.

When night had fallen on the eve of Passover, Jesus reclined at
the paschal meal with his circle of twelve. It was to be his last supper, and though his audience was awed by Jesus' words and poetic
paradoxes, they understood little. Nevertheless, all those present
would have recounted the story of Passover from Moses' Torah;
they would have remembered Moses as a worker of words and signs
like Jesus. In the ancient freedom won from Egypt, it was Moses'
task to free his people from mental slavery as well—and Jesus spoke
of a similar freeing of the individual body and soul.

Soon after, in the nearby garden of Gethsemane, Jesus was
arrested by the Temple guard of the Sadducees. He was brought to
the Sadducee high priest, who ruled at the pleasure of the Romans.
Still, there is no record he ever turned over a fellow Jew who threatened Rome. In his role as Temple guardian, however, the Sadducee
priest would have been confused and insulted by Jesus' willingness
to be arrested. But the trial that is about to take place is unlikely to
be historically true. His followers, and even Jesus himself, understood that the Jewish Temple guardians had no power to physically
punish or kill him. Only the Romans could do that.

By that point, when Jesus was ready for his ultimate confrontation, he was as much in the hands of God as Moses had been when
he was prohibited from entering the Promised Land. Moses was
prevented from finishing his story as a writer, and Jesus too knew
that his story could have no earthly closure. His life's journey had
established the core text: it would be a new testament, just as Moses
had founded the original testament of the Hebrew Bible.

That Jesus had a Jewish trial is doubtful, as we have established;
and the Pharisees would not have been part of it. But he was brought

to the high priest's chambers, where those who gathered were Sad-ducees, members of the Temple committee. The sayings of Jesus during this interrogation were not even as aggressive as the typical Essene attacks on their Jewish brethren who controlled the Temple. More hostile comments by rabbis about the Temple guardians are to be found in Talmudic sources.

So it is unlikely that this informal interrogation convened by the high priest after hours can be considered a Jewish court. Certainly, it could not have found Jesus legally guilty of blasphemy for his say-ings, nor did it have power to condemn a Jew to death. Most telling, the whole proceeding as sketched in the Gospels was devoid of the most basic Jewish understanding, for the grace of biblical interpre-tation is absent.

The outlook of Jesus was close to that of the Pharisees, and he regarded them as the true successors of Moses. Like Jesus, the Pharisaic school of Hillel was devoted to love of one's neighbors, whatever their origin. Hillel had expounded upon the concept of lovingkindness rooted in the Hebrew Bible, interpreting it as God's love, and Jesus plumbed its depth: one's enemies, too, must be loved. Yet this form of inverting a principle was familiar in the midrashic sayings of rabbis, and the method went back through the Hebrew prophets to Moses and his God. When he needed the principled authority of God's name, Moses recorded that God answered paradoxically: "I am that I am." And among the Jewish Essene writings that Jesus studied and that we can now examine in the recovered Dead Sea Scrolls, unambiguous parallels to loving one's enemies have been discovered.

The Romans, on the other hand, had already crucified hundreds of Jews for encouraging Jewish power. While Jesus and his follow-ers did not seek power, the Romans would not have understood the Jewish spirituality of his parables and sayings. Talk of kings and messiahs sounded provocative to them, and they were uneducated in Hebraic wisdom and prophetic traditions. Some recent histori-ans, upon investigating imperial Roman practice, have suggested that Jesus may have been arrested by the Temple guard to protect him from the Romans. In any case, the Gospels imply that Jesus anticipated his death.

The cruelty and meanness of Pontius Pilate, the governor who had Jesus executed in the most brutal way, is recorded in Roman history. After the crucifixion, Jesus' tomb was found empty. The discovery was interpreted by his Jewish followers to confirm the expiatory power of Jesus' martyrdom: like all Jewish martyrs, he atoned for the guilt of man and nation. At the same time, also in the Hebrew prophetic tradition, Jesus questioned the very meaning of guilt, atonement, and sacrifice. However, in the manner of YHWH's spellbinding revelation of his name to Moses, Jesus stood the conventional meaning on its head.

How does the worldly and mythic idea of the hero achieve higher authority as a biblical redeemer? The active role is translated into a biblical writer's authority: his text outlives his death sentence on Earth. But the cruelty of the Roman execution reflects a worldly law bereft of the biblical writer's moral vision. That vision places supreme value on a human life and its birthright: to be educated, which means to read, interpret, and be profoundly transformed. The biblical life of Jesus in the New Testament is not one of a classical hero, his gospel triumphing over law. It is quite different and resembles the writing Psalmist who rejoices in the law recorded by Moses, along with the grace of interpretation. The hearing of the transcendent law was, as it were, the very first gospel, as written by Moses and grounded in Earth. And the later gospel that tells the life of Jesus is of a piece with it.

V

·THE·DUAL·BIOGRAPHY·OF·
·MOSES·AND·JESUS·

When Moses was brought into the huge complex of the Egyptian court, the princess of Egypt took the infant in his basket cradle to her family's lodging. There were hundreds of princesses at the Egyptian court—daughters and sisters, along with their families—who had married into the royal caste or been born there. The princess who had found Moses, along with her family and servants, would bring Moses up among this elite, educated Royal class. He would be sent to school along with many other children of the court, and like them he would also have his private tutors.

And just as his Hebrew mother, Miriam, had been hired to nurse the child, it is natural to expect that among his tutors would be at least one Hebrew—even if just to translate between Miriam and the others. So as we look more closely into the details that shaped Moses' sensibility, we'll come to understand how his education developed in Egypt, starting with what languages he learned as a toddler. First, however, we need to come closer to his surrogate mother herself, the princess. She was the one from whom Moses would learn sophisticated ways of speech and manners. And she was the one through whom Moses would meet his peers at the royal court.

Perhaps the most crucial thing to know about the Egyptian princess—and one of the first things Moses would comprehend as a child—is that she had her mummy. For all the royals, transformation of their bodies after death—into mummies and elaborate burial houses—was not an end of life but rather a continuation into an eternal Egypt. The child Moses would certainly have visited the mummies in the burial houses of his surrogate mother's family. There he came face to face with the gorgeous countenances of his royal relatives, painted and bedecked with golden ornaments on the exterior of their sarcophagi. From his earliest years, therefore, Moses would have understood that neither his Egyptian mother nor he himself would have to die. Instead, a transformation would take place—hardly more miraculous than his becoming an Egyptian prince.

Now what about Miriam, his Hebrew mother? He would not have known her as a mother, of course, but rather as a servant, until much later in life. But she too may have had her own mummy, as even the Egyptian lower caste did—much humbler, and buried in open sand, yet still a part of the Egyptian cosmic theater encompassing natural and heavenly Egypt.

It would be a long time before Moses, in his youthful maturity, would confront a different kind of death—that of a man he would kill himself, and later, those his Hebrew God would allow to be slain in the last of the ordained plagues. It is only at that point in his life, already mature in years and about to leave Egypt forever, that Moses as well as we readers will begin to know Miriam, his brother Aaron, and the rest of Moses' Levite Hebrew family. At that same point in time, we will also lose track of the princess, Moses' surrogate mother, and all his Egyptian relatives. So we must learn what we can about Moses' life while he was growing up in Egypt.

Moses' Egyptian education is our key to understanding the outward consciousness and inner life of Moses. The knowledge of the world and heavens that he would acquire begins at the age of four, when he's taken with his young classmates to the Temple precincts and shown the historic scenes and hieroglyphic commentary adorning the walls. Back at the palace school, he would read and draw his first hieroglyphic words and phrases.

In these early years of school Moses would also learn the basics of mathematics and the Egyptian sciences. He'd first encounter the imposing statues and ubiquitous artworks, the breathtaking architecture and the splendor of religious and political ritual, the gorgeous jewelry and decorated housewares—all of this a visual feast with elaborate, hidden meaning, just as found in the hieroglyphic writing that was more than a thousand years old.

In contrast to this visible world, the biblical text asks us to re-member the Hebrew voice of Moses' early servant, his true mother, Miriam. It is only a voice that Moses would remember. No visu-als, no spellbinding images, no complex architecture of thought. Just the voice of his Hebrew mother, who was already becoming an absent mother. Perhaps there would be some stories, some lyrics and lullabies, that would remain unforgettable in his ears . . .

· · ·

When Jesus returned to Nazareth with his young Jewish mother and father, he would grow up among relatives and neighbors whose Jewish religion required an early education. In order for a Jewish boy in Nazareth to become Bar-mitzvah at the age of twelve, he would have begun to read and write the biblical Hebrew language at the age of six. So at twelve, young Joshua, as Jesus was called, would already know the written script of the Aramaic language spoken throughout Israel at this time and much of the Middle East, an ancient language very close to Hebrew. The Jews wrote Aramaic with the same alphabet as Hebrew, and many Hebraic words and phrases had been incorporated into their local dialect of Judeo-Aramaic. Thus, it would not be long before Joshua was bilingual in Hebrew and Aramaic; and soon enough, he would add knowledge of the Hellenistic Greek that was the official language of the country.

We now know that the Galilee region that included Joshua's town of Nazareth was diverse in culture—the nearby city of Sepphoris, just a long walk away, held a majority of Greek-speaking peoples, including assimilated Jews. The Sepphoris synagogue where young Joshua studied was just around the corner from a Greco-Roman gymnasium attended by Hellenized Jewish children. What would Joshua have absorbed of Hellenistic culture at this early age? Prob-ably of more significance is the understanding he would have inter-nalized of the boundary between Jewish and non-Jewish cultures.

However exotic the Hellenistic culture appeared to young Joshua, his Jewish education encouraged a resistance to its charms. And a multitude of charms it no doubt held for a youth of the time, because unlike the Jewish world, its cultural face was more richly painted and its communal body more invested in public ritual and daily drama. A child at the gymnasium knew not only his local and national public figures, but also the painted portraits and seductive statues of emperors in Rome and other places. In contrast, the Jewish teachers talked of the sages and ancestors of the Hebrew Bible—they were heard from but not seen.

But this deeper Jewish history found its origin in a single overwhelming voice. It was the voice of the Creator, translated into written words by Moses, and elaborated into the Hebrew Bible by the ancient poets and writers in Jerusalem and Samaria. One of the late tendencies of these original biblical writers was to prefer human dreams as the vehicle in which the Creator's voice was heard. Back in the earlier day of Moses, however, the face as well as the voice of his Creator was still present in real time. It was as if God's voice was more palpable than his own father's. We hear little of Moses' biological father, even less than of his mother. The Creator's voice has replaced the father's—and with a greater intimacy than most fathers command.

For young Joshua, the Creator's voice was already on the lips of his early teachers in Nazareth. His father, like Moses', remains a distant one, and we will hear much more about his mother, Miriam, than his father, Joseph. There is no question that Joshua's ultimate intimacy becomes one with God the father. And eventually, the voice of Jesus himself will supplant the entire Hellenistic culture and religion, just as Moses had supplanted the ancient Egyptian.

Both men, Moses and Jesus, struggled between family voices and the text that represents the Creator's voice. This conflict was already well under way when young Joshua was sent to Sepphoris for his bar mitzvah studies. Prime among these studies was the prophetic portion—known as the Haftarah—that the young boy chants on his special day. Like the prophets themselves, Joshua was now moving beyond the realm of his family and its history in Nazareth. When, years later, Jesus returned to Nazareth as a rabbi-teacher in his own right, this conflict became full-blown, as the citizens and presumably some of his own family rejected his teaching.

Which Prophet of the Hebrew Bible would Joshua have committed to memory at this early age? We don't have an explicit answer, but we can make an effort to discover it in the prophet-like role that Jesus takes on. In the second chapter of the Gospel of Matthew, concerning the birth of Jesus, we read: "After Herod's death, the angel of the Lord appeared in a dream to Joseph and said, 'Get up, take the child and his mother with you and go back to the land of Israel, for those who wanted to kill the child are dead.'"

The family returns to Nazareth and Matthew comments, "In this way, the words spoken through the prophets were to be fulfilled: He will be a *Nazarene*." That word was a term for the early Hebrew prophets, establishing a biblical lineage for Jesus' calling. In the same way, Bethlehem was established as the birthplace of Jesus, as it had been for Israel's first king, David, and this represented a Hebraic lineage of "God's anointed"—and the hope for anointing a kingly Messianic successor.

Although the text tells of an angel that speaks to Joseph in a dream, we do not hear of angels very often in the life of Jesus. Why? Because Jesus has recourse to the Creator's voice instead, in his detailed knowledge of the entire Hebrew Bible. We will see evidence of this in almost every saying attributed to him, and that is why we begin with his education.

Once he completed his bar mitzvah studies, Jesus was sent to further study with a rabbi and his circle in Capernaum, a main cultural center in the Galilee region. We must assume that Jesus displayed an unusual intelligence, since it was not uncommon for such children to leave their families for the surrogate family of a rabbinic circle. No doubt the model for Jesus' own circle of disciples was based on this Jewish custom.

Once in Capernaum, Jesus would be reading Moses' words of the Torah and be taught to comment upon them. The biblical commentary at this time usually took the form of interpreting the kind of life that a Jew needs and the natural laws that underlie it—in order to be on intimate terms with a father-like Creator. This Hebraic commentary eventually evolved into the written texts

of the Mishnah and Talmud in later centuries, but for now it consisted of dialogue and argument among the rabbi and his disciples.
When rabbis would meet among themselves for study, these dialogues were maintained on a higher level. But the style was already
accessible to the young Jesus: a style that would come to be called
midrash, in which biblical passages are elaborated into story and
history.

Meanwhile, at this same time in the first century AD, Jewish writers living in the great cultural center of Alexandria, Egypt (as well
as other cities throughout the Greco-Roman Diaspora and within
Israel itself) were writing in a different style. Their language was
Judeo-Greek—that is, the Greek of the time infused with Hebrew
and Aramaic phrases—but they also read and drew upon the classical Greek texts. Prominent among them was Philo of Alexandria,
who published a "Life of Moses" that tried to explain not only the
significance of Moses as a man but also as a writer of the Torah (the
Five Books of Moses). Jews in Israel who were literate in Greek—a
significant elite—would be reading this book along with the larger
non-Jewish audience of the Greco-Roman empire to which it was
addressed.

Did Jesus learn to read Greek also? It is a question we will ask
again, when Jesus comes into contact with the Greek- and Latin-
speaking ruling class in Jerusalem. Certainly he read in his mother
tongue, Aramaic, an older lingua franca of the Middle East. Most of
the Jewish writers in Israel at the time, even those who read Greek,
wrote their books in Aramaic. For now, we note that Jesus knew
of this Aramaic literature, and thus would have been familiar with
the work of Philo, since many of these Aramaic texts would have
glossed Philo's work in Greek. His "Life of Moses," for instance,
was controversial among Jews for the scope of its biography.

Moses as a writer, as Philo depicted him, told something new
about the life of a Jewish prophet. The Torah was still understood as
a sacred text, a translation of the word of God by Moses. And yet, in
Philo's terms, Moses was a "writer—a flesh-and-blood creator." In
other words, the act of writing, apart from its later status as revela-

tion, was embraced as an enabler of profound interpretation. As the interpreter of his Creator, Moses the writer was responsive to the moment, the physical and historical moment in time in which he lived. That is, he was responsive—but not *responsible* for it. As a writer, his responsibility was to interpret what has happened in terms of what must come next. He is thus a historian of his own life, and as such was held out to the educated readers of Philo's world as an example of Jewish genius—and unlike any previously known.

The Greco-Roman reader was to be persuaded that Moses' books were numinous—written in the presence of God—because Moses himself was a new kind of writer. And since they were reading the writer Moses, and not simply an anonymous sacred text, the non-Jewish reader would be forced to ask about the Hebraic culture in which Moses was educated in his later years, along with his innumerable descendants among the people of Israel. Before Philo published his "Life of Moses," the Greek translation of the Hebrew Bible (known as the "Septuagint," after the apocryphal committee of seventy Jewish sages who authored the translation) was widely read. In fact, it may have been the only text known to Philo himself, since there is little evidence he was fluent in Hebrew. But now, Philo's reader was being asked to see the text in a new light, one that would illuminate the hand of the writer as well as the original nation for whom it was written.

We must also be aware that Philo would have known the Aramaic translations of Moses' Torah, and he would have considered these much older translations as less authoritative, less modern than the Greek Septuagint. Yet these Aramaic translations from the Biblical Hebrew, known as the *Targums*, were at the core of Jesus' education. Although the Hebrew text was primary, the main educational aid to reading it consisted of the Aramaic translations. And then, as a mature man and a rabbi about to form his own circle, Jesus would come upon Philo's Moses as the embodiment of a striking new idea. So when Jesus began to think of himself as "speaking" and writing in the prophetic tradition, he would now have to reckon with the original prophet, Moses, as more deeply original than had been realized. At this point, Jesus saw himself as also embodying the figure of a biblical Hebrew writer—in the sense of being an originator of numinous texts.

The rabbis who wrote midrash and the Hellenized Jews who wrote biblical "Apocalypses" and "Testaments" (Aramaic and Greek imitations or pseudo-books of the Bible) do identify themselves as authors, either in their own name or in the pseudonyms of biblical characters. Accordingly, Jesus would have been quite conscious that his words would be set down as authored, whether by himself or by his disciples. Yet none of this contemporary Jewish writing was to be considered numinous in itself—it was all extrabiblical. Only the new idea of Moses the writer would move Jesus to envision his own words as numinous. And what would be more spontaneous than to see himself in the image of Moses the writer: the original Jewish figure who inscribed his own numinous life and that of his times. But only Jesus' sympathetic familiarity with the Jewish texts, rooted in his education, could allow for such originality.

. . .

Before Moses, ancient civilizations saw time without beginning, middle, or an evolving idea of the future—a future that would end in a new species of human being. In short, our Western idea of a world with a creation, a salvation story, and a messianic resolution was created by the hand of Moses. (Although exception might be found in classical Sumerian literature, it is the exception that proves the rule, for the later civilizations of Babylon and Assyria diluted and disfigured the original genius of Sumer.) But Moses used his ancient Egyptian education to embody a new idea that no Egyptian had dared to dream: he gave *voice* to the visual idea of the eternal mummy and thereby bequeathed to his descendants a Hebrew tradition of writing, interpretation, and a future of progress.

Today, if we can imagine Moses' Torah in the figure of a mummy—a way of envisioning a text never before imagined—we can see that it is the communal *audience* of Israelites who keep the Torah alive and preserve its voice. Nowadays, not only are the scrolls dressed in garments and breastplate, they are kept in an ark, a portable sepulcher, as was carried by Moses and the Israelites through the wilderness years and into the land of Israel. Everything that was changeless in Egypt is now movable; the eternal verities have become a journey of new history and its development. The Egyptian afterlife of the body became voice and memory in Moses' scrolls, and the afterlife trials of the Egyptian eternal body became the fraught journey on earth of the Israelites. By the time of Jesus, the Jewish idea of Moses' text gave to the Torah its numinous quality—as if the Torah scroll was an eternal mummy brought perpetually to life. It was no accident, therefore, that Jesus would come to equate his own body with that of the word of God, as contained in Moses' written text.

So the text written and carried to the people by Moses the Israelite had roots in Egypt. We are only beginning to realize how even Egyptian mummies are a serious factor in the development of Jewish and Western civilization. Without them, the voice of the ultimate father's face, the God of Moses, might not have been imagined— though we are prohibited from conceiving of it visually. It started with the face and it continued with God's voice, and as it entered human language it could become a personal dialogue reaching into the inner life of the individual as well as the outer world of public life.

That is why Moses' journey is set down as history rather than myth. The written scrolls based upon this history amounted to a will and testament for an entire community, and even the whole world. In place of being buried like a mummy in its inscribed case, the Israelite was now born into human history, like Moses floating in his basket. But first Moses had to grow up within the intellectual milieu of royal Egypt. Although the historical drama of Moses and the escaping Jews in Sinai would be rooted in the Egyptian drama of personal immortality, the eternity of the mummified body was an *ahistorical* extension into the future. Moses was capable of transforming this drama into a historical one, because in his maturity he came face to face with events so real they could not be denied.

Moses, a man by now, set out at this time to visit his countrymen and he
saw what a hard life they were having. (Exodus 2:11)

Here is the first shock of recognition, as recorded in Exodus. If
this was the first time he met his people, we can imagine how painful it was to see them enslaved. Slaves had to work on the Sabbath . . .
It began to dawn on Moses that somehow the word of God commanding the observance of the Sabbath would have to become
written. But how? The answer unfolded as a biography of a man
and his people. And more than a thousand years later, in the New
Testament, it was still remembered that "Moses was taught all the
wisdom of the Egyptians and became a man with power both in his
speech and his actions" (Acts 7).

Before the question of what to do and how Moses' education can
help him, history steps brashly in. There is no time for Egyptian
wisdom.

And he saw an Egyptian strike a Hebrew, one of his countrymen. Look-
ing round he could see no one in sight, so he killed the Egyptian and hid
him in the sand. On the following day he came back, and there were two
Hebrews, fighting. He said to the man who was in the wrong, "What
do you mean by hitting your fellow countryman?" "And who appointed
you," the man retorted, "to be prince over us, and judge? Do you intend
to kill me as you killed the Egyptian?" Moses was frightened. "Clearly
that business has come to light," he thought. When Pharaoh heard of the
matter he would have killed Moses, but Moses fled from Pharaoh and
made for the land of Midian. (Exodus 2:11–15)

Killing and burying. Followed by shocking self-recognition and
fear. To his fellow Hebrews at this time, Moses seemed only an
Egyptian prince, a grandiose figure of contempt. Furthermore, his
Egyptian identity had also become contemptible, to the point where
he could have been killed as a criminal—just as he was first targeted
for death by Pharaoh, when he was abandoned in his infant basket

on the Nile. This will not be the last time Moses is threatened with death, but it is the imminent threat of extinction that drives his life forward. Nothing can be more historical than that, and we shall see how the threat of extinction to the entire people of Israel propels their journey into and through the desert.

Again, more than a thousand years later, we must note that the New Testament records how "Moses refused to be known as the son of Pharaoh's daughter and chose to be ill-treated in company with God's people rather than to enjoy for a time the pleasures of sin" (Acts 11). But Moses had actually remembered it differently when he wrote the Torah. He did not "choose," nor did he "enjoy" anything. For Moses would be writing history in which events are primary—not premeditated thought and action. "Moses was frightened," and "Moses fled," is how it is written in the Torah. He acted as a man overwhelmed by events. Now, his Hebrew education would really begin, and only after many years would he be ready to return to Egypt and convince his enslaved people that they must also flee toward the same wilderness where he now found himself, the land of Midian, in Sinai.

And as we follow the initial flight from Egypt by Moses, soon enough we find him fondly taken in by the Midianite priest Jethro, who was perhaps as impressed by Moses' Egyptian manners as by his Hebrew integrity. So Moses married Jethro's Midianite daughter, Tzipora. They had a son, but he was not named as a Midianite. Gershom means a "stranger in a foreign land." Now we know that Moses is not going to forget where he came from, either as an Egyptian or as a Hebrew.

There would be much to learn from an educated Midianite priest such as Moses' father-in-law, Jethro, and much of that would entail knowledge by the Midianites of their Canaanite neighbors, the early Hebrews. Midianite culture absorbed their historical contact with the Israelites even before they became enslaved. By the time the Hebrews fled famine for Egypt, the sagas of Abraham, Isaac, and Jacob (Israel) would have been known to them. So not only does Moses learn more of his Hebraic heritage from a foreign people, but he learns what the Hebrews enslaved in Egypt may have already forgotten.

Then one day, while Moses "was looking after the flock of Jethro, his father-in-law, priest of Midian," a bush blazing in flame stopped him in his tracks. Now YHWH spoke to him: "'I am the God of your father,' he said, 'the God of Abraham, the God of Isaac, and the God of Jacob.'" Clearly, YHWH expected that Moses knew the history of the Hebrew patriarchs, just as might any educated Midianite. But now, God spoke only to Moses. Here is what the Creator wanted Moses to know: he is well aware of his people's sufferings in Egypt and he plans to deliver these people, "the sons of Israel, my people," to the land of Canaan. Much later in history, the New Testament would put it this way: "I have seen the way my people are ill-treated in Egypt, I have heard their groans, and I have come down to liberate them" (Acts 7). But in fact, it is Moses who first "sees" the condition of his people. And now Moses will "hear" what he must do: "I send you to Pharaoh," says YHWH.

Moses will return to eventually redo the accidental killing of the Egyptian officer whom he had seen beating a Hebrew—for in the end, Pharaoh's son will be struck by YHWH's Angel of Death, in order to make possible the exodus. And this time, Moses' second flight to Sinai will bring out the entire people. But before any of this can happen, Moses has to agree to go back to Egypt, and it's not surprising that he's reluctant. He knows that returning to Pharaoh is like his own death sentence, since no one has forgotten him.

"'Who am I to go to Pharaoh,' protests Moses, 'and what am I to tell them?' And God said to Moses, tell them my name is: 'I Am who I Am.'" Now, instead of Moses acting on his own "seeing," he has become a witness for YHWH. In the same way, Jethro and the Midianite culture had served as Moses' witness to knowledge of the historic Israelites. In becoming a witness for YHWH, Moses now listens before he acts. And in this listening, he has become a Jew again, as when he was born.

What Moses literally sees and what he hears has become one, for the visible sign he now encounters, the burning bush, contains the voice of YHWH. We need to dwell on the significance of this sight to Moses, whose Egyptian education rests upon the singularity of the High God, Ra, the sun. The suppressed Amarna religion of King Akhenaten, also known to Moses, turned the High God into the One God, though still represented by the sun. Thus, the fire that faces Moses in the burning bush is no strange sign to him; neither is the singularity of the voice of the Creator, though no Egyptian had heard it.

But what about the name? Perhaps its first significance lies in the fact that YHWH is not only a Hebrew phrase, but also a severe poetic test of Egyptian belief: Unlike Ra, the God of Abraham is invisible, hidden in an uncanny phrase, "I Am That I Am." Thus, the Creator's words are more deeply elemental than any visible object. It is the voice, and the Hebrew words it utters, that make possible a new history, one that can be written down and responded to, in the human words of dialogue, interpretation, and commentary.

"I am the Son of God . . . ," though never uttered, becomes the vatic voice of Jesus in the Gospels, echoing the name of the Creator, *I am that I am*. But long before this, Jesus would first have to discover his voice as a rabbi. This could only happen in a submersion from the visible world into the water of baptism, the sign of invisibility that Rabbi Yochanan reinterpreted—a cousin of Jesus, known to us in translation as "John." Baptism had been a Jewish purifying ritual for many centuries before John added his own interpretation. And when Jesus encountered this new meaning, he found his own unique voice as a rabbi.

It was the invisible realm of YHWH in which he could now move as a representative voice. As if he had crossed the sea parted by God, as Moses and the Israelites had, Jesus heard this voice: "This is my Son, the Beloved." That is how King David was known, the original messiah figure, "Beloved of God." All this Jesus would have known from his Hebrew Bible studies, and his words from now on will echo through the entire written history of Israel.

In the very next sentence following his encounter with John

the Baptist in the Gospel of Matthew, Jesus would be "tempted by
the satan"—after he had "fasted for forty days and forty nights,"
a direct reminder of the time Moses had spent with the Creator
on the mountain, listening to YHWH's words. In response to the
satan, Jesus says to him:

Man does not live on bread alone.
But on every word that comes from the mouth of God.

This echo of the manna-bread that YHWH had provided for the
Israelites in the desert (the scene with the satan also takes place in
the desert) further reinforces the written authority of Moses' Torah.
Now Jesus directly quotes the Torah to the satan: "You must not
put YHWH your God to the test." Such scenes with the satan are
further evidence of Jesus' familiarity with the entire Hebrew Bible,
where they are found in the Prophets and the Book of Job. In the
latter instances, the scenes also involve a test devised by the satan,
but they are intended less as historical events than literary visions.

In reality, Jesus began a journey in Galilee, speaking of the
invisible realm in synagogues. Before he could return to John, his
compatriot had been arrested and would soon be executed as a
revolutionary by the Roman-appointed king, Herod. From then
on, Jesus would slight the power of the king by beginning his sermons with the poetic phrase, "the kingdom of heaven is close at
hand." This invisible realm of YHWH's heaven is precisely what
John had raised the Jewish rite of baptism to—by reinterpreting
it as an otherworldly submersion. For most Jews at the time, and
even today, this purification rite, whether in streams or an enclosed
"mikvah," prepares one, especially a woman, to reenter the daily life
of human history—rather than a vision of heaven. But in the same
way, one reenters human history via the liturgical reading of the
Torah in the synagogue, just as Jesus did in his day.

· · ·

At the burning bush, Moses is being instructed for his mission—
just as Jesus was inspired by John to begin his mission in Galilee.

God tells Moses to tell the people of Israel: "YHWH, the God of our fathers has appeared to me—the God of Abraham, Isaac and of Jacob." And just as Jesus would say "the kingdom of heaven is close at hand," YHWH tells Moses not to worry about the king of Egypt because he will be "forced by a mighty hand"—the power of heaven, more than a thousand years earlier than when Jesus came to face King Herod and the Roman authorities.

This power of YHWH comes from our beginning to understand history as including more than we can know, as having been negotiated, covenanted, on earth. It can be invoked by Moses and Jesus because the Covenant had already been accepted by Abraham centuries before. One of the first things the mature Moses would learn about Hebraic culture is the nature of the Covenant.

Beginning with Abraham's knowledge of Mesopotamian contracts, which he brought with him when he left Ur for the Promised Land, the Covenant was negotiated as a means to bring supernatural God and natural man together on equal terms. That is, God must take care not to injure or even scare his human partner, and man must pay attention to the needs his God presents. We see the results of this negotiation when God and man are already speaking the same language and responding to the same Hebraic customs. And so we can only imagine with what complexity the Covenant evolved to the point of easy, if tense, dialogue. Not only the Mesopotamian but the Canaanite notions of contract and political covenant went into the early development of the Hebraic Covenant with YHWH. And then, Moses would study all this and bring to it as well his Egyptian education in the occult Wisdom tradition, which entailed centuries of nuances in an imagined communication with the gods.

Finally, in his growing self-awareness as a Hebrew, Moses added a new knowledge of the self. Every Hebrew regardless of social status had his or her role in the People of Israel and its history. That role would begin to be elaborated in all the events that accompanied the forty-year journey in the wilderness. As Moses would interpret these events, such as the disastrous making of the golden calf, the

Israelites would learn from Moses how to be involved in dramatizing the Covenant with YHWH by struggling to internalize its laws of the human condition.

· · ·

Jesus would learn this resourceful struggle to interpret the Covenant from reading Moses' Torah, along with the later centuries of Hebraic commentary and prophetic interpretation based upon it. By the time of Jesus, the Covenant had been made far more complex by its layers of interpretation and the events of Israel's history. On the other hand, the Covenant with YHWH was familiar, a concept lived and breathed by each individual Jew. Thus Jesus, as many rabbis of reform in his day, would feel quite natural in textual dialogue with Moses' God—cutting through the centuries of commentary to Moses' negotiation at Sinai, as we shall see.

It would have begun for Jesus in two sources that were in creative tension: his Jewish family and the Hebrew Bible. While he was growing up in Nazareth, the history of his wider Jewish family, cousins and ancestors, was embodied in the stories told around him. This family history influenced his being chosen for extended school studies—and ultimately his leaving home altogether. But at the same time, the stories of recent generations would have been read back into Israel's history: how the Covenant was brought closer or pushed further away.

At first, the family was not prepared to see something special in Jesus; the event of his birth in Bethlehem was long ago mixed in with the terror of flight at that time and now forgotten. Neither did Jesus see himself as special. Not until his being chosen to continue after his Bar Mitzvah studies with a rabbinic circle in Sepphoris did he comprehend that his family recognized his intelligence. Now, between the ages of thirteen and eighteen, Jesus would learn what it meant to be a historical Jew in the mirror of his classical Jewish studies. Immersed in the idea of what it meant to be a Hebrew prophet, he would come to realize that his Bar Mitzvah Haftarah— the portion of Isaiah he committed to memory—spoke to him in terms as familiar as a brother.

So a year later, when he had a substitute family of colleagues in his rabbinic circle, he could imagine himself standing in relation to the historical prophets he was studying. They too would become like family—like brothers in dialogue with the same heavenly Father. The tension between leaving his natural family and the mysteries that still lay hidden behind the Mosaic text that he would study for many years began to dissolve. For there were also mysteries and unexplained events that characterized his own family in Nazareth—mysteries that few of us ever completely unravel in our own family history—but these receded as the place of his natural family in the history of the Jewish people began to come clear.

It went back to Moses and his unique ability to get it all written down. And what was it? A record of a journey in real time toward not only the place of Israel but also the idea of Israel's significance in the world. Yet without successive generations of children to study his words, Moses would have become embalmed in legends. Indeed, many legends have arisen around him; but still, each child in every generation forms his own internal dialogue with the Mosaic text.

And had the text itself not been written, it too would have been engulfed in supernatural legend. As a record of a historical journey, however, it calls each reader to find his place in the trek as it continues to unfold in time. That is why Jesus' early rabbi and teacher in Capernaum would have seen himself in a dire historical situation. He would have been a Pharisee, a recent tradition of teachers who were in conflict with the political and temple sect, the Sadducees.

The Sadducees were a ruling class of priests and politicians certified by the Roman power in the land. They established Hellenized schools where their Jewish children learned to become good vassals of Rome. The Pharisees, on the other hand, avoided these schools and taught in synagogues and their own homes. Like the Hebrew prophets themselves, the Pharisees were actively engaged in interpreting the Hebrew Bible in the historical circumstances in which they now found themselves. They weren't satisfied with the literal codification of Moses' words that the Sadducees followed. Jesus' rabbi-teacher, as a typical Pharisee, brought the Hebrew prophets back to consciousness, unlike the Sadducees who preferred to forget them.

This does not mean that Pharisees and Sadducees were in direct conflict, any more than the Reform and Orthodox movements of Jews are in conflict today. They shared and gave allegiance to the same Jewish history and Hebraic culture, and they would recognize each other as Jews just as a Catholic and a Protestant would hold their Christianity in common today. However, there were many other Jewish movements and traditions in play at the time of Jesus. One of these, the Essenes, would come to hold Jesus' particular interest. It is enough for now to say that each tradition had its own schools and customs of education.

The most crucial element that binds Jesus to an early Pharisaic education is the recognition of Moses as the first in a line of Hebrew prophets that would extend down the centuries. Jesus would eventually identify with Moses as a reinterpreter of history, in line with the Pharisaic emphasis on Jewish history. The Pharisees were worried about the mental as well as physical dependence of the Jews on Roman ideology. They saw themselves as providing a way out of this mental slavery and into a restoration of the Covenant with YHWH. And so it would be genuine for Jesus to see himself in brotherhood with Moses as a leader toward the Promised Land—as it was meant to become: a land free of pagan influences.

It is no simple matter of describing "this" as pagan and "that" as Jewish. The land of Canaan to which the Israelites arrived after the death of Moses was diverse in culture and history. To label it all as pagan would be a gross injustice. What the Israelites now brought with them, however, was a new type of light (call it a spiritual fire) by which to see and separate the natural world from supernatural interpretation. The Hebraic covenant clarified the long-held confusion about supernatural influences to which cultures to that date were bound. In place of temple statues, the Hebrews carried within their portable Ark a written text of Moses.

And from this text, they interpreted moral laws about how to live as if the entire creation had only one Creator. Thus, there were no gods to appease—in fact, appeasement was no longer the way—but instead, only the truth of the Creator was to be studied and thrown as a light upon the nature and problems of society. To keep this light intense, the early Hebrew tribes would remain separate from their Canaanite neighbors and in enduring intellectual conflict with them. It was as if the Israelites were in confrontation with a world empire of far greater worldly power—just as Jesus and the Pharisees would find themselves resisting the clutches of Rome.

But the original, imagined negotiation with a Creator who represents all that is unknowable to us had changed the way of thinking about history for the Jewish people. Jesus grew up in this original way of thinking about the world, coupled to a tradition of study and interpretation. There were also the disciplines of meditation and prayer, just as there were in all religions. And thus, too, there were also supernatural legends and expectations. Yet there was one big difference. The miracles and legends were merely signs to the Jewish way of thinking, not to be understood as events unto themselves.

Even the miracles and healings that Jesus would later perform were meant as signs of his role in interpreting the Hebraic Covenant—they were not intended to display supernatural power in itself. They were signs to the Jewish people, just as the plagues that YHWH delivered upon Egypt were intended as signs to the Egyptians, not supernatural punishments. The signs needed to be interpreted and thus they became words through Moses, both spoken and written. Not the words of soothsayers and magical healers, but a written text of historical events that would bear study and interpretation into the future—however it unfolded.

That is why Jesus in his latter-day interpretation of history remained in tune with Moses and the Hebraic covenant. The miracles associated with him were signs no different than those associated with Moses: they were merely indications of the central importance of the written texts to come, the testaments of the Covenant between YHWH and the Jews. Neither the word nor the significance of the term *Christian* was ever known to Jesus. He saw for the Jews what Moses had first seen: a way to continue the trek out of slavery, mental and physical, in order to bring the new light of Jewish thought to the world.

In the days when Jesus studied the background of the Covenant, the reinterpretation of it was a common theme. A popular collection of the sayings of rabbis (a precursor to the Talmud chapter, *Avot*, "Fathers," and the adjunct "Sayings of the Fathers") was edited by the Pharisees. In it, the covenantal dialogue was conceived as one between "Israel" (rather than Moses) and its fathering (rather than legislating) God. So now, the Chosen People are not only a sacred audience for the Torah or a "nation of priests" but are represented as incarnate by the term "Israel." It would be a short step from this incarnate Israel to the incarnated Jesus, embraced by his Jewish disciples and followers as the "Son of Man." When Jesus referred to himself in this way, he would be extending the idea of the covenanted Israel to himself.

The complex historical education that allowed Jesus to negotiate his relation to the Covenant was founded on Moses' envisioning of the future. For Moses, the Torah text marks the Covenant with an Israel-in-the-land that is yet to be—they are still an assortment of tribes in the wilderness of Sinai. But Jesus is already the fruit of the Covenant as a Jewish citizen in the land. Yet when he reads and studies the Torah, as if written by Moses, he is also witness to the creation of Hebraic culture that elaborates the Covenant into the many more books of the full Hebrew Bible, down through the centuries. It is within this Hebraic culture that Jesus can conceive of himself as creating additional text to parallel Moses—when engaged in interpreting the Covenant.

For it is there, in the Hebrew Bible's Book of Daniel, that the concept of a "kingdom of heaven" was read by Jesus, suggesting that the boundary between man and God, namely the Covenant, had now been extended. In other words, the realm of God could be conceived of as pushed further into the realm of man. The "king of the universe" could further elaborate his kingdom by extending Moses' journey on earth into one of Jesus walking it as a rabbi interpreter.

The Book of Daniel was composed not long before the Maccabean revolution that restored Israel's sovereignty. Less than two
centuries before Jesus was born, a Jewish sect of ancestral rabbis,
known as the Hasidim, explored the ideas of an afterlife and a kingdom of heaven. These newly elaborated Jewish ideas reinforced the
desire for the nation's freedom, in which Jewish culture could be
rejuvenated. Thus the Hasidim of this time prepared the ground
for the Pharisees and other Jewish movements that would project
a heavenly Israel and therefore a redeeming afterlife.

The Maccabeans made of this influence a mix of religious and
political redemptive ideas that reinterpreted the Covenant, and it
was in this spirit of reinterpreting that Jesus was born. Centuries
before, an explicit afterlife attached to the martyrdoms suffered
by Hebrew prophets, so that by the time of the figure of Daniel,
the idea had become palpable of a Messianic leader who was both
a political and a spiritual one. The time of Daniel found the people
of Israel in peril, per usual; this time, from the invading Hellenic
kings installed in Syria on their northern border. The Book of
Daniel encouraged the Jews to envision their eventual triumph—
but in order to disguise this from their enemy, the history and
politics in the book were submerged into a prophetic vision of the
future, complete with signs of miracles and divine intervention.
The book would thus appear to the Syrians mere mythic fantasy, as
if modern science fiction. But these were the signs that Jesus would
himself use in his own ministry. And in order to use them as he did,
a deep Jewish education was first required.

When we go back to Jesus as a boy making his first trip to Jerusalem, with his parents Mary and Joseph, we learn what they are about
to learn: Jesus already had the temperament of a biblical scholar. In
the second chapter of Luke's gospel, we're told that this trip was
a Passover pilgrimage. As the events unfold, we can assume that
it was Jesus who urged his parents to take him to see the Temple.
No doubt Jesus had been encouraged by his rabbi-teachers in Galilee to visit not merely the awesome sight of the Temple and its sur-
roundings, but also the many circles of rabbis and students who

would congregate in the holy city at this time. What happens next is described as an "accident," but we readers have been prepared for its larger significance.

It was time for Mary and Joseph's family, which included many relatives and their children as well, to return to Nazareth, and they began their journey. After less than a day, Mary discovered that Jesus was not with them; his absence had been overlooked in the hubbub of leaving. Mary and Joseph returned to Jerusalem and after desperate searching found Jesus "in the Temple sitting among the teachers, listening to them and asking them questions." Clearly, Jesus was at home in the Temple, and also at home in the depths of Jewish study.

So it is not very likely that Jesus was apprenticed to his father as a carpenter, though he would no doubt have helped out. During these periods of helping his father in the district of artisans near the main street of Nazareth, Jesus would become comfortable and familiar with all types of workingmen and tradesmen—and not like a boy who grew up in a rabbi's family. If we consider the boy Moses at a similar age, his studies in the royal school would include the science of medicine, an Egyptian field that would bring these elite Egyptian royals into contact with ordinary people and their various wounds and illnesses. Thus Moses, too, was never uncomfortable among common people.

Still, even in the realm of medicine, the most vital focus of study for Moses was on texts. We know this today from the recovery of Egyptian medical scrolls. One in particular, which was displayed at the Metropolitan Museum of Art in New York several years ago, extended over so many walls that it could hardly be thought of as a single volume. There were chapters on how to treat and heal every type of disease known to the ancient Egyptians; there were also chapters with explicit and complex instructions on how to perform operations and all manner of surgery. In addition to the text, written in an Egyptian shorthand rather than classical hieroglyphics, there were accompanying drawings of medical procedures as well as of medicinal plants and mixtures.

These illustrations were most exquisite, in colored inks and ample detail. Parts of the body and its internal organs were also visualized, and thus we can imagine the visual acuity that Moses would later bring to the building of the Tabernacle in the desert, as described in the Torah. We can also understand how the plagues of disease that Moses brought to the Egyptians (and would later encounter among his own people in the desert) were not unfamiliar to him. The laws of diet and the strictures of purity that are part of the Mosaic text were also health measures that Moses had studied in Egypt—and which he now transformed into a moral dimension in the Torah, imbuing the Israelite society with a scientific spirit. The elaboration of this moral law was not only studied but still argued among Jewish sages at the time of Jesus, and the questions Jesus brought to his rabbinic circle—and also answered of them— were likewise imbued with moral and spiritual dimensions.

Jesus had a cousin, a young man of his age from Mary's family, named Yochanan, translated as "John." It is unlikely that he went by the name of John the Baptist in his time—baptism was already a common Jewish custom going back many centuries. John was also a rabbi, and as we have seen he gave to baptism an interpretation additional to its common one of purification. According to John, one could now be purified in the "kingdom of heaven," in addition to reading about this idea of heaven in the Ancient Hebrew prophets. "Make a straight highway for our God/ Across the desert," echoes through the Book of Isaiah.

In other words, the boundary between natural and supernatural will be pushed clearly into the landscape, and Israel will become the "kingdom of priests" that was promised to Moses in the Covenant. So John was making the Prophet's metaphor literal, suggesting that the kingdom of heaven was at hand. And Jesus would act on that suggestion, turning his ministry into an acting-out of a Mosaic journey toward a promised kingdom of heaven.

Even before Jesus visited him, John anticipated a living figure in the form of a messiah. "Israel" had already become personified in the Hebrew prophetic writings, described as the eternal or heavenly

Israel that God could speak to as if it were a person. The Prophet
Isaiah in the sixth century BCE had anticipated the appearance of a
messiah who would represent the kingdom of heaven—someone
descended, in fact, from King David. So when Jesus goes to meet
John, the latter recognizes in him such a messianic figure. Not a
supernatural one—not a changing of the Covenant—but a man
who could found a new way to teach and write about the kingdom
of heaven.

So there it was: in the meeting of John and Jesus, the first sign
that Jesus could embody the personified figure of Israel written in
the books of the Jewish Prophets. But on a more literal level, here
were two cousins discovering that each had traveled a similar road
in his Jewish education. There would be one obvious difference.
John, in his ascetic ways, had probably been a member of the Essenes, but in a more extreme form than Jesus had encountered in
Galilee. John had lived in a commune with monastic Essenes, Jews
who were actively living out the concept of a "kingdom of heaven"
in the form of intense study and worship. But John became an outcast from these monastic Essenes, leaving the communal life to
teach among the common people.

Much of the Essene teaching was in line with the Pharisees,
whose interpretations of Moses' Torah were intended to draw out
meaning that was already there—and not to invent a new religion.
In the synagogues in which each would have studied, the cousins
Jesus and John found "Moses' seat," a literal thronelike stone chair.
Here sat a man who would deliver the sermon interpreting the
Torah portion read on Shabbat (the Sabbath). This was a Pharisaic
custom, and thus the Gospel of Matthew refers to the Pharisees as
"those who sit on Moses' seat."

A short while after their meeting, when Jesus heard that John
was in prison, he returned to Capernaum in Galilee, a town in
which he would have earlier studied in a rabbinic circle. And as he
began to teach in Galilean synagogues, Jesus gathered disciples in a
circle of his own. He developed a following, much of it based upon
word of his healing practice. Many rabbis engaged in healing as a

form of affirming the natural power of the Hebrew Bible's text. This
was not magic; it was simply testimony, and the powers ascribed
to Jesus in the Gospels are signs of his textual knowledge. When
the Gospels state that, for example, "he cured them," we are in the
same realm of biblical writing as when Moses worked his miracles
in Egypt. It is a realm of signs that show YHWH participating in
the history of the Jews.

However, YHWH still observes the Covenant and does not
cross the boundary from the supernatural; instead, his interpreters, Moses and Jesus, take the common conventions of their
day—supernatural signs and healings—and reinterpret them
as testimony of YHWH's words in the Bible. This is the way the
Gospels wrote it, as if the crowds that formed around Jesus were
drawn by his supernatural powers. That is the way it was done
in writing, but what happened historically was that the interpretive powers of Jesus were given mythical dimension (in line with
those of Moses) in order to heighten the drama. Because immediately after we read in the Gospel of Matthew that Jesus is drawing crowds, we are confronted with the major text associated with
his life: the Sermon on the Mount. News of this dramatic speech
he delivered in Galilee, echoing Moses and the Jewish Prophets,
would travel far and wide.

> *Happy are you when people abuse you and persecute you and speak
> all kinds of calumny against you on my account. Rejoice and be glad,
> for your reward will be great in heaven; this is how they persecuted the
> prophets before you.*

Jesus is speaking to his new disciples as well as to the crowd in
the Sermon on the Mount, but why would it make sense to refer to
abuses and slanders that had not yet happened? First, the passage
is not unlike one of many ancient Hebrew psalms known to the
audience. In the psalms, it is YHWH whose name is slandered—
or else it is a common Israelite who is abused by others, for calling on YHWH's name. But the psalm reminds the Israelite that he

will have his reward. And so, it will not be long before Jesus in his new ministry will return to his hometown, Nazareth, where he is welcomed to teach in the synagogue. When they heard him, however, this particular audience, made up of people who had known Jesus from childhood, "were astonished." They thought his words and allusions to scriptural power unbelievable. He was the historical son of a carpenter, not of a priest or a powerful rabbi. Yes, they knew he was sent to study in rabbinic circles, but instead of coming home as an ordinary rabbi, he was speaking like a man possessed. "Is not his mother the woman called Mary, and his brothers James and Joseph and Simon and Jude? His sisters too, are they not all here with us? So where did the man get it all?"

So Jesus would have to leave his old friends and neighbors, and even his parents and siblings, precisely because his human history was too well-known to them. Neither his mother nor his father nor any of his family would follow him out. What a terrible blow it must have been. The Gospel of Matthew records that "he did not work many miracles there because of their lack of faith." It could not be clearer that Jesus' "miracles" depended on the willingness to believe of the audience. Without that, the wonders of Jesus dissolved into what they actually were: signs that interpreted the depths of the Hebrew Bible. However, what the Gospel now records is not the dejection of Jesus but rather his comment to the hometown audience as he departs:

"A prophet is only despised in his own country and in his own house."

Here Jesus is echoing Moses, who doubts that the Israelites "will believe me or listen to my words," as he put it to YHWH. Many Hebrew prophets who came later recorded a similar scene of being disbelieved by those who knew them best—that is, those who knew them as ordinary human beings like themselves. By quoting one of them, the Prophet Jeremiah, Jesus has acted like any Pharisaic rabbi, referring his audience back to the authority of the biblical text. In other words, Jesus was not simply referring to himself as the

prophet in "a prophet is only despised in his own country..."—and
yet the audience that knows him misunderstands, and assumes that
he is calling himself a prophet. But he is not; he is instead interpreting a numinous text of Jeremiah in which he's been educated. So
educated, in fact, that those who do trust his words will find themselves caught up in the biblical drama of the kingdom of heaven.

Yet before all this has happened, we must return to the Sermon on the Mount, in which Jesus already anticipates those who
will disbelieve him. And more than that, he already expects to be
persecuted—probably because of what had happened to his cousin,
John the Baptist. (Jesus has not yet learned the details. The public renown of John had caused political ripples that reached King
Herod, and seizing on the occasion, Herod's wife asked for John's
head.) At this point in time, before the Sermon on the Mount, however, Jesus knew only that John was imprisoned, though that was
certainly persecution enough. Jesus would also have known that as
he became a more public figure, the same ripples would spread to
no good.

About to give his most public speech of all, there could be little
doubt that a public Jew with a considerable following would come
to antagonize the Roman authorities and their anxious Jewish dep-
uties. Thus Jesus is already anticipating the precursor of Roman
anti-Semitism that Jews throughout the empire—and later, the
Jewish-Christian sects—would suffer. We shall come to understand how Jesus was also a victim of anti-Semitism, long before the
Gospel writers would accuse a hypothetical Jewish court of disputing the Messianic authority of Jesus.

But now, at the Mosaic mount—really a hill—that Jesus and his
disciples ascend before the Jewish crowds of Galilee, Jesus speaks
as a proud Jew. He opens by quoting lines from several Hebrew
Psalms: "Happy are those who are persecuted in the cause of
right:/ Theirs is the kingdom of heaven." It is a direct evocation
of his cousin John's fate, for it was John the Baptist who took the
doctrine of the Essenes on the afterlife and made of it a metaphorical kingdom that could touch the hearts of the common people.

Nevertheless, it is the sovereign kingdom of God and his earthly Chosen People that holds the center of Jesus' thought here, just as it had in the Jewish prophets before him. It is this root in Israel's earthly kingdom that reveals Jesus as what we would call today a Zionist. For it is only in their promised land of the Covenant that Jews can fulfill the ideal of Moses' Torah, even for Jews in Alexandria and Rome; and embodying that prophetic tradition, the "light to the nations" for Jesus shone from Mount Zion.

Among the many lines quoted from Psalms, Jesus opened his discourse on the Mount with this one: "Happy the pure in heart/ They shall see God." This is also an echo of the historical record of Moses' journey with the Israelites toward the Promised Land. As recorded in the Torah, concerning Aaron and a crowd of Israel's leaders whom Moses gathered around him,

> *They saw the God of Israel beneath whose feet there was, it seemed, a sapphire pavement pure as the heavens themselves. He [God] laid no hand on these notables of the sons of Israel: they gazed on God. (Exodus 24:9–11)*

Here is the Mosaic prefiguring of the Sermon on the Mount: the audience of Israel gathered to hear God. Jesus next reminds us in his sermon of the psalm that makes the promised land personal for all those "pure in heart." And then, Jesus will compare this purity with those "scribes and Pharisees" who will "never get into the kingdom of Heaven." The impurity he ascribes to the Pharisees (the "scribes" referred to here might simply be called lawyers) is that of power—the political power of their accommodation with the Romans and their kings. For immediately afterward, Jesus is speaking as if he were the purest of Pharisees himself when he quotes the Ten Commandments from Moses' Torah. "You must not murder; and if anyone does murder he must answer for it before the court." Further, "You have learned how it was said: You must not commit adultery. But I say this to you: If a man looks at a woman lustfully, he has already committed adultery with her in his heart."

Is Jesus here demanding a greater purity than any person could rightfully fulfill? Is he not out-Phariseeing the Pharisees? But it is not as it seems. These are the words of a powerful writer who is playing with the conventional beliefs of his audience. For in the very next sentence, Jesus instructs: "If your right eye should cause you to sin, tear it out and throw it away." None of his Jewish listeners are going to be tearing out any eyes; instead, they are hearing that the Creator's great power exists in their own minds and hearts, just as the Psalms had sung, and just as Moses had demonstrated when he threw the Ten Commandments against the rock, smashing them.

And what had the Israelites done that was impure? Why, they had fashioned a pure idol, the golden calf. From the historical record in Moses' Torah to the words of Jesus on the Mount: "If your right hand should cause you to sin, cut it off and throw it away." This is visionary writing, not literal lawmaking. From the Torah itself, we learn that a remnant of idolaters had to be "cut off"; they were the exiles who could not bear to leave Egypt and needed an Egyptian representation of heaven. For that is what the "Heavenly Cow" (not literally a calf) actually was: a deity of compassion, but not the one waiting for us in the singular kingdom of heaven that Moses inscribes and Jesus interprets. We need to know more about the Egyptian "Heavenly Cow," since it would have been part of Moses' education in Egypt, but for now we are beginning to encounter and understand the passionate writing of Moses and Jesus.

Jesus elaborates: "You have learnt how it was said: 'Eye for eye and tooth for tooth.' But I say this to you: Offer the wicked man no resistance. On the contrary, if anyone hits you on the right cheek, offer him the other as well." Again, we know that Jesus is not asking his audience, or the Pharisees in general, to literally cease their resistance to Rome. What the words tell us is what a great writer is doing when he magnifies the written words of Moses and renders them indelible.

Indeed, to this day there is scarcely a person on the planet who has not heard of the improbable gesture of "turning the cheek." Yet even as Jesus uses this term, he has taken it from an older Hebraic source. And even as Moses had written, "Eye for eye and tooth for tooth," that saying came from a much older code of law that Moses was raising to a personal level, just as each Jewish individual was to personally inscribe in his or her heart the Commandments. It was not to be taken literally; the Jews did not go about taking tooths for tooths. Instead, they did the exact opposite: they inaugurated a moral code of law that would evolve through a hundred generations until it became the early form of the Mishnah—that Jesus himself would have studied among the Pharisees.

By taking the Commandments personally, as Moses taught, it was to become the task of the Jewish people to interpret and elaborate from them a moral life. In this way, even the individual Israelite was uniting him- or herself with the writing of God, as Moses inscribed it in the Torah. It does not matter whether God had a pen in his hand or a sword when "His mighty hand" helped deliver the Jews from Egypt. What matters is that Moses and Jesus will go to any length to impress upon their audience that the moral law can't be changed, either by the fashion of the times or the particular culture in which it is interpreted. If "eye for eye" suggests revenge for a loss, Moses has already turned this archaic saying on its cheek by making it clear that this law could no longer be applied. Instead, each specific case of social conflict had to be understood and interpreted on its own merits.

Suddenly, the right of the individual had overturned the law of the powerful. Each individual, however poor, had recourse through a body of interpretation and refinement of the law that would eventually fill countless volumes. Indeed, the Jew who followed the Torah found himself in a new world of rights and privileges that had a moral foundation. For this, he would need a land and a Hebraic culture—precisely the direction that Moses was showing. And when Jesus turned his cheek, he was also following Moses, who had turned the laws of the powerful into the laws of the individual heart—as if it were a kingdom of heaven rather than a kingdom of corruptible power.

As we return to the Sermon on the Mount, Jesus is saying: "You must therefore be perfect, just as your heavenly father is perfect."

Aside from quoting the Torah again, Jesus affirms but also goes beyond the understanding that we are made in the image of God; he interprets that we must strive to better ourselves as that we must become like God. It will only be a natural progression from this idealization to the looking at Jesus as godlike. But again, Jesus the writer—the interpretive reinscriber of the Covenant—is not using words that are simply literal, nor does he mean that if you are "imperfect" you are a total loss. Jesus in this context is an author, and he is echoing a numinous text, that of both Moses and the "heavenly Father" who has called himself YHWH.

According to the interpretation that Jesus would learn and that later became part of the Mishnah (the rendition of the Law in the Talmud, linked to the Covenant in being called an "Oral Torah"), God enters the world through the original written Torah, so that Israel's history is his. It's a common mistake, however, to think categorically that an "Oral Torah," like an oral literature, comes first, prefiguring a written one. In fact, the concept of an Oral Torah developed almost a millennium after the written one. It was Moses' written Torah that offered us the chance to learn YHWH's desire, and one of the commentaries on its code of moral law became the Oral Torah tradition—to be elaborated in Jesus' day by the Pharisees.

As the author of his sermon, Jesus embodies that learning of the Torah. That is why he speaks to his audience in the same way that God speaks to Israel: Moses had already shown that the Covenant will unfold for each individual citizen of Israel to feel connected to those who saw and heard God at Mount Sinai. After Jesus' death, as the Gospels were beginning to be written, Peter emphasized to Paul that the meaning of Israel includes the followers of both Jesus and Moses. In other words, the Jewish followers of Jesus would remain tied to Moses, in creative tension within the Jewish community. Although it did not turn out that way and the Christian movement left its home behind, we can feel that creative tension in every word of the Sermon on the Mount as it echoes Moses' Torah.

And as the sermon continues, its Jewish audience recognizes that the insight Jesus is expressing comes from a close reading of the Hebrew Bible. Phrases from the Book of Job, the Book of Psalms, and the Book of Jeremiah are behind the following passage, which is typical:

> *Do not store up treasures for yourselves on earth, where moths and woodworms destroy them and thieves break in and steal. But store up treasures for yourselves in heaven, where neither moth nor woodworms destroy them and thieves cannot break in and steal. For where your treasure is, there will your heart be also.*

Does this mean one is not even to open a bank account? Of course not. Jesus speaks as an educated man—and that means, like the Pharisaic rabbis, he teaches us not to take things literally. If there is anything literal here, it is the insistence on our own deaths. The moths and woodworms testify to that; the worms will even break into the grave. In contrast, the world of the spirit is represented not only by "heaven" and "heart" but by these very words themselves, indestructible after many centuries, taking us back to the writers who completed the Torah in Jerusalem, building upon the words of Moses.

Nobody in the audience in Galilee on that day was going to go home and disperse their worldly goods. Neither was the town police going to stop chasing thieves, or owners remove the padlocks from their stores. No matter how primitive this audience in Galilee is portrayed, Jesus speaks to them as educated Jews who understand that behind the literal story and its disturbing news of death and loss, there lies the Mosaic joy of a numinous text: the one being written as a sermon by Jesus and the one he echoes in the Hebrew Bible and its origins in Moses.

It was just so when Moses copied down "Eye for eye and tooth for tooth." It was not YHWH that he was copying but rather an older text which he would now reveal needed reinterpretation. There were few among Moses' educated audience who did not hear the echo of the archaic *lex talionis*, and also hear the way Moses and his God play upon it—a spiritual play of words. "Thou shall not commit murder" is followed by the people saying, "'Speak to us yourself,' they said to Moses, 'and we will listen; but do not let God speak to us, or we shall die.'" Here is an early justification for the author Moses to be a writer. The primitive fear of dying in the literal presence of gods was a superstition held long before. So what is the spiritual play that Moses makes of it in the Torah we still read today? He will do the "speaking" himself, which for mankind is precisely the civilized act of writing: no one has died from reading.

Thus, "You shall not murder" sounds radically new because, unlike "a tooth for a tooth," a situation where human beings no longer commit murder is unheard of. Except, that is, in a revelatory poetic vision such as the Torah has provided at the foot of Mount Sinai, and which Jesus would later echo on his mount. In place of literalism, the authored quality of Moses' text and Jesus' text demands from its audience a knowledge of sources. In order to know that Moses did not invent the phrase "eye for eye," the educated Jew had to know history—just as the original Jewish audience for Jesus knew the older biblical texts that he echoed.

. . .

Let's pause a moment at this crucial point, right here at the mountains of both Moses and Jesus, because it suggests an early source of anti-Semitism. It has everything to do with resentment of the written Torah and of a Jewish education. It coalesces around the falsehood that the Jews who followed Moses as well as Jesus were so primitive that they did not understand the writerly authority of these men. In other words, that the biblical audience was so uneducated in the Bible itself that they might assume that "eye for eye" was God's law—instead of actually being the spiritual expansion of it, as expressed in the Torah. We saw the same misunderstanding in the caricature of Shylock, which Shakespeare used to expose literal-mindedness in the audience for his *Merchant of Venice*. It would be no different if non-Christians were to accuse Jesus of primitive violence, since he wishes to "tear out the eye and throw it away" of those who look at a woman lustfully.

So when Jesus had finished his sermon, "his teaching made

a deep impression on the people because he taught them with authority, and not like their own scribes." *These* scribes are not to be thought of as writers; they are mere copiers, and because they are only copying, they can serve to flatten and literalize the text. In contrast, Jesus woke his audience up with a true writer's *authority*. For what has been described as Jesus' authority is his spiritually joyous play with words and Jewish sources. It is the same authority the Jews requested of Moses when they begged him to please get the words from God on his own and then bring these words to them. Clearly, these Galilean Jews listening to Jesus were moved by the interpretive power of his words, and how else could this be known to them without a knowledge of the text that was being interpreted? Only resentment would lead to the falsehood that Jesus was making up his words out of thin air.

. . .

Before Moses returned to Egypt to speak to Pharaoh with the words of YHWH, he said: "I am slow of speech, why should Pharaoh listen to me?" Critics have argued about just what this said about Moses, but it doesn't really matter. It might even mean that he was worried that the biblical language of YHWH would be difficult to understand by an Egyptian. Regardless, YHWH says: "See, I make you as a god for Pharaoh, and Aaron your brother is to be your prophet." Well, if God has a prophet in Moses, then Moses must have his own prophet if he is to be godlike—that much is clear from the text. But what irony or humor can we be missing here?

Only if we forget that this text has a human author will we miss the authority that its Hebrew writer is expressing. Once again, it is a display of spiritual joy in the words as well as with the characters in this numinous drama of God and man in a contest of wit. Yet even the downtrodden former slaves that will follow Moses into the desert are possessed of a metaphorical wit. "To Moses they said, 'Were there no graves in Egypt that you must lead us out to die in the wilderness?'" If his slave followers can speak with such a quick wit, what chance would Moses have with them if he "was slow of speech"? Obviously none, and thus we have yet further proof that Moses had to be recognized by all as an educated man. And so too were so-called sons of Israel to a significant degree, because soon they would recite along with Moses a great poem of victory after crossing the Sea. It is a poem made of a metaphorical wit that is kin to—and part of—the Jewish education of Jesus.

. . .

This is a good point at which to remind ourselves of just how complex a character Moses was, and how much that complexity has been lost. The contemporary literary critic Adam Kirsch, in a recent review of a book about the death of Socrates, states that "Socrates has been, and should be, the most revered figure in Western culture, only Jesus excepted." But why is Moses missing here? Perhaps it's obvious to say that both Socrates and Jesus chose their own deaths. And in that choice, there is the irony of the deathlessness of their words and ideas. There is further irony in their most famous sayings, whether it be "turn the other cheek," as we have already heard Jesus say, or Socrates, speaking of the eternal soul as a type of student: "She has been a true disciple of philosophy and has practiced how to die easily. And is not philosophy the practice of death?" Neither Jesus nor Socrates appears simply fearless in the face of death; rather, they collaborate with it, and make of their own deaths a drama filled with anxiety—in addition to the triumph of an unflinching life in the face of death.

In contrast, it seems that Moses' life (as seen through the prism of Christian Humanism) is one of great drama that is nevertheless subordinate to God's presence. Thus the image of Moses as merely "God's secretary" has mistakenly taken hold in our liberal education. But the time has come to change that perception. We have just seen God speaking to Moses with great irony, telling him that he will play the god and Aaron will play the prophet. We don't really need to hear Moses' reply, because there can be no doubt that he understood and embraced such irony. He will use it himself when he speaks to Pharaoh as well as his own people.

Further, when we arrive at the "Song of Victory," recited by Moses and the people after crossing the Sea of Reeds unharmed, there is a sublime irony that attests to Moses' authorship:

Through the power of your arm they [the Egyptians] are still as stone
as your people pass, YHWH,
as the people pass whom you purchased.
You will bring them and plant them
on the mountain that is your own ...

The contrast between the Egyptian army "still as stone" and the
Israelites "planted" on a fertile mountain is exquisite irony—for
stone is no doubt what the mountain is made of. Out of this stone
will come the stone tablets. There is irony as well in God's "purchase" of His people, since it refers to the very human transaction
of redeeming property (almost as commonplace as going to a pawn
shop). And indeed, this redemption is rendered all the more sublime by YHWH's human-like participation in the scene.

Earlier, YHWH had instructed Moses to request of the Pharaoh
that his people Israel be let go "three days' journey into the desert,"
in order to worship him at his mountain. In fact, the mountain here
referred to is a Midianite site, of which Moses would have learned
from the Midianites. Their god spoke in a volcanic speech of flame
and thunder—suggesting the mountain was formerly a volcano.
But when we go back to Moses' Egyptian education prior to his
flight to Midian, we find a similar deity who is worshiped as the
supreme—and only—high god. In one Hymn among hundreds
sung to the creator-god, Amun-Ra, we hear:

People fall down immediately for fear
that his name will be uttered knowingly or unknowingly.
There is no god able to call him by it.

So it was no problem for Moses to accept a god whose name was
ineffable, based on his Egyptian education, just as he could envision a god speaking on a mountain, based on his Midianite education. The huge Book of Hymns in the Egyptian canon—a far larger
book than the Hebrew Bible's Book of Psalms—contains the further poems of Akhenaten's monotheistic revolution, the period that

lasted but sixty years, yet ended only a generation before Moses was born. Moses would have learned of it among the Palace teachers and Temple priests. Because even though Akhenaten's religious innovation was now suppressed, knowledge of it lived on, as did some of its texts. The single god of this monotheistic revolution was represented by the sun, yet he was no typical sun-god. He was the creator of life but he was also a hidden god, and his invisibility was manifest in how dangerous it is for a human creature to stare directly into the sun.

> *Though you are far, your rays are on earth;*
> *Though one sees you, your strides are hidden . . .*
> *You who made seed grow in women,*
> *Who make water into men;*
> *Who vivify the son in his mother's womb,*
> *Who soothe to still his tears,*
> *You nurse in the womb!*
> *You giver of breath . . .*
> *How many are your deeds,*
> *Though hidden from sight,*
> *O Sole God beside whom there is none!*

Although the influence is plain, there is no need to say that Moses borrowed from Egyptian religion—or from Midianite religion or any other tradition. The Israelite revelation is unique because it has transformed rather than borrowed the earlier sources that Moses would have known. The Israelite culture itself absorbed Egyptian knowledge during its four hundred years of living in Egypt. We will see how Moses was able to transform his education once we've grasped what was taught in the ancient culture of Egypt. But we won't find direct reference to it in Moses' Torah because the great revelation in Sinai has no need to remember it.

We can find memory of Egypt in the text when we read it now, however, just as the repressed memory of his Hebrew people returns to Moses only when he is a mature adult. Only then would he learn of the far older Covenant between God and Abraham in the promised land. Most likely the Israelites themselves had repressed it during their many centuries of captivity. For they never speak of it to Moses, nor does he refer to it before the exodus from Egypt.

Still, this knowledge returns, probably because the remnant of Israelites who never left Canaan and were never enslaved held on to the earliest Jewish sources of their written text. Moses would have known of them, either through the Midianites or through direct contact during the years he was in flight from Egypt. When the burning bush revealed its voice, it was also a shock of recognition to Moses. The voice of Abraham's God returned to awaken Moses' repressed memory of his Israelite origins. Building on his Egyptian education, Moses elaborated this voice into a dynamic physical presence.

For instance, in Egypt Moses learned a love of the face, as it is represented on the mummy case—and this he would transform into the crucial "face-to-face" encounter with YHWH at Mount Sinai. And from the Egyptian Akhenaten religion he was able to reinterpret the Canaanite origin of the Jews, transforming it into a facing of the entire cosmos: YHWH ruled everywhere, above and below, and most crucially, unlike the Egyptian sun-god, he desired to be intimate with human beings, and to speak with them about establishing his eternal Covenant.

The continuing record of the journey with YHWH in Sinai is taken up in the Book of Deuteronomy, the fifth Book of Moses. It is this book that is "rediscovered" in a forgotten archive by King Josiah of Israel in the eighth century BCE. For the history of the Jews, this would be the most significant return of the repressed, because Deuteronomy amplifies the moral law in the Book of Leviticus (or at least a portion thereof) that Moses was writing during the long years of the Sinai journey. Deuteronomy would be appended to the earlier books attributed to Moses, and it would be forgotten that they were all completed in their written form in different periods after the founding of the kingdom of Israel in Jerusalem. Whatever the sources of Moses' actual writing that survived into the Hebraic culture, they were taken up and written down once more by the great Jewish authors who came in the centuries prior to King Josiah's rediscovery of them. Together, these books of Moses' Torah constituted a small library testifying to the origin of human history and the Jewish discovery of God—and most significantly, the Covenant written and rewritten that was created out of this discovery.

· · ·

And just as we can rediscover today the Egyptian education of Moses, we're also able to explore the Jewish education of Jesus in Galilee—and to recognize its dependence upon what Moses transmitted and wrote. We do not expect to find the Egyptian texts that Moses studied within the Torah itself, and we will not find in the Gospels of the New Testament an account of the rabbis and texts among whom Jesus studied. The historical life of each man is dramatized by the journey he takes, and not by the experience from which he comes. This is not the way we write biographies today, nor is it the way our universities teach, but we must encounter the original context. In academe today, it is more usual to generalize from the facts rather than to dramatize them. We do not go to the university for theater, although the cosmic theaters of Greece and Israel are studied there.

Yet without the dramatic, we lose the sense of how history could be embodied in a man. It is not a radical innovation that Jesus was seen as God incarnate, for it was quite common that prophets and later Jewish sages were viewed as the Torah incarnate. The Torah itself is a numinous text: it is already an incarnation of the encounter with the Covenant. Certainly the incarnation of Jesus goes further, since it is not only the Torah that he represents but also the God speaking in it. Nevertheless, the numinous scenes of Jesus among his disciples and followers are rendered as drama and not in terms of academic knowledge. The more we are aware of the difference between intellectual generalization and the cosmic theater that Moses and Jesus embodied, the more we will understand how it happened. It took the form of a journey through time and personal experience, but the drama was enacted on the invariable stage of the Covenant.

The models for Jesus' journey did not come solely from Israel's prophets and their dramas of speaking truth to power in their time. The pioneering sages of the Mishnah, who studied and reformulated Israel's history in dramatic fashion, provided the model of an educated man. The Talmud, which later evolves out of the Pharisaic sages, is also not an academic text; it does not merely generalize about what has happened. Rather, it re-creates the drama of thinking and encountering the Covenant. It preserves the Hebraic cosmic theater and all that flowed from it.

What we are beginning to learn about the actual history of the Pharisees changes the picture we're given in the Gospels of a movement inclined to codify law based on the biblical text. Instead, we find they are devoted to interpreting the Bible. Since Jesus is primarily represented as an interpreter, the Pharisees as codifiers rather than interpreters come off badly. But when we now look at the Gospels from the perspective of how and when they were written, the relation of Jesus to his mentors, the Pharisees, changes.

The Gospels come into their final written form just after the fall of the Temple in Jerusalem and the destruction of the Jewish nation by the Romans (70 AD). This was not a catastrophe that could have been anticipated by the Pharisees, and it is only *afterward* that the emphasis on a moral code became crucial to Israel's survival as a religion. So this is what the Gospel writers saw: the beginnings of the Mishnah, Jewish moral law, were being written in their day by surviving Pharisees. But it is not how the historical Jesus knew the Pharisees, among whom he studied and was called rabbi. For in Jesus' day, before the Temple was burnt and leveled by the Romans, the central concern of the Pharisees was the Jewish education of the majority of Jews who were not of the aristocratic and ruling classes.

It was an education in reading and interpreting the Hebrew Bible that is absent from the picture of the Pharisees given in the Gospels, where precious little about the ideas and programs of the Pharisees is emphasized. Indirectly, however, we do learn from the Gospel of Matthew that they attend synagogues, are called "rabbis," and "proselytize"—that is, seek to educate. We can also discover, in Mark and Luke, that they are particular about who they eat with (suggesting they kept kosher, at least some of them, some of the time); they do not work on the Sabbath; they wash their hands before eating; and they allow for divorce. Further, although it is not emphasized, it's evident the Pharisees believe in a kingdom of heaven or afterlife that is not at odds with Jesus and would have influenced him.

It was only after the destruction of Israel (Jesus himself had died almost forty years before) that the Gospel writers would have forgotten the vanishing Sadducees and resented the surviving Pharisees for their prior devotion to the Temple (even as they built synagogues throughout the land) and their insistence on strict interpretation of such ideas as incarnation. However, Jesus' education was dependent on those synagogues, as well as the Temple, where he will go to state his truth among the priesthood that is not all that sympathetic to the Pharisees either.

We must consider how distorted the history of Israel could become in merely fifty years after Jesus' death—and how that distortion survives today. A popular current dictionary defines *Pharisee* in this manner:

> *A member of an ancient Jewish sect, a lay democratic party among the Jews, whose legalistic interpretation of the Mosaic Law led to an obsessive concern with the mass of rules covering the details of everyday life; anyone more careful of the outward forms than of the spirit of religion, a formalist; a very self-righteous or hypocritical person.*

Yes, the Pharisees respected the daily Temple rites, and yet they also worked against them by democratizing education. Jesus, too, was no disrespecter of the Temple, only of some of the customs associated with it. We could say that his critique was quite Pharisaic in its desire for reform. Yet by focusing upon the exaggerated "obsessions" of the Pharisees, the New Testament encourages further caricature. No mention is made of the Pharisees as teachers of reading and writing. Since writing is associated with power, and what Jewish power there was under the Romans is used as a foil for Jesus, we rarely hear of Jesus as a reader and writer himself—as if he would be tainted by the power that writing (and its prevalence among the aristocratic rulers) bestows.

Nor are we allowed to imagine that Jesus' disciples and followers are literate, though many prove to be. We can now estimate that almost a million Jews in Israel at the time of Jesus were reading and writing. Even the ongoing Jewish biblical commentary that developed into the Talmud was based on the idea of an "Oral Torah"—for the same reasons that Jesus' teaching was represented as oral. Writing, after all, was at this time associated with the Roman Empire, with its pagan sources and written mythic traditions. If power corrupts, then writing might also, or so it might have seemed to the early Jewish-Christian sect.

. . .

It is perhaps easier to understand now why Moses, too, is not pictured as a reader or a writer in his Egyptian and Midianite education. Egyptian power was not only symbolized by its monumental engineering and art, but also by its sacred writing and text. However, we may rediscover today how the Torah transforms this aversion to writing into a new kind of writing—one whose incorruptible power is anchored in a worldly, thorough, and comprehensive moral law. And further, we can witness the coming into being of this written document—as it unfolds to become Torah and Hebrew Bible—in dramatic narrative and poetry. And it is Moses who is rendered foremost a writer at its origin.

Through the biblical books ending with Deuteronomy, Moses is seen writing the narrative and the laws he has absorbed in Sinai—and this is exactly what the people of Israel expect of him. In various renditions of this same description, we read, "These are the words of the Covenant which YHWH ordered Moses to make [that is, 'write'] with the sons of Israel . . ." As here in Deuteronomy, and all the way to its last paragraph, the figure of Moses the writer is crucial. The final paragraph begins: "Since then, never has there been such a prophet in Israel as Moses, the man YHWH knew face to face." Yet what survives are not scenes of YHWH and Moses "face to face," which would constitute the numinous meeting between God and man, but rather the text itself of which Moses wrote the original sources in Sinai. Thus the Torah itself is numinous, raising the power of writing to the equivalence of eternal survival. If the Covenant is true and the Chosen People are to survive, then the written Torah ensures it—for it is both a record of witness and the text of witness itself.

There can be little doubt that much later the largely Jewish writers of the New Testament understood that they too must have a written text that is numinous. In their case, however, it is not the writing which becomes so; instead, it is the portrayal of Jesus as supernatural that lends the scenes in which he appears a numinous quality. He is, in other words, the "torah" incarnate. It might not have been such a problem for the Jewish sages of his time to accept this rendition—if only Jesus, like Moses, had been represented as a writer of his own words.

But this did not happen. Jesus was rendered by the writers of the New Testament as an embodiment of a Torah that needed no words of further interpretation, superseding the written Torah of Moses. In essence, Jesus represented the end of writing as a numinous interaction with the Covenant, and with both Jewish and human history. We might say he was the last Jewish writer of the Covenant in the line of Moses, except that the Gospel writers were not as devoted as was Jesus to the written authority of Moses. Other Jewish sages before and after Jesus were understood as incarnating the Torah, in the sense that they read and interpreted its numinous text. Yet the Gospels prefer a Jesus who is no longer a reader or writer in any sense.

This is not, however, a sudden break. In fact, it was commensurate with the real "break" in history that all Jews of the time were experiencing: destruction of the nation and the seeming end of its history in 70 AD. Nevertheless, it was not to be the end. It actually resulted in a new beginning for Jewish texts. The Pharisees had begun to compose an "Oral Torah"—originated by Moses but not written down by him—that would frame the Torah and the Covenant with a new written text, the Talmud. So we can see now that both the New Testament and the Oral Torah were becoming rival texts whose authors were thought of not as writers but as "witnesses."

For the Jewish-Christian sect, their new "torah" witnessed to the life of Jesus and his disciples. And for the new efflorescence of Judaism, the Talmud was also represented as a witness, though of a very different kind. What the sages who speak and write in the Talmud (which includes the written law of the Mishnah and "Sayings of the Fathers") are providing are words of witness—not to the life of Moses or any of the prophets who descend from him, but to the written text itself, the Five Books of Moses and all the commentary to come after, down to our present day. Just as we find the "Sayings of Jesus" central to the Gospel history, the "Sayings of the Fathers"—the Jewish sages, among whom many lived at the time of Jesus—parallel the New Testament.

Yet the historical scenes these Jewish sages or rabbis portray are a written record of the drama taking place after the death of Jesus and after the fall of the Temple. It's a drama that anchors the Covenant in a moral interpretation, but it is always based on an interpretation of the biblical text. As we are coming to see, the New Testament is also built upon interpreting the Hebrew Bible, yet to a different purpose: it wants to remove the burden of interpretation and replace it with the life of Jesus. To the extent that we can recover these parallels between the re-forming Jewish people in their post-Temple exile and the Jewish-Christian sect, we will see how Jesus more and more resembles Moses as a figure who interprets, writes, and inspires biblical text, rather than stands apart.

As the figure of a writer, then, we're forced to refocus the historical scenes in the life of Jesus, especially his education. And this becomes a further mode of interpretation—one Jesus has left to us, just as Moses had done. When we return to the biography of Moses, its relation to the biography of Jesus can be further considered.

How did Moses come to speak the words of God to the Egyptian Pharaoh who was, for all intents and purposes, his adoptive father—or one of that father's sons, who would then be as a brother to Moses? If what is written in the Torah didn't happen like real life, and if it wasn't framed in scenes of real life, it wouldn't have had the staying power to become the backbone of Jesus' education.

So the ultimate question about how Moses' text survived is also about how the Jewish people survived. It is their survival that is dramatized in the Torah, and the life of Moses is the paradigm of survival beyond death: he lives in the concept of an eternal *written* Covenant. For this, Moses must have an education, and now we must begin to recover it with the aid of contemporary ideas of history. How does a founding writer, and even such a great personality as Moses, come to be?

. . .

The available facts about the period of Moses' growth and maturity are few; instead, there is a wealth of cultural and literary contextual knowledge that is beginning to be applied. In the same way, it has been common for biographers of Jesus to admit that few facts about his life can be substantiated. Yet the historical work goes forward, because so many aspects of daily life at the time continue to be unearthed, weaving an indelible background for Jesus' actual circumstances.

To compare Moses and Jesus in terms of how they are remembered in the Jewish and Christian religions means acknowledging that the Jewish writers of both Hebrew Bible and New Testament would have left out much—simply because they assumed it was common knowledge. We've lost sight of these essential details by now, knowledge that was gone with the fall of the Roman Empire and even before.

We do have new ways for recovering such information, however, ways of reading the texts and reimagining what the authors knew as well as what sources they made use of. So as we reenter the lives of Moses and Jesus, we are also engaging the history of the authors who followed them, writing and elaborating the biblical text. But the biographies have remained so slim because no one has recovered the thing that both men had in common, their complex education. To say, as many have said recently, that Jesus was a Jew must be more than an ecumenical gesture. It is rarely if ever acknowledged that Jesus came from a Jewish culture and was educated in one, which means a living Jewish culture of the time. And we're just beginning to do the same for the slender biography of Moses.

An educated man at the time of Moses was one who could read and write. Since literacy was more common in the time of Jesus, there were at least two versions of what constituted "an educated man." One version was the man of the Roman Empire who received a Hellenistic education in Greek and Latin; the other was also a citizen of the empire, but educated within his or her local culture. In most cases, these local cultures throughout the empire were considered inferior both in the depth of their history and the worldliness of their literature. Israel was an exception; its history was deeper and its Hebrew literature embraced the history of the entire human race.

A rabbi in Israel at the time of the Pharisees would be considered an even more "educated man" than his Hellenized counterpart. Not by the Romans, of course, but it is the Jews who will determine the fundamental meaning of education—and not only going back to Moses, but also under the influence of a rabbi named Jesus. Even in the United States today, we recall that our oldest universities were founded by Christian denominations that instilled the significance of religious history in any serious culture, especially a democratic one. However, when we reconsider the educated man in ancient Egypt, a man or woman who could read and write received a broader education than most of us do today.

In addition to literature and the arts, religion and history, law and diplomacy, the educated Egyptian studied the sciences, including a hands-on knowledge of the healing arts. There was astronomy; there was engineering and architecture. All these were included in a ruling-class education—acquaintance with several other languages included. So we must remember what Moses might have put aside when he reconnected with an Hebraic education in Midian, after fleeing from Egypt the first time. Perhaps he did not so much give up the knowledge he'd acquired in Egypt, but rather applied it toward conceiving of Hebraic culture in new ways.

Most commentators do not consider what Moses left behind when they describe the special attributes and mission of Moses. They find that Moses' original reluctance with taking on God's mission—as it first came to him from the voice in the burning bush—has only to do with Moses' character. But let's take another look at the way Moses first responds to YHWH and the idea of his special mission.

At least four times, Moses offers a different argument for why he is the wrong person for this mission. First, he says he's just not capable of it; not up to it, not good enough, not smart enough. Then, he asks YHWH what his name is, to see if the Israelites will respond to that. After YHWH tells him his name and its derivation, Moses insists that the Israelites won't listen to him. And finally, Moses complains, as we've noted, that he can't speak well—that he is "slow," not smooth-tongued. But YHWH is very patient with all this, and we hardly know why. In the end, YHWH offers to provide the words himself and all Moses will have to do is utter them in a human voice.

And what is it he must say? He needs permission from the Pharaoh to let the Israelites have three days off, in order to go on a "three-day journey into the wilderness" to make a brief sacrifice, in worship of their God. No great sacrifice for the Pharaoh, since his slaves will return and work even harder. You don't need to be an elite lawyer to argue such a case. In fact, it makes more sense that one be a humble underling, except that in this case it is Moses' education and background in Egypt that confers his real authority with Pharaoh. But Moses continues to balk. He even makes YHWH angry, though just for a moment; and then YHWH offers to make Aaron a spokesman for Moses (presumably Aaron will be a more polished "prophet"—with Moses as his soft-spoken god).

So the character of a humble Moses, terribly sincere and without personal ambition, is the one preferred. But the commentators
cannot tell us why this is so, other than suggesting that God had his
reasons for choosing Moses. Yet if we consider the historical situation, it becomes clear that the reticence of Moses was buttressed
by a deep Egyptian education. It was a background that forced him
to think about how he could accomplish what Pharaoh Akhenaten
had failed to do with all his kingly powers, just a generation or so
earlier. Over a period of sixty years, Akhenaten and his queen,
Nefertiti, established a monotheistic order in which the creator
god, represented by the sun, was the only god—and a god who
spoke to his royal servant Akhenaten, just as YHWH was speaking
only to Moses.

And with all the power of Egypt under his control, Akhenaten
still could not ensure that his people would not rebel. That they did,
with a vengeance, tearing down the new monuments to the one
god. Knowing this, how could Moses think to succeed as an outcast
Israelite where Akhenaten had failed as a Pharaoh? Moses' Egyptian education supported him in doubting and resisting the mission
of YHWH. Any other man called in this way, even Moses' brother
Aaron, might not have refused, and might have embraced the mission without reservation. YHWH must have understood that he
needed the strong education of Moses to accomplish the mission.
And now, we can see that, beyond the journey itself, YHWH needed
an educated man who could write down the Covenant as well as
interpret it.

YHWH also needed an educated man who understood the work-
ings of government and society, a leader who could draw upon not
only his Egyptian education but also the Midianite one, knowledge
that made him familiar with the Sinai and its geography and history. Further, Moses would have learned during his many years
in the "land of Midian" that Israelite history gave him foreknowl-
edge about the Promised Land. Israel—then called Canaan—was
a land that already had a covenantal history with Abraham and

generations of forefathers. It was not a new land in the Israelites'
eyes, but a land to be "restored" to its original promise. Only an
educated man could both contemplate this restoration and mold a
new nation in the wilderness.

However sympathetic it is to contemplate the humility of Moses
and other character attributes, it is his education that allows it all to
happen, as we shall see. For the moment, we shouldn't forget that
Freud was the first to address this issue head-on, just seventy years
ago. Crucial for Freud was the paradox of the Jewish anti-myth
of Moses: he was brought up in royal wealth and then returned
to the poverty of his people, rather than being the typical mythic
king or savior who starts as an outcast. Unfortunately, Freud had
begun his Hebrew education as an old man. His late work, *Moses
and Monotheism*, fulfilled a lifetime of study in the cultural effects of
collective repressed memory, in which there seemed sublime logic
to Moses having been an Egyptian. But Freud, lacking a Hebrew
education, could not imagine one for Moses, nor could he read the
Bible's paradoxical myth of Moses as intended to acknowledge his
Egyptian *education* rather than covering over an Egyptian origin.
Perhaps had Freud been younger, he would have investigated the
even greater paradox of the biblical Jewish writers who came after
Moses—yet who found their authority in Moses as a model of the
Jewish writer itself.

. . .

For three separate biblical authors, known to scholars as J, E, and
D, writing in different centuries and at least three centuries after
Moses, the story of his life and complex education had solidified
in them a uniquely Jewish worldview. These later writers of the
Torah, already living in the nation of Israel, with its own kings and
Temple, also understood that Moses was not the first anti-mythic
Jew. In fact, it was Abraham, who came from a world cultural capi-
tal in Mesopotamian Ur that prefigures Moses' Egypt, and who
also left behind a settled and well-off family, as had Moses his
Egyptian family. Like Moses, Abraham headed into the seeming

wilderness of an unknown land, Canaan—only to find it well settled. In recent years, the considerable education of Abraham has also come to light.

So the worldly educations of the biblical writers at King Solomon's court and at the courts of Israel's later kings gave them access to Mesopotamian and Egyptian sources. They themselves resembled Moses in this vital way: in order to write the history of their people, they had to enter into a frame of mind that left their known world behind. As a result, the crucial things that happened to the Jews in the Bible appear to have never happened this way before to another people. True, isolated tribes and nations had thought of themselves as chosen ones, yet the Jews were not isolated; rather, they were deeply educated in the world's knowledge. Thus their concept of being chosen had to be a conscious choosing, and more importantly, a consciousness of a new beginning.

Like Moses, the writers who came after him described the Covenant stories as founding a new way of living, based on ongoing investigation into moral truths. Yet it began with proscription and renunciation: thou shalt not murder, and also, thou shalt not covet. And even further: no gods, not even those of the world's great civilizations. One creator, one author of life. The story will expand under endless interpretation and hundreds of Jewish writers, but it will remain a historical beginning that is written down in antimythical fashion.

Thus the Chosen People were stuck with the burden of proving their case in world history by survival—surviving the larger world's invariable return to mythic views, right down to the revolutionary myths of the twentieth century's treacherous ideologies. In every generation, even among the Jews themselves, historians and archaeologists try to change the biblical story back into one of ordinary mythic origins. Recently, some archaeologists described the entire Torah as a mythmaking extravaganza of Jewish kings commissioning the history of made-up kingdoms of David and Solomon. King Josiah, for instance, who lived more than three centuries after King David, is said to have needed these myths to buttress an agenda for reform. If this were true, then the Jews blend into history like everyone else: they have their political agendas and their reformations. And most essential, they have the common myths of a "glorious past," just like any ordinary people. Even the miracle of their survival over so many millenniums turns out to be just an accident of history.

It is understandable why some concerned academics would want to "normalize" the Jewish experience, lifting the burden of being special from Jewish shoulders. We have even seen Moses himself refusing the special mission that YHWH was asking of him. At least four times, as I counted them, Moses offered a different argument for why he was the wrong person for the mission. For his first argument, he said he wasn't capable of it, not up to it, not good enough, not smart enough. If Moses were these things, he might really have been an ordinary man. But since he is holding his own, he must know with whom he is speaking, based upon his considerable education. He knows, but he asks for the mission's details; and when he is immersed in the working out of the Covenant—the dramatic boundary between himself and the Creator's supernatural realm— he argues them just as Abraham had.

"If you are the God of truth and justice," Abraham said, "why would you destroy the righteous along with the wicked, in your anger at Sodom?" This was the question of an educated man, as was the intricate "Why send me?" of Moses. It seems clear that YHWH needed such educated men because the entire mission in the history of God and his Chosen People was an education in thinking about civilization. Can it thrive under the constant threat of backsliding toward myth? That's why it needed forty years in the wilderness. And that's why their survival depended upon the written text dramatizing the Covenant, one that could be expanded and elaborated through the centuries.

The beginnings of that written text are put into an ark and surrounded by the rituals of approaching and interpreting it—in other words, a new cosmic theater in which the writing becomes the main action. Although Moses and the elders have witnessed God on the mountain, Moses is bringing down to the people a text that requires them to accept a God that cannot be seen. YHWH is an invisible God, and therefore a further transformation beyond Akhenaten's, which represented the one Creator by the sun. YHWH will not be known by visible rays of light or heat; he must be internalized by interpretive power, so that making the case for moral law becomes the internal stage of the biblical cosmic theater, represented by the ark carrying the text. The outer stage remains the journey through time and space: forty years in a wilderness landscape, for starters. But this outer journey will now be paralleled by an inner one that interprets the new text of Moses.

Before this can happen, Aaron and the people have a more immediate idea of how to grasp an invisible God. They built a golden calf—Moses would recognize it as the Egyptian Heavenly Cow, as we shall see—to be a pedestal for the invisible YHWH. It would be a mistake to think the golden calf was worshiped in and of itself; it was not really an idol, but rather a frame in which to hold in mind an invisible God. For this was not an uncommon motif in the most ancient civilizations, in Egypt as well as in Mesopotamia; the difference here is that the god is now invisible. So this calf-pedestal is not a refusal of YHWH but rather an aid to the beginnings of sublimation, the external Creator internalized as invisible. Why then did Moses react as if betrayed?

The answer is that the crucial act of sublimation, or internalizing of the Creation, required the new cosmic theater of writing and interpreting—inscribing on parchment, not carving statues. What Aaron had allowed in the golden calf-pedestal was a remnant of the old Egyptian cosmic theater: a visible and physical drama of making the calf-pedestal and then dancing around it in the old ways. But there were to be no compromises in Moses' eyes. The entire cosmic theater of visible drama in the Torah would be sublimated and transformed into the service of the new written text.

The term we are using, *sublimation*, was rendered popular barely a hundred years ago by Freud. And in his last written work, Freud explains how an invisible god who must be internalized also increases the intellectuality of a culture. Yet it also adds a new tension that can manifest itself as rebellion. Time after time on this journey in the wilderness, the people will rebel against text and law. When they are hungry, they will ask for visible food, and when they are thirsty, they will demand real water in the desert. But the payoff, Moses teaches, comes in the service of higher ideals. The Chosen People will bring a new dimension to human culture, a new way of exploring the boundary between the known world and the unknowable: a new cosmic theater of journey is created. The Hebraic cosmic theater, unlike any before, will be a portable one, beginning with the ark in the desert and reaching a realm of prophetic interpretation that addresses the entire world.

"You shall not make for yourself any image of god"—this is the revolutionary idea that Akhenaten brought into the world in Egypt, overturning and erasing all the Egyptian gods in the generation before Moses. It had not lasted, and was repudiated by the time Moses began his education in the royal palace. But Moses would transform this idea into a comprehensive way of thinking about the world: a whole new approach to knowledge of the natural world and of what may lay beyond it. This knowledge would become text and commentary available to each Israelite individual. In the beginning, however, the portable Hebraic cosmic theater still held vestiges of a visible stage. Above the ark, YHWH was imagined to be seated on the outspread wings of cherubim, mythic figures, half man, half beast.

The ark, in effect, was YHWH's footstool, where he was metaphorically invited to invisibly stand and be brought into battle. And when not embattled, YHWH spoke with Moses from the "mercy-seat," the winged throne created by the cherubim (Exodus 25:22). It may sound like another framing of the invisible God, similar to the golden calf-pedestal, but now it is something totally transformed. This dramatic representation of the ark and its invisible guest was now secondary to what the ark itself contained and all that would flow from it: the written text embodying the Covenant. We can recognize this as a Mosaic transformation because the crucial text for

Akhenaten was the king's physical body itself; the body had a mind, yes, but its intellectual elaboration was missing.

So now, the Creator internalized in a written history of covenant-making was a formative transformation, allowing the numinous Torah of Moses to become the center of the Hebraic cosmic theater. From the Ten Commandments onward, YHWH's moral require-ments for truth and justice had to be translated into a social theater of how to live. Belief in visible attributes of God was not required, and neither were demands about how to observe the Covenant. Instead, the Covenant evolved into moral demands, and these would need human writers and thinkers to dramatize in a narra-tive cosmic theater. It was an inner journey that opened out toward progress in knowledge of human nature and in societal norms.

The narrative itself, including the entire Mosaic journey in the wilderness, would be outwardly dramatized by the lives of the later biblical writers themselves. Although we have no biographies of the great Torah writers that followed after Moses, we nevertheless have their invisible presence manifested in the imagination they brought to witnessing the scenes and overhearing the dialogue between Moses and Pharaoh, for instance. Let's follow their intentions now in the story of Moses approaching Pharaoh and the dramatic messages of the Plagues he would deliver. We will then be able to compare the Mosaic scene with a startlingly similar scenario when Jesus enters the Temple in Jerusalem and violence ensues.

But let's start with an objective view and admit that the plagues visited upon Egypt—and the threats of them made by Moses—were violent acts. People died in large numbers, along with their cattle. The narrative doesn't dwell on this, and part of the reason is that the personality of Moses stands in the way. Here is a man educated at the royal court, yet he is returning to Egypt in all humility as a sheepherder-in-exile. We already know he is "slow of speech" and thus his character serves to mollify the violence he must threaten. Not to mention the fact that he is merely making a nonviolent request: three days for his people to worship their god.

Consider now the third plague: the mosquitoes.

Then YHWH said to Moses, "Say this to Aaron, 'Stretch out your rod and strike the dust on the ground: throughout the land of Egypt it will turn into mosquitoes.'" Aaron stretched out his hand, with his staff, and struck the dust on the ground. The mosquitoes attacked men and beasts; throughout the land of Egypt the dust on the ground turned into mosquitoes. The magicians of Egypt with their witchcraft tried to produce mosquitoes on their own and failed. The mosquitoes attacked men and beasts. So the magicians said to Pharaoh, "This is the finger of God." But Pharaoh's heart was stubborn and, as YHWH had foretold, he refused to listen to Moses and Aaron. (Exodus 8:16)

Aaron *struck* the dust: the mosquitoes *attacked* men and beasts throughout the land. So Moses in his mildness is not even capable of striking the ground—it is Aaron who must do it. Egyptian magic couldn't do this because clearly it was not magic; instead, it was a natural sign from YHWH that he is the Creator—as if he were Aten, the singular creator-god of Akhenaten returned again. And yet: "This is the finger of god," say Pharaoh's minions. The plagues are as if YHWH is writing in the landscape with natural signs. It is his "finger" doing the writing, just as it may also aid Moses on Mount Sinai—and, "as YHWH had foretold, Pharaoh refused to listen." We can only imagine that Pharaoh had all the doors and windows sealed and was content to remain indoors until the mosquitoes died.

So what was the point, since YHWH already knew that Pharaoh was not going to listen? The point was the writing itself: YHWH's finger in the landscape, and Moses' hand in the narrative. Each plague renders another aspect of Egypt useless. In this case it was the court prophets or magicians. And the next plague, the infestation of gadflies, invading even "the palaces and all the houses of the Egyptians," is so dire that Pharaoh relents. You can sacrifice to your God, says Pharaoh, but do it in Egypt. Moses explains that the animals to be sacrificed might be considered sacred to the Egyptians, so in order not to offend, the people must go into the wilderness. Again, Pharaoh reneges, regardless of how many Egyptians were going to die of starvation and disease. And what livestock would be left in Egypt would all die in the next plague, "horse and donkey and camel, herd and flock."

Though Pharaoh will continue to refuse, we see that each plague shows his royal power to be useless, other than to submit to Moses and YHWH. In his eyes, it would be a submission, since the Pharaoh is the representative on earth of the Egyptian gods and their powers. Yet Pharaoh cannot even keep the flies out of his own room. This "writing" of YHWH is actually the steady dismantling of Egyptian power for which only an educated man, like Moses, would understand the necessity. In the end Pharaoh will be so reduced that not only is his kingship useless but he is only half a man. The royal power to slay the firstborn of the Israelites, invoked when Moses was just born, now will kill Pharaoh's own son and heir to the throne.

True, Pharaoh had the power to enslave the Israelites and to multiply their suffering after Moses' first request for his people to worship YHWH. Now, not only can he not lift a finger against the Israelites, the entire cosmic theater of Egypt has been reduced to a shell. And even what sign is left of Pharaoh's authority is about to drown in the Reed Sea, chasing after a futile obsession with his Israelite former slaves. Ancient Egypt will ignore this and go on—the episode is probably forgotten—but the Israelites have been definitively shown that the long-running cosmic theater of Egypt must be left behind. Because what the plagues and the negotiations with Pharaoh demonstrate is that the Israelites were in grave danger of mental slavery as well as physical.

Let's go back a moment and listen to the negotiations. After Pharaoh has seemed to acquiesce, letting the Jews go for their allotted three days' worship—but "not very far"—Pharaoh renegotiates, allowing only the males to go, ensuring their return. After further plagues, Pharaoh's negotiating position continues to retreat. He agrees that the women may also leave, but the animals would have to be left behind. That cannot be, says Moses, because the animals are necessary for the sacrifices.

In particular, after the plague of gadflies, when Pharaoh has suggested the Israelites may go, "provided you do not go far," he makes an additional request: "Pray for me," or "intercede with your God," as most translations have it. Are we thus meant to believe that Pharaoh has now accepted the power of YHWH? Or, is he being slyly ironic, as negotiators must often be? The Hebraic author of this narrative, known as E and writing in the northern Israeli capital of Samaria in the eighth century BCE, probably intended both meanings—a sly Pharaoh, but also one beginning to understand that his own cosmic power was drying up. Yet he could not admit this to Moses, of all people. For Moses had been a prince in his palace and his education was more than equal to the Pharaoh's. It would have been of no use for Pharaoh to call upon his own Egyptian gods, either for help or advice, because Moses was as familiar with them as he was.

If we have any doubt about why the Egyptian gods are never heard from in this negotiation, this must be the reason. And this would be the reason that YHWH sent Moses; had it been Aaron, the lifelong Israelite, he would have been subjected to all the sophisticated intimidation that the gods of Egypt could bring to bear. For instance, Aaron might have taken Pharaoh literally when he asked Moses to "intercede for me with your God." Indeed, that is how some academic scholars also read it, offering the historical detail that high priests of pagan gods acted as mediators and that Moses was seen as such a mediator. But Moses is no Aaron; he is equal to the Egyptian subtlety of Pharaoh.

If we think back to the beginning of this negotiation, we recall that Pharaoh not only refused the request of Moses but also flaunted his power: not only will you not be going anywhere, Pharaoh suggests, but now all the slaves of Israel will have to work twice as hard. "Up to the present," Pharaoh says to his overseers, "you have provided these people with straw for brick-making. Do so no longer; let them go and gather straw for themselves . . . Make these men work harder than ever, so they do not have time to listen to glib speeches." Thus we can see how Pharaoh's disbelief in the power of YHWH would progress to the point of asking for prayer on his behalf, even if insincerely. He knew he was speaking with an educated man in Moses and that this continuing drama of plagues and negotiations was revealing his own intellectual inadequacy.

In the end, after Pharaoh has lost his symbolic mental and physical power by having allowed the death of his own firstborn, the heir to his throne, he is left with only the accoutrements of power, his armies. When he goes back on his final agreement to let the Israelites go, there is no thinking left in him. He charges incautiously after the Israelites as they are crossing the Reed Sea, and naturally his captain's chariot's wheels, like all the others, are stuck in the mud. In the traditional understanding, the story of plagues and of Pharaoh's obsession with holding on to the Israelites is mistakenly reduced to a parable. Slaves are freed by the God of all men, and brutal tyrants receive their just desserts. "Let my people go" is the rallying cry and it is made possible by natural events that seem supernatural: the sea parts, the pursuing Egyptians drown. But what we have in fact read is a complex negotiation that reduces Pharaoh's spiritual and intellectual authority, and allows us to recognize the complex authority of Moses and his God.

The echo of parable, however, adds another level. In many other ancient literatures there are stories of difficult crossings, even miraculous crossings of rivers and seas. We find it written down in the cuneiform records of Mesopotamian kings, who miraculously crossed the Tigris or Euphrates rivers in their victory campaigns. We will even hear an echo in the complicated crossing of the Jordan River by the Hebrews later on. Yet rivers do flood and dry up, and the tributaries of the Reed Sea do the same. There are marshes and there is the mud of drying marshes. These natural phenomena do not change the fact that the escape of the Israelites was miraculous. Rather, we must now see that the later biblical writers and readers of the Torah were capable of comprehending that there was something special about themselves as well, about their particular historical experiences and their intellectual and spiritual growth. Beyond parable, Moses' encounter with Pharaoh tells a nuanced history.

. . .

Ultimately, the larger story unfolds to show a coming to terms with
YHWH's desire. It began with a voice calling from a burning bush
in the wilderness and it continues in the voice that Moses consults
while he writes during the later years in the wilderness. Clearly,
YHWH needed a writer, and he needed one with the worldly education of Moses. The story of the Exodus and the journey to the Promised Land is dependent upon the life of Moses—the full biography,
as it had been understood but never fully written. An educated man
requires a fertile culture in which to grow, both intellectually and
among his people in a fertile land. The fact that Moses could not
cross over into that fertile land with the Israelites is the supreme
irony of his biography and the catharsis of his people's journey to
freedom. For the real fertility that YHWH desires is not the physical landscape of Egypt's Nile Valley or the Jordan Valley; rather, it
is the fertile mind of Moses, stripped down to its bare essentials of
a writer. In the wilderness, in such utter isolation, Moses had no
pharaohs to talk to, and no land to inhabit. It was only in such isolation and such perilous freedom that the education of Moses could
continue—and YHWH could find his writer.

The result of the Israelite march to freedom is that a text is produced, and we can now see that the core of the Torah embodied
YHWH's desire. It was a desire for more than moral and worldly
education, and more than an education in survival, which forty years
in the wilderness was sure to provide. It was an instilling of desire in
the Israelites to create a Hebraic culture in Israel that would allow
ongoing biblical writing and thinking. Perhaps the most significant
quality of the written Torah is that it reduces dependency upon a
worldly theater of kings, tyrannical and otherwise.

There's another way to think about the spiritual isolation of the
Jews in the wilderness and their escape from civilized Egypt. The
Israelites' isolation was comparable to what we now know as the
conditions for natural evolution. When isolated, a species must
explore, adapt, and evolve. In contrast to the similar isolation of
Moses and the Jewish people in Sinai, it was the empire of Pharaoh

and all the riches of ancient Egypt that were revealed as a dead end. Moses and the biblical writers dramatize how Pharaoh was unable to conceive that all his beliefs and powers were being dismantled, one after the other, by Moses. We have also seen the absolute necessity for the humility of Moses, as it was developed by transforming an Egyptian education into a Hebraic one.

· · ·

Now we can discover the same quality of educated humility in the biography of Jesus. We confront it in the story of Jesus' last journey to the Temple in Jerusalem, where he will enter and overturn the tables of the moneychangers. There are parallels to the life of Moses here that have rarely been drawn. Recall that the raison d'être presented to Pharaoh by Moses was the need to carry out sacrifices to his God. Consider that the moneychangers serve the Temple sacrifices. In fact, the moneychangers were the representatives of the poorest and most precarious citizens of Israel. They allowed those who could not afford it to exchange a pledge for the money necessary to purchase a portion of the sacrificial animal. Only with their participation could the community of Israel be whole, leaving no one isolated. So why would Jesus want to dismantle this symbol of unity among all the people of Israel, especially the poorest ones?

Certainly no one at the violent scene would have understood, not the moneychangers and not the priests. In fact, it was not about money at all or about Temple worship. It was rather a symbolic act for the benefit of Jesus' disciples—or more accurately, for the writers and readers of the Gospels who would come later. The contemporary scholar Jacob Neusner connects the overturned tables with "setting up another table," namely the Passover table of the Last Supper (*Judaism in Monologue and Dialogue*). At that Passover meal with his disciples, Jesus equates the matzah of the flight from Egypt by the Israelites with the wafer of the Eucharist. The symbolic relevance of the humble matzah is that all of Israel took part in leaving Egypt and all were provided for. And then, the institution of the Eucharist turned this humble bread into the symbolic inclusion of all the followers of Jesus.

Thus Jesus, serving—or serving as—God, dramatizes a new journey in which all the experiences are symbolic. Instead of the Promised Land, there is the symbolic Kingdom of Heaven, and instead of the Temple there is the heavenly Jerusalem of the afterlife. And since the journey this time, to the "kingdom of heaven," dramatizes the afterlife, the Temple can also be rendered symbolic—and reinterpreted in the New Testament. In fact, the Temple had already been destroyed by the Romans when the Gospels were being written, but even if that actual history was in the minds of the New Testament writers, they rendered the Temple as a symbol rather than in its historical reality.

But the Jews who survived the Roman catastrophe continued the historical journey of the Jewish people—extending the original Mosaic narrative, commentary, and interpretation of the moral law underpinning human society. At the same time the Gospels were being written from Jewish-Christian sources, the Jews were writing the origins of the Talmud, a library of interpretive books that would continue being written for centuries. Rather than a break with Moses, the Talmud would conceive of an "Oral Torah" that Moses also transmitted. What we need to ask now is if the symbolic action of Jesus' overturning the tables in the Temple, which we have just focused upon, really conveyed a break with the Mosaic Torah.

But how could it, if we remember that Jesus' symbolic acts were in the tradition of the Hebrew prophets, and Moses himself? It was Aaron, not Moses, who stood at the symbolic head of the sacrificial tradition associated with the Temple that the later prophets sometimes criticized. They did not conceive of an end, however, to a consciousness of sin and its need for expiation. Neither did Jesus, for those who could not participate in Temple sacrifice could partake of the Eucharist, just as the Talmud was written for all Jews to study and even comment upon. What we learn here is that the humility of Jesus comes not from his humble background but rather his Mosaic education. He is angry when he overturns the tables in the Temple, just as Moses had been when he smashed the tablets upon seeing the golden calf. In both cases, it is the prophetic anger of an educated man faced with the people's misunderstanding of how the journey from mental slavery in Egypt must continue and cannot stop.

The actions of Moses and Jesus were not about the people itself; they were symbolic acts. Moses understood that the golden calf represented not a rebuke to him or YHWH but a wish to include everyone, from the poor to the pagan. It had been made of gold and included even the outsider in its celebration, just as the money-changers served to include the poorest Israelite. Yet both Moses and Jesus realized that the journey had to continue, that more had to be written, and that the text could not stand still and the interpretation could not stop. The journey required a deeper elaboration of the individual's place in society and responsibility for self-improvement—there was no improved understanding to be gotten from the golden calf. The individual Jew had to be made aware that the ritual act was not enough.

This awareness of intellectual rigor would be "inscribed" into the text: instead of literal freedom, the ritual of the Passover meal became a revelation of freedom from mental slavery especially. And the Passover text from Exodus (elaborated further in the Hagga-dah) sustained the revelation at Sinai, where the Israelites arrived at last and received the Torah. It was the revelation that inspired Moses to go on writing it, which is how Exodus began to be written down. This was the freedom to think in terms of the Hebraic cosmic theater—that is, to think about what needs to be revealed because it's beyond our creaturely limitations to know. It was a freedom that would continue to inspire Jesus in his symbolic acts and, at the same time, to inspire the Jewish sages who would continue to write the Talmud.

This education in YHWH's text—the cosmic theater of journey and continual interpretation—is not something the educated Egyptian in Moses' day would have understood. His world was set, timeless. And it was hardly different for the educated Roman or Hellenist in Jesus' time: their world of power and inquiry had arrived and was not meditating on the journey. That is why Philo

of Alexandria, as he seeks to explain Moses' Torah to the wider
Roman world, has a problem in representing anything but the
unruffled serenity of Moses.

We see this explicitly in another life of Moses, provided by the
eminent Jewish historian writing in Rome not long after the death
of Jesus, Josephus. In order to be comprehensible to the Romans as
a great man, Moses was described as having a noble lineage: a man
whose birth was predicted, whose childhood was heroic, and who
was exceedingly handsome. He is the ideal of a military general
and his spiritual knowledge is based upon great insight into human
nature. He never gets angry, because he approaches every situation
with wisdom. For these reasons, therefore, Josephus had to completely leave out the golden calf episode and Moses' confrontation
with the people over it. Neither could there be a smashing of the
tablets, for this would have seemed an undisciplined impulse to the
Romans. They would not have comprehended its symbolic aspect
as an insistence upon further and deeper education, beyond natural
and mythic worlds and into the still-being-written moral law.

An educated man would not act upon his anger, not without
reflection—that's how it would have seemed to the Romans. The
Hebraic Moses would be an anomaly to them. Yet this is precisely
the manner in which Jesus also acts when he overturns the tables.
Jesus is hardly a vision of Roman wisdom and yet he will ultimately
educate Christian Romans, because they come to see him not as a
great man but rather as not a man at all. When seen as a god incarnate, however, Jesus' symbolic acts, even when seeming angry, were
to be expected.

· · ·

YHWH himself seemed capable of anger, at one point ready to
destroy his own people in anger at their misunderstanding of him.
Moses is able to dissuade him—but only by threatening to sacrifice his own life: "Block me out from the book you have written,"
Moses threatened, if YHWH cannot forgive the sin of the golden
calf. And as we have just seen, it is not simply a sin of disobedience
about making an image of a god; it's a refusing to accept the deeper

knowledge that the journey must continue, more must be learned, and the Torah will provide its basis. It is the Torah then, internalized as knowledge, which makes Moses and Jesus into remarkable men. They stand apart from any previous notion of an educated man.

And standing halfway between Moses and Jesus in historical time is the Hebrew prophet Isaiah, whose portrait of YHWH's "Servant" is unlike any leader we would expect. Isaiah's picture of this Suffering Servant, which we will examine later, seems to resemble neither Moses nor Jesus in the historical sense. Yet this ideal suffering prophet that Isaiah depicts provides an *inner* vision of the mind and heart of Moses and Jesus. How could these charismatic leaders also be so broken inside? It is almost as if we're carried back in time to the Moses who returned from his encounter with God to be confronted with the golden calf: we can imagine the devastation inside, the sense of betrayal.

And how must Moses have looked to the people who broke his heart? He might resemble the Freudian archetype of the vanquished father, except that Moses turns out to survive and to be stronger than anything we might expect. Here we are drawing closer to YHWH's desire for humble servants who are also deeply educated and therefore unusually strong-minded.

Here is how Moses would have spoken to the people from the strength of his inner life, beginning with the announcement that "things hidden" will now become public knowledge. It's easy to imagine that Moses is referring to Egyptian religion, since the priests were keepers of secret wisdom. This does not mean, however, that Moses is drawing upon Egyptian sources but rather that the people would have common knowledge of this reference to Egyptian religion.

> *Now I am revealing new things to you,*
> *things hidden and unknown to you,*
> *created just now, this very moment,*
> *of these things you have heard nothing until now,*
> *so that you cannot say, "Oh yes, I knew all this."*

But in fact it is not Moses who has written this; it is the prophet
Isaiah, who is speaking and writing more than half a millennium
after Moses—but like him, he is also denied the Promised Land,
since he is writing now in the Exile of Babylon. The "hidden things"
are now necessary to explain the inexplicable: How YHWH could
have allowed his Temple to be destroyed, and how this new exile
to Babylon continues the journey through history of the Jewish
people. By this time, however, the Hebrew prophetic literature
had developed the idea of the soul, or inner life, and it is identified with a personification of Israel—the entire community, giving
further meaning to the concept of salvation (also personified as a
messiah). This messiah figure can speak in the name of YHWH as
did the prophets, but now he can also speak in the personification
of Israel:

> *Islands, listen to me,*
> *pay attention, remotest peoples.*
> *YHWH called me before I was born,*
> *From my mother's womb he pronounced my name.*
>
> *He made my mouth a sharp sword,*
> *and hid me in the shadow of his hand.*
> *He made me into a sharpened arrow,*
> *and concealed me in his quiver.*
>
> *He said to me, "You are my servant (Israel)*
> *in whom I shall be glorified";*
> *while I was thinking, "I have toiled in vain,*
> *I have exhausted myself for nothing."*

Already, five centuries before Jesus would be born, the prophets are writing in parables. And there is the additional paradox
of a humbled, even despairing servant, who is to think of himself as becoming "glorified." It is the same paradox of the humble
Moses, "slow of speech," chosen to be a strong leader. Here too,

the strength lies in an education: since Israel is the personified servant, we cannot ignore the education and Torah of its long journey.
Without such an educated history behind it, Israel could not have
survived in its Babylonian exile. But now it is more than surviving;
it is renewing the Covenant with God—a YHWH who can be anywhere in the world now, including Babylon.

All of this Jesus had studied in his own Jewish education. Furthermore, he would have internalized the following lines from Isaiah:

> *On him lies a punishment that brings us peace,*
> *and through his wounds we are healed.*

. . .

Not only will Israel survive its punishing exile, but the suffering
will yield new insight into the Torah. Knowledge of the text itself
provided healing. Yet this personification held stronger echoes in
the time of Jesus, when many Jews were being killed and crucified
by the Romans.

> *By force and by law he was taken;*
> *would anyone plead his cause?*

The law was now Roman. And the cause? A redemption or healing, and also the Hebrew prophetic concept of YHWH's lovingkindness. Since it is the voice of the soul that is also represented as
speaking, the contrast with the suffering body is clear: it is the soul
that survives, whether we are speaking of death or of the ongoing
journey of Israel in time. That this "Suffering Servant"—Isaiah's
figure for Israel—was also a figure of the Jewish messiah is not
a surprise to Jesus, when he reads this in his youthful education.
Even a century before Isaiah, the Book of Deuteronomy made
use of poetic allegories. "I will raise up a prophet like yourself for
them from their own brothers; I will put my words into his mouth"
(Deuteronomy 19:18). It is Moses to whom God is speaking in this

passage from Deuteronomy, so not only would Jesus recognize his image here, but this passage will be later quoted by authors of the New Testament. The words that YHWH promises to suggest to his prophet are poetic words. They are the words of a writing prophet, who in this time wrote in poetry.

The words "come to" the writer, in a classic figure for inspiration. As Moses had written the narrative of a journey, and as Isaiah dramatizes the suffering servant of Israel, Jesus too, in his day, would "speak" or write in poetic parables. While the writer is passive, in that he is receiving or conceiving the words, a parable is also "reading" a text, and almost always the Hebrew Bible. The parable "reads" in the sense of unfolding the text into the future; that is, projecting new meaning. But there are many kinds of parables, and indeed many were used by Hebrew writers long before Jesus. But especially in the time of Jesus and the years that would follow, these parables provide narrative material in which God can continue speaking, even though he no longer speaks directly.

In the continuation of the Hebrew Bible for Jews that would become the "Oral Torah" and the Talmud, God continues to be personified in the narratives. Instead of secret knowledge, however, God speaks like a Jewish sage, as an interpreter, a clarifier of the text. Actually, it's as if the "Holy One" were a writer himself, though in less dynamic a presence than Moses. To take one example among thousands, we can concentrate on the following text as it fortifies the Hebraic tradition in which God has always and continues to be personified:

> *Rabbi Simeon bar Yohai taught, "The book of Deuteronomy went up and spread itself out before the Holy One, blessed be he, saying before him, 'Lord of the world! You have written in your Torah that any covenant, part of which is null is wholly nullified. Now lo, Solomon wishes to uproot a Υ of mine.' Said to him the Holy One, blessed be he, 'Solomon and a thousand like him will be null, but not one word of yours will be nullified.'" (y. San. 2:6.II.AA—DD)*

The rabbi referred to here in the Talmud was a contemporary of Jesus, and this parable itself may have been written at the time of the Gospels. God clarifies the meaning of the Covenant here; he does not make it a secret knowledge. Yet many of the parables of Jesus are described as meant for his disciples alone—not expected to be understood by his Jewish audiences, as he traveled and spoke in the Galilee region of Israel. Nevertheless, this form of parable had been used before by Jewish sages. The most common characteristics of the personified YHWH in this time are represented as a sage, in order that human recognition of him come through a relationship—in this case, that of a student to his rabbi. That is why later, Matthew in his Gospel tells us that Jesus is teaching his disciples by parable. And just as God had long been personified as a social being, it's not so surprising that Jesus would see himself or be seen as a personification of a messiah figure in relation to God—in the same way that he figured as a sage in relation to his disciples.

But the parables also need a writer, a passive writer who conceives the inspiration of "YHWH's desire" in a text, as had Moses and the writing prophets that followed. How did this fit into Jesus' experience? To receive these words required a discipline of "waiting"; that is, waiting for the inspiration that would apply the Jewish education of Jesus to the text, in order to see what might happen in the future. It is precisely this condition of waiting that Jesus refers to many times with his disciples, even as they fail to understand. For Jesus tells them that they will see what will unfold if they allow themselves to wait, rather than jump to conclusions. And this quality of waiting was just as deeply embedded in the Jewish tradition that continued after Jesus, and that continued to conceive of a messiah. Yet this ongoing "Oral Torah" tradition of Judaism was not about a messiah, but about how to live while *waiting*.

Unfortunately, as the Jewish-Christian sect broke away, it tended to characterize Judaism as having ended with the Hebrew Bible. In fact, the anti-Semitic implications of this claim (Why should Jews continue to exist?) would only grow stronger in the centuries to come. At this time, however, when the Gospels were just being writ-

ten, the Jewish-Christian sect could not yet foresee how powerful
and rejuvenated the Jewish Covenant with God would become as
the Oral Torah became written down in the Talmud and the commentaries. So the "waiting" aspect of this renewed Judaism in its
second Exile (just as Isaiah had envisioned the future survival of
Israel in the first Exile in Babylon) would be interpreted as a form of
healing. And this second journey in exile from the land might more
properly be called the third: the exile of the Hebrews in Egyptian
slavery is the first one, and the redemptive journey into Sinai (along
with the beginning of writing the Torah) begins the healing.

Back in Sinai, the redemptive figure of Moses was not about a
messiah but about Moses writing the moral law of how to live in
the world—and how to continue to interpret YHWH's desire for a
world of "truth and justice," however long it takes. Jesus, too, wishes
his followers to continue interpreting his words and his personified
journey through history that his historical life represented. It is true
that the Gospels are not written as history but rather as meditations
on the life of Jesus, thereby emphasizing the Hebraic inspiration
to write a continuing text of commentary on the Covenant. That is
why we should not be held back today from observing the historical life of Jesus with the same seriousness as was given to the life
of Moses in the Torah and throughout the Hebrew Bible. Without
Moses, Jesus would be unthinkable.

. . .

The life of Jesus, to the extent it was modeled on the life of Moses,
tells the implicit story of a man waiting and then finding his moment
in time to act. I have compared the acting to writing because the significance of each event cries out to be written down as a milestone
in a journey. Until we witness Jesus meeting John the Baptist in his
thirtieth year, his life has appeared to be one of waiting—a waiting
filled with an education. The same was true of Moses, whose life
only begins actively when he is similar in age to the Jesus we have
just described (mistakenly cited as forty years of age by certain commentators partial to the number forty).

When Moses is called by YHWH, we learn how God preferred

a man outwardly humble while inwardly strong. The Moses who struck an Egyptian soldier in anger later becomes a man who controls his feelings. Jesus too becomes such a man after he has overturned the tables and is ready—even waiting—for the end of his life.

What would the young Jesus have thought when he read of Moses' smashing of the tablets in the Torah? Superficial commentary describes Moses as angry, but he would not have appeared so in the eyes of Jesus. Like many of the more sublime commentators, Jesus would have envisioned Moses in a manner similar to Michelangelo's depiction of him in a famous sculpture in Rome. Here is how Freud describes the sculpture, suggesting the kind of insight that we would have expected from the historical Jesus:

> *[Michelangelo] has added something new and more than human to the figure of Moses; so that the giant frame with its tremendous power becomes only a concrete expression of the highest mental achievement that is possible in a man, that of struggling against an inward passion for the sake of a cause to which he has devoted himself. (Imago [1915])*

The cause for both Moses and Jesus was the enactment of YHWH's desire: a perfected truth and justice. Moses has successfully rejected the golden calf because he recognized it as the Egyptian Heavenly Cow. The way he rejected it was to transform the rebellion of the Egyptians as it took place in their ancient sacred text, "The Book of the Heavenly Cow," and project it upon those rebels among the Jews who had turned away from the cause of truth, wishing to return to pagan Egypt.

Isaiah, too, presented the Suffering Servant as Michelangelo would represent Moses: a man who outwardly projects the imperfection of truth and justice in the world by his vulnerability. The Servant of YHWH suffers the wounds of being vulnerable to the cause of truth. Yet his inner strength survives, as it does in Moses and as it will in Jesus some five centuries later—and all because these leaders successfully struggle against the anger of rebellion.

The "Israel" that the Suffering Servant represents will likewise suffer the destruction of its nation. Isaiah and other Hebrew prophets interpreted the loss of Temple and nation as punishment for the sin of what we can paraphrase as "taking it too much for granted." By taking the nation for granted, the responsibility for its survival grew lax. The nation had, in these terms, lost its inner strength— if not its desire to survive. Throughout the Hebrew Bible, there is a focus upon those suffering remnants of Israel who will always survive and renew Judaism. And in those renewals, the Covenant survives, carried down through history in a story of journey.

But this was not the interpretation of some later Christian commentators, nor is it always implicit in the Gospels. Like those earlier Hebrew commentators who were quick to attribute simple anger to Moses smashing the tablets, these later Christian ones, the second-century Egyptian scholar Origen among them, took it for granted that the Jewish nation as a whole rejected the Messiah— and showed their anger by "killing" him. It is easy to see why they would want it so. In their eyes, Jesus represented an end to the need for survival, and thus an end to the journey through history of the Jews and the education in Torah it required. Jesus had rendered history complete, by his advent.

True, these Jewish-Christian commentators expected an imminent end to the world as we know it, and they should have seen how the lives of Moses and Jesus refute that prediction. Yes, there is a Promised Land and yes, there is a Kingdom of Heaven, but because Moses and Jesus were educated men, they understood that these were not to be taken for granted. The survival of the Covenant that is embedded in a Jewish education as it travels down the generations from sage to Jesus' disciples requires an immense responsibility: not to forget the suffering that upholding the truth can command. The Jewish slaves suffered in Egypt, and in the wilderness, and in the struggle for the land, and in exile and destruction. As represented in the figure of the Suffering Servant, it's clear that Jesus too was taking nothing for granted and was willing to suffer the consequences of his devotion to the truth.

It is not hard to imagine the young Jesus as a student in his rabbinic circle, questioning his rabbi about the Servant figure in Isaiah. The Servant was also the face of our Exile, his sage might have answered. That is why he can represent a message of hope as well, for the Suffering Servant is proof that Israel will survive and will return to its land. And when the Gospels were being written, at the time of the fall of the Second Temple, the Jewish sages who survived were already compensating for its loss (and the end of animal sacrifice) by formulating the Mishnah and its elaboration in the Talmud. The New Testament writers rendered the loss of Temple and sacrificial rites in another way: as if the need for the Temple had now been superseded by the sacrifice of Jesus.

Yet a Jewish education, then and now, shows that the Romans who destroyed the Temple and nation were very much like the Egyptians who pursued the escaping Jews. They represented a physical power incapable of withholding their anger from those devoted to a more complex inner life. The ancient Egyptians and the Romans had no use for suffering; in fact, the torture of Roman slaves in the coliseums could even be an object of entertainment to some. But a Jewish education interprets suffering without rejecting it. Instead, its meaning is transformed by a willingness to find complex meaning for the physical journey through time and space that we are still embarked on. There's every reason to expect that Jesus would have asked his rabbis the historical questions to which the Torah implies an answer: the journey through history is a cosmic theater of coming to grips with the Covenant.

The original Hebraic audience would not have needed to be told this, so it falls to sages and writers of later generations to provide historical interpretation. For instance, once we have accepted the details of Moses' education in Egypt and later in Midian, it still must have appeared puzzling to a man like Jesus how the impoverished Jewish slaves were capable of comprehending a man like Moses. However, today we know from Egyptian sources that it was their common practice to allow talented men and women from among their slaves to be educated and to hold important positions. There were no doubt many such educated men among the Jews escaping Egypt, and they complemented those others who had held on to ancient Israelite learning through the centuries and remembered Joseph's rise to power in Egypt. Although Jesus' rabbi would not have known the historical facts of Egyptian custom, he might have explained, as in a common midrash, that a rabbi always finds his necessary disciples. Certainly when the time came, Jesus had no problem finding his disciples.

It had been no different for Moses, long before. The Midianite priest Jethro, Moses' father-in-law, returned to his side during the wilderness journey and patiently tutored him in how to appoint justices to help govern and educate the people. No doubt Jethro had tutored Moses like this before, during the many years Moses had spent as his foreman. Jethro, priest and leader among the Midianites, had much to teach Moses. And now, the judges to be appointed in the wilderness would later serve as a model for Jesus, when he would appoint his disciples.

In the Book of Deuteronomy, Moses writes about his people: "How can I bear unaided the trouble of you, and the burden, and the bickering. Pick for your tribes men who are wise, discerning, and experienced, and I will appoint them as your heads ... You shall not be partial in judgment; hear out low and high alike. Fear no man, for judgment is God's. And any matter that is too difficult for you, you shall bring to me and I will hear it." These judges Moses now appoints will also become interpreters of Moses' Torah to the people—just as Jesus will later instruct his disciples to interpret his words to the larger world. In almost the same words as Moses, Jesus tells his disciples to fear no man and to be ruled only by God's judgment, or YHWH's desire for truth and justice.

Jesus speaks to his disciples as a writer would, so that they will be educated in how to interpret his words. He tells them: Those "who will not receive you, will suffer worse than Sodom . . ." But the disciples will learn to understand that this does not mean cities will be destroyed like Sodom, but rather that it will be men's souls who suffer for rejecting the news of them (their souls) and the fact that these souls are now being spoken to directly. Jesus explains further, "Fear not them which kill the body but are not able to kill the soul." Since the soul is what belongs to the Kingdom of Heaven, Jesus instructs his disciples to live *as if* the "Kingdom of Heaven is at hand"—as if "this day." That is why he can tell them, when they ask what they should say to the people they meet, that it will not be they who are speaking, it will be YHWH's words.

After all, this is precisely what Moses was answered when he asked YHWH what he should say: he learned that YHWH's words would be in his mouth. The difference here is negligible, for Jesus has learned from Isaiah and other Hebrew prophets before him that in order for the soul to survive death it must ensure its survival by following YHWH's desire, his words.

> *Lift up your eyes to the heavens,*
> *look down at the earth.*
> *The heavens will vanish like smoke,*
> *the earth wear out like a garment,*
> *and its inhabitants die like vermin,*
> *but my salvation shall last for ever*
> *and my justice have no end.*
>
> *(Isaiah 51:6)*

When he read these words in Isaiah during his youth, Jesus was not thinking that the end of the world was at hand. Nor does he think it later, as he instructs his disciples. For Jesus, like the Hebrew prophets before him, interpreted YHWH's desire as to live *as if* the Kingdom of Heaven was coming—just as Moses instructed his people to live *as if* "YHWH dwells among you." This is how the Hebraic writer writes, provoking the students of his text to make the leap between the literal and the envisioned—a leap that only the will to do so can make, if it is dedicated to YHWH's desire.

Jesus asks his disciples, "Who am I?" One answers: "A prophet." But Jesus says no, he is the Messiah—which means, in the context of Matthew's Gospel, that he is "delivering" YHWH's words, not his own, and that he is thus a Hebraic writer like Moses. When Jesus tells his disciple Peter that he is delivering the "keys of the Kingdom of Heaven," he is teaching how a writer conflates time and space to imagine a future—as if it existed "this day." Yet Jesus is not expecting the history of YHWH and his Chosen People to end. He tells Peter that history will continue anew in the church he must found. It will be up to Peter, however, and the other disciples to interpret their messiah-writer, and to hold in mind the literal reality as well as the *as if.*

When the Gospel writers later depict Jesus as deriding the Pharisees, it is only because he now views those rabbis, among whom he had studied, as too literal-minded in their interpretations of Moses' Torah. Jesus was more attuned to the words of Moses, according to the Gospels, because he was focused on reinterpreting the Hebrew prophets. That is why the Gospels are intent on putting the words of Isaiah and other Hebrew prophets in Jesus' mouth. Nevertheless, his life comes closest to Moses when Jesus instructs his disciples to "go into the city"—meaning the cities of Israel—and speak YHWH's words. For they will be familiar words to the Jewish people, although now reinterpreted by Jesus' embodiment of the Kingdom of Heaven.

Of course some cities would resist, just as Sodom had resisted YHWH's desire, and just as souls may rebel against the difficult journey that YHWH's words entail. The Jews who followed Moses into Sinai would later follow the original Joshua (if we recall that Jesus' name in his day was Joshua) into Canaan, in order to conquer the cities that might resist YHWH's desire. Certainly this required more suffering. On a simple level, we could say that God was with the Israelites in their battles just as YHWH's word, through Jesus— known to them by his Hebrew name, Joshua—was with the disciples as they entered strange cities.

The disciples were called by Jesus "fishers of men"; in other words, fishers of souls, who would encounter dangerous times, just as the Israelites had found in Canaan when Moses writes in the Torah: "Many will try to entice you: 'Come, let us serve other gods.'" Of such men, Moses counseled: "You must not give way, nor listen to him . . . you must not conceal his guilt." Even in the promised land, in the cities of Canaan, it would be a struggle to the death for men's hearts and minds.

It is this to which Jesus refers, when Moses foretells in the Torah how critical it is to be educated in the words of YHWH, crucial for the journey through history to continue. Those who cannot hold in mind YHWH's desire to live a moral life, following his words— at the same time as they conform to custom, which usually means the "old ways"—need the further interpretation of how to live in the civilization and nation coming-into-being, Israel. But if they remain literal-minded, seeing only that custom rules, and are comfortable knowing there is not more to know, they cannot properly read the Torah, a work that holds past and future in mind at the same time.

This is what Jesus means to teach his disciples, and it is how he answers them when they ask literal-minded questions. He is teaching them to read him, just as *he* reads the Torah, by holding past and future in mind, as the prophets had. That is why Jesus, when Peter says to him, "You are the Son of the living God," replies: "It was not flesh and blood that revealed this to you but my Father in heaven." That is to say, Peter now could read the words of YHWH on his own and not as just the literal words of a flesh-and-blood teacher—in this case, Jesus. For now, Peter is making his own interpretation of Jesus as a messiah figure, just as Isaiah had done with the Suffering Servant. In both instances, the crucial message is that YHWH's words—whether written and interpreted by Moses or Jesus—are numinous, existing outside time or outside "flesh and blood."

For Moses, the emphasis had fallen on "outside time," in that Israel's journey through history would eventually arrive at a just nation and world, the embodiment of YHWH's timeless words. But for Jesus, as for some of his Jewish contemporaries among the Pharisees and Essenes, the emphasis fell on "outside flesh and blood," or beyond death, where the soul's survival is equated with the survival of Israel, as promised in the Torah.

. . .

Apart from dramatizing a Covenantal journey that can be imagined to arrive beyond time or beyond death, a fundamental question remains: What is on the stage of the Hebraic cosmic theater
that precedes the Covenant itself? It is the voice of YHWH that is
found center stage and it allows dialogue to begin. The stage must
now be completely cleared, as the second of the Ten Commandments requires: "Thou shalt not make . . . any likeness of any thing
that is in heaven above, or that is in the earth beneath, or that is in
the water under the earth." That is, no image on the cosmic stage.
Does this mean that the stage is empty? Can this be a stage on which
a man is seen in conversation with an invisible God, rendered just
by a voice?

In fact, there are no voices; there is simply a man at a table,
writing. It is Moses on the Plain of Moab, as described in Deuteronomy, "writing the Law." What is in his mind is capable of being
read by any person and in any age, for it is becoming a narrative in
which the journey of the Israelites is a negotiation through time
and space. The record of this new negotiation—namely, its history
as it becomes writing and as it becomes the Hebrew Bible—will also
be read one day by Jesus, who will reinforce and dramatize it like
this: "the Kingdom of God is not coming visibly. Nor will one say:
Look, here! Or: There! For, look, the Kingdom of God is within
you!" (Matthew 24:23).

With these words, we see Jesus embodying the Jewish writer that
Moses first characterized, a writer for whom what is being said and
written must be intelligible to all men and women. No ivory tower
priesthood. The sacredness of language must no longer be secret,
the province of clergy only, as in Egypt. Language has been rendered physical, a text that can be written and carried and stored and
copied. And even as it contains the supernatural voice of YHWH,
the drama remains the human one of retelling, reading, and
interpreting.

The Israelites become an audience when they are asked to "Hear,
O Israel" (the *Shema*, or hearing, that confirms the invisibility of

God) as they are about to receive the beginning of the Torah, the Ten Commandments. Nevertheless, Moses is still represented as a writer. What Israel *hears* is already a text that Moses may "teach" from. In Deuteronomy, Moses describes it as a text "that I am teaching you to observe"—and this is the text of laws that Israel will live and think by. What will be taking place on the stage of this new cosmic theater will be the envisioned journey of the writer and reader as the mind is explored: What is it we are reading and how do we interpret it?

The question applies both to the text of the Torah and to the physical text of our journey through space and time. The Jewish writer interprets both at the same time, and in order to do this, the cosmic stage will become a *bimah*, the Hebrew word for stage that is at the center of every synagogue where the Torah is read. Like prophets and rabbis before him, Jesus will act on that stage of the synagogue as an interpreter and something more. He will embody the writer, like Moses, as he pushes further toward the boundary between God and man, between human thought and what is unknowable to the human mind. And thus, thinking, as represented by numinous texts, transforms the entire visual world.

Now, the golden calf can be internalized and understood for what it was: As the Heavenly Cow, it is not simply representing the Egyptian afterlife but a vision that Moses has transformed. For "The Book of the Heavenly Cow" reveals that heaven nurtures us, but that after death we remain as we are, encased as mummies on the Earth, witnesses to a vision of the future that is indeterminate. Once again, we must think of the mummy—and we must be never far from thinking of it—when we confront Moses' education. The mummy carries the identity of the person that has died into the future, so that even today, in an Egyptian museum, we may gaze upon the remarkably vivid face of the young king, Tutankhamen—a Pharaoh who lived and died while the Israelites were building his pyramid. And it is not only the image of a face but the face itself, as God created it.

This pharaoh has journeyed into an indeterminate future that the contemporary museum director describes thusly: "With the latest climate control technology we should be able to preserve it forever." The Israelis have done no less with the Dead Sea Scrolls, preserved today in Jerusalem. What we need to know is how the inspiration provided by the mummy became transformed into Moses' inspiration to write a *text* (rather than embalm a body) that would journey into an indeterminate future itself.

In the time of Moses and the Israelites in Egypt, the visible mummy was everywhere, for every person who died, even the lowest, would be mummified. The mummy—that is to say, a living person transformed—was not worshiped in itself. It was not even venerated the way Lenin's or Stalin's body lies entombed in glass to this day in a Russian monument, the face perfectly preserved and visible to all. No, each ancient Egyptian person, even while alive, prepared for and then carried on after death into an indeterminate future—in the form of his or her mummified body.

And yet all this was transformed in the Torah, so that each person's death holds a meaning in the narrative journey that the Covenant unfolds. In the Torah, the voice of the Creator is represented as eternal and to be carried forward into the future in its very own words. The written text itself, the very scroll, becomes almost like an eternal mummy: it could be written down in conversation with men like Abraham and Moses, as if the voice of the Creator was not forbidding—and no more numinous than the text itself. And it was a text to be cared for like a mummy, carefully tended, encased, and sheltered. So if even YHWH's voice can be both eternal and temporal, both holy and familiar as a mummy, then the power originally represented by a person's mummy is something we must understand more deeply.

Moses had nothing to say about it because the mummy would have been central to the lives of all the Israelites who left Egypt. The Egyptian cosmic theater, even though left behind, was internalized. We will soon see how the Hebrew prophets developed the idea of the individual's soul, whose life and afterlife would continue to remain part of Israel's journey into the future. But for now, let's look more closely at what lies at the heart of an Egyptian education such as not only Moses received but even the poorest slave: the mummy. For the human face is still with us at the heart of a Jewish education: It becomes the faces of the forefathers and foremothers brought to life in the Bible, and it also becomes the faces of the sages who interpreted it. It is the face of individual thought: no longer were the priests to do all the thinking for us.

. . .

In the time of Jesus, priests in the Temple, the Essene monks and nuns in their religious communes, and the Greek-reading upper class all had their own special languages for engaging the Torah. The Pharisees alone sought to use the common Judeo-Aramaic vernacular, and since Jesus was educated among them, it is no surprise that his words, as quoted in the Gospels, are plainspoken. Yet they are highly literary: paradoxical, punning, and ironic—precisely what might impress both the Pharisaic leadership and his common audiences in the synagogue. As we have already seen, it is a mistake to imagine that either Jesus or the majority of his audiences was uneducated. Yet even the most recent scholarship tends to assume exactly what Hollywood movies have shown us for decades: an illiterate Jesus preaching to street people or facing an overly refined complement of accusers, invariably defined as Pharisees.

And yet the Pharisees included the Jewish sages who spoke and taught in the simplest manner, although they might write differently. Like Hasidic rabbis in the last few centuries of our own day, their teaching remained humble and plainspoken, while their writing was highly stylized, just like Hasidic tales full of paradox and ironic twists that echo back to the Pharisees and Jesus himself. It was a style generally known as midrash, most commonly used in sermons, dramatizing the week's Torah portion and often creating a buzz that the synagogue audience would carry home. The midrash also retold its portion of the Torah in terms of local color and daily life. Thus it is not unexpected to find among Jesus' words a predominance of local life and country scenes.

It is easy to forget this aspect of Jesus' Jewish education, or for those who have been raised with a strictly Christian education to have never known this. There are passages in the Gospels that seem to want to cover up this knowledge. For example, the Gospel of Matthew quotes Jesus: "Woe to you, Pharisees, for you love the place of honor at banquets and the front seat in the synagogues and accolades in the markets" (Matthew 23:23). Yet here, Jesus uses the term "Pharisees" as one might address "Christians" today: "Woe to you, Christians, for you love to appear on television and drive to ostentatious churches and hear yourself honored for your generous monetary contributions." Does this mean that the Christians addressed here are to be detested? Of course not, and neither would Jesus have derided his own teachers.

Nevertheless, the point being made here in the simple language of a Jewish sage (or even a Jewish prophet writing centuries before) is that living in this world is a perilous journey. It is to be contrasted with the Torah's journey to the Promised Land—and, as both the Hebrew prophets and Jesus would characterize it, an inner journey to the Kingdom within, what Jesus referred to as the Kingdom of Heaven. By "Pharisees" Jesus might also intend that movement's leadership, just as we refer to the leadership when we might invoke "those Democrats," or "those Republicans." If we have any doubt that Jesus has internalized the Kingdom of Heaven, he makes it clear that he identifies with the Hebrew prophets and his contemporary Pharisees about the importance of the inner life. It is worth quoting again:

> Asked when the Kingdom of Heaven is coming, he answered them and said: The Kingdom of Heaven is not coming visibly. Nor will one say: Look, here! Or: There! For, look, the Kingdom of Heaven is within you! (Matthew 24:23)

But Jesus can be far more scathing in his irony when he invokes the inner life in the common language. Consider this single sentence, also from the Gospel of Matthew (24:28): "Wherever the corpse, there the vultures will gather." There's a corpse, there's a funeral, and there are the self-interested attendees—a scene from social life, highly stylized. Yet for Jesus and the audiences to whom he spoke regularly in the synagogues—the majority with a Jewish education—during his year of journey through Galilee and adjoining cities, this comment would invariably echo a passage from the Hebrew Bible's Book of Ecclesiastes, where the pithy saying went: "Better get thee to a house of mourning than a banquet." Jesus does not intend to contradict Ecclesiastes; instead, he is viewing the scene from the perspective of the inner life.

The "vultures" are not gathering to mourn the corpse but rather to feast upon it. Real vultures will do that, but here we are facing the metaphor of selfish interest. Only an educated man like Jesus could have thought of such a midrashic insight—as if the Book of Ecclesiastes was the weekly Torah portion read in the synagogue. And indeed, on the festival of Sukkot, Ecclesiastes is read as a scroll to accompany the Torah portion.

And further, for Jesus the inner life that this quote contextualizes takes precedence over the afterlife. Perhaps if the corpse had been an Egyptian mummy in the time of Moses, it actually would be the afterlife that we are being confronted with. An afterlife, that is, which Moses transformed into the journey of thinking and feeling that Israel's progress in history represents. Probably Jesus did not know about the significance of the mummy in ancient Egyptian culture, but he did imbibe Moses' transformation: the journey of each Israelite and each inner life continuing on to an indeterminate future. For the reading of Moses' Torah embodies that journey, just as the mummy was imagined to set out on an eternal journey into the future.

And perhaps Jesus had to explain his midrash for his disciples— but probably not. It was not his intention to make scholars out of his audience, and this is where he differed from many of his own teachers. Rather than scholars, he preferred to make prophets out of all his disciples and even all those who followed him. Or not prophets exactly, but rather the taste or sensibility of a prophet, especially one who would be reading his words in the future.

A disciple is not superior to the teacher. It is enough for the disciple that he become like his teacher. (Matthew 10:24)

What sort of education is this? It is one in which the conventional saying—just like the one from Ecclesiastes, though that itself was a play upon convention—is turned inside out, or, as we have termed it when engaging Moses, is transformed. To become like his teacher, Jesus, his disciple or reader must also become humble. Not, in other words, as outwardly smart as his teacher, but one who recognizes the inner life, just as Jesus could identify with Moses as a writer who serves the Covenant. If we can read like Jesus, we are also exploring the boundary between inner and outer lives—and that boundary became most evident in Sinai, when God and man settled upon a text.

Superficially, we may think of Jesus as claiming credit for who he was; as a devout Jew, it would have seemed blasphemous to him to claim to be God. He suggested God spoke through him, as had Moses, so that his words were those of a writer, one whose deeds and acts are also inscribed in his text of a life's journey. But for all those who misread him, and who are blind to the way that both Moses and Jesus transformed their education into a journey to a deeper Jewish education, they blur the historical boundary that is the Covenant, reading literal interpretation in place of numinous presence. As a result, the literal reader can't read the parables, which have to be turned inside out. It was the Covenant that created the dramatic stage upon which this could happen: whether in Sinai in the wilderness with Moses, or reading Moses' Torah through the inner life, as represented by Jesus.

So one must become a historical reader, but know that as a Jew or a Christian, one is reading a numinous text. It is not unusual for nonbelievers to point out the hypocrisy of what they read in a literal-minded way. Even in regarding Egypt they might say: "Oh that mummy is just a sack of bones. Whoever that person was, the only heaven for them is an exhibition case in a museum today. Only a fool could believe in heaven." Here is our uneducated reader bereft of knowledge about how the Covenant—no less than a mummy—transforms the human concern with death and survival into a drama of how to live. Yes, there are requirements ("commandments") that focus human society on truth and justice, but they also concentrate the mind.

· · ·

The historical lives of Moses and Jesus do not adhere to a chronology of events but rather to a development of thought and feeling. When we confront the mind of Moses or Jesus, it is interpreted in some episodes more than others, often in the form of dialogue and speeches given by these figures. This is how a writer reveals character today, and it was no different in the time of Moses, who himself described the presence of God on Mount Sinai in vivid, visual terms—as well as in "remembered" dialogue with the Creator. We now know that later Hebraic writers in Jerusalem were doing much of the writing; nevertheless, they did not get in the way of the crucial image of Moses as writer. It allowed them to continue revealing how he thought—or more precisely, how his memory was alternately seared by events and worked to interpret them.

Now at daybreak on the third day there were peals of thunder on the mountain and lightning flashes, a dense cloud, and a loud trumpet blast, and inside the camp all the people trembled . . . The mountain of Sinai was entirely wrapped in smoke, because YHWH had descended on it in the form of fire. (Exodus 19:16)

This is a visual record, and the description continues as "the whole mountain shook," the thunder grows louder, and Moses was called to come up. Now, it is not hard to imagine that some months or years later, Moses wrote down these experiences. However, he might as well have been writing at the very moment when the Creator said: "I am YHWH your God who brought you out of the land of Egypt . . . You shall have no gods except me" (Exodus 20:1). It renders the words indelible, the words of the Ten Commandments that Moses brought down from the mountain. However, if

Moses wrote this experience down some years later, while writing the Torah, we must trust the accuracy of his memory.

Yet what we can now discern actually happened is that the Hebraic writer more than two centuries later in Jerusalem wrote this down, perhaps based on earlier written or oral sources. And even these earlier sources must have had an authentic authorship to be so trusted by the writers in Jerusalem.

Nevertheless, today we have found that the description of violent atmospheric events on Mount Sinai is very similar to those written down by writers and poets in other ancient cultures and in earlier centuries. So we may assume that these are poetic images of a writer, even in the Torah—but with a crucial difference. Because we have a writer at the scene—Moses as at least a figure of a writer—we can understand that these powerful images are used consciously to evoke God's presence. For even the most literal-minded reader is not thinking about whether these are natural manifestations, whether it be a volcano or some other upheaval. For unlike the pagan gods, YHWH, especially as represented in dialogue with Moses, was wholly independent of nature; the image we are presented is purely a poetic sign that his presence has been felt. Not seen, that is; not made visible, but rendered in the same poetic idiom that earlier civilizations had used in a more literal manner—since their gods were, in fact, present or directly represented in nature.

Now, for the first time in history, we are conscious that the Hebraic writers in Jerusalem were deeply educated, no less than Moses. They were able to transform mythic beliefs that depended upon gods inhabiting nature, and change them utterly, in order to convey that the transcendence of YHWH nevertheless remained in touch with the history of civilization as it unfolded over time. Of course, we don't expect the recently freed Israelites in the wilderness to have studied Ugaritic (a Canaanite literary language that even Moses might not have known, but that contains some similar poetic images to what is found in the Torah). And certainly the Israelites would not have recognized the experience of their journey as a literary projection. They were witnesses, not writers, and what was important to them was not description but the words that came down through Moses from Mount Sinai.

So at least Moses, as writer and educated man, would have known that the trembling of nature was common to ancient pagan literatures. Certainly, the educated Hebraic writers at the royal court in Jerusalem centuries later knew this, but more importantly, they would have assumed that Moses knew it also. Actually, the description before and after the first statement of the Ten Commandments in the Book of Exodus (it will be restated and reformulated in the Books of Leviticus and Deuteronomy) places it in a narrative context that closely resembles the ancient legal covenants of older civilizations. In the mind of a writer, using such ancient archetypes can further confirm the integrity of the work if it is the *transformation* that holds us—and not the knowledge of common sources.

So when we look at the Covenant at Sinai today, grounded in recent historical studies, its resemblance to Hittite (Asia Minor) treaties of earlier centuries is at first almost shocking. There is a preamble, identifying the treaty author—and now it has become, "I am YHWH your God . . ." After this, the Hittite treaty reviews the history of the parties involved—and now it has become, "who brought you out of the land of Egypt . . . ," reminding us of past history. There is a Hittite list of stipulations—and now it has become, "Thou shalts," and "Thou shalt nots." There is a copy of this covenant that must be kept in the Hittite party's sanctuary, from where it must be brought out and read publicly in the future—and now it has become, "Put into the Ark the tablets" and "Every seventh year, at the Festival of Booths . . . you shall read this aloud in the presence of all Israel" (Exodus 25:16; Deuteronomy 32:1).

And then there is a list of witnesses to the Hittite covenant— and now it has become, "I call heaven and earth this day to witness against you" (Deuteronomy 4:26). And to end the treaty there must be some serious curses and blessings—and now these have become, "If you do not listen to me . . . I will inflict on you a fever that wastes the eyes away and exhausts the breath of life" and "If you live

according to my laws . . . I will turn towards you: You shall eat your
fill of last year's harvest, and still throw out the old to make room
for the new" (Leviticus 26:10). Several more curses and blessings
are listed in the Mosaic books of Leviticus and Deuteronomy.

The model of the Hittite treaty was made between kings and
their subordinates. But now it has been transformed into something never before imagined, a Covenant between the natural and
supernatural worlds, between God and man, in a historical narrative of cosmic theater. It is now a numinous text: a form of treaty-
making transformed into a negotiation that is divine. There were
other law collections from ancient civilizations that contained
many of the stipulations we find in the Ten Commandments, such
as the sins betraying one's parents, stealing, adultery, murder, and
bearing false witness. Even the stipulation against taking the name
of one's god in vain, which is found in the Egyptian "Book of the
Dead."

Yet a poetic leap is required to comprehend the transformation
of these stipulations into the Torah. Here, they become part of a
narrative in which an eternal Covenant is being negotiated for the
first time. Much of the Covenant has been revealed before, as when
Abraham first heard of the Promised Land. And much will happen
in the ensuing years of journey in the wilderness, all of it to add context to the meaning of a negotiation between natural human beings
and supernatural Creator. Yet this does not take place in some
trance or supernatural transaction; rather, a history is recounted
of how a complete corpus of laws comes to be written in the Torah,
and it remains a further negotiation of the Covenant.

Moses, whose name is associated with the Torah's laws, is not the
source of this Covenant, like pagan kings and pharaohs had been.
He merely writes them down, and in the process presents a figure
of a great writer that will be interpreted and emulated throughout
many centuries of Hebraic culture—all the way down to the first
century AD, when Jesus begins to speak in the writerly parables
found in the New Testament.

At the end of the Book of Deuteronomy and the Torah, and just before Moses must die, we read: "Moses wrote down this Teaching and gave it to the priests, the sons of Levi, who carried the Ark of YHWH's Covenant—and to all the elders of Israel" (31:8). The "Teaching" itself has taken up most of the book, in the form of narrative and instruction; much of it had already been written during the wilderness years. We have seen Moses set up his table outside the Tent of Meeting during those years. The books that come before Deuteronomy, Numbers, and Leviticus, must also fall under this heading of "Teaching." Nevertheless the real teaching begins when Moses' written text is read to the people, who are instructed to hear and study it every seven years, and to know it well enough to teach their children.

So although the priests and the "elders" are in charge of the written text, the entire people are to become literate in it. This has never happened before, as far as we know, because all other sacred books, whatever their religion, were to be used only by the priests. And now these recently freed slaves are not only to "read" (hear) this voluminous text of Moses but to learn how to interpret it and all its laws concerning justice and how to live, as well as history. Furthermore, aside from the priests, those of the intellectual class who could read and write, or those born into a class of spiritual or hereditary elites, are now responsible for the entire people being taught their history and their God's laws. Everyone will know their rights and what is required of them—not just the leaders. Starting in Exodus, parents must teach their children, for the Ten Commandments and the Book of the Covenant that originally elaborated it are meant for the people as a whole, even the lowliest, and including women, children, and strangers!

Since all the people are to hear it read aloud, the assumption has been that until recent times, when books became affordable and the congregation could follow the writing, oral teaching was the mode of literacy. But I believe that is a mistaken assumption. Scrolls would have been copied in abundance in Jerusalem, when the Books of Moses were completed by the writers at the Solomonic royal court (and later, in Samaria, the capital of the Northern

kings). Not only prophets and students, including those hundreds
or thousands whose names are now lost, had scrolls to read. For
learning to write often began with the exercise of copying. Kings
David and Solomon and those who came after had their archives
and libraries; any student could read there, with permission.

Of course, there were no such libraries in the wilderness of Sinai,
but the first thing we learn from Moses' text is how to understand
history as a journey from period to period, and from place to place,
and from ignorance to knowledge. When it comes to the laws, they
are not merely stated but we are made conscious of the audience
of witnesses. So in most cases Moses' text elucidates the law's
meaning, especially its ethical points. All the events of the journey
in Sinai, going back to the deliverance from Egypt, have become
historical in Moses' writing hand—so that they can stand for experience, the kind that makes the necessity for moral law apparent.
Both the problems in grappling with the new faith, and the laws
meant to reinforce it, are described and taught against the background of an arduous journey in which an entire generation must
die in the desert. So the Torah provides not only the writer and the
text but also the living audience.

Just as historical events are used to elucidate Moses' text, the
same text will be used to imaginatively interpret the sermons delivered in the synagogues of Jesus' day—and there, the writing of the
rabbis will be known as midrash. Yet we can see that from the beginning in the Book of Deuteronomy, Moses himself was already writing in a midrashic frame of mind.

So in a way it is mistaken to refer to "laws." They are more like
what is desired by YHWH to make the Covenant valid than commands to subjects, and Moses elucidates them as an interpreter or
writer. The latest scholarship asserts that the later Hebraic authors
of Deuteronomy were of the educated class, writers at the royal
court of a seventh-century BCE king—just as the writers who complete Exodus were attached to the royal court in the tenth century
BCE. Clearly the literary quality of Deuteronomy requires an educated writer; who else could draw together the many layers? And

yet it can remain a question only because Moses himself, in whose name the later authors seem to write (it is just as likely their names were known before they were lost), has not been more directly faced as an educated man himself.

The emphasis in Deuteronomy on teaching love for God would inspire later generations to "serve Him with all your heart"— further democratizing Moses' text (as against the priestly elite's concern with Temple and sacrifice). It is in the same spirit that the Pharisees confronted the attachment to Temple ritual by making the Torah available to all—and thus ensuring that it underlies Jesus' education. And since his education was Pharisaic, let's look more closely at it.

The Pharisees taught the Torah by transmission from rabbi to disciple, in circles and schools resembling the Greek philosophers who established their own schools. It was not only father to son, as it had been in the priestly tradition. Neither was it the province of an aristocratic class or any other hereditary caste. So it would be hard to believe the Pharisees did not read some Plato, as the Hellenists did, and be inspired by his perpetual influence among teachers and students. Thus, when Jesus instructs his disciples to privilege their "family" of rabbi and disciple, he is not out of step with prevailing custom. In fact, we can imagine that the Pharisees were even more egalitarian than the democrats of ancient Athens, since the latter still depended upon their aristocratic class for interpretation of sacred customs.

Like any rabbi influenced by the Pharisees, Jesus would have turned his disciples into a "school" that would perpetuate and interpret his words. But it also reflects an acquaintance with Greek philosophy, as it was known in the Israel of Jesus' day, and this could be found in the Hellenistic education that was available in most of Israel's cities. And that would include Sepphoris, the Hellenized town a short walk from Nazareth, where Jesus probably studied in youth, albeit in a Jewish circle of Pharisaic teaching. But whether Plato or Moses is taught in Sepphoris, the work attributed to each man is considered, in the words of Cicero, a renowned Roman author of that day, "a precious possession," insofar as Plato and Moses are understood to have founded a school of thought.

In the same way, the Pharisees transformed the Greek notion of the soul into a resurrection of the dead, as well as the day of judgment at world's end. Shortly after his death, the Greek influence would intensify upon Jesus' disciples and we see it more clearly in the Gospels, which echo the Platonic intellectualizing of the Roman author Plutarch—who in the time of the Gospel authors was known as an exemplary religious writer. Surely they would have been acquainted with Plutarch's genre of biography: the brief lives he wrote of famous Greco-Romans. While recent research has shown that the original written text of the first, or Ur-Gospel, now lost, was probably written in Hebrew or Aramaic, it most likely resembled a text of "Jesus' teaching" rather than a biography. It was only in its later Greek-language evolution that the life of Jesus in the Gospels took narrative shape. Plutarch was perhaps at the margins, but the Jesus we find in the finished Gospels of the New Testament is much less like a noble Greek or Roman—and far more like the humble and deeply educated Moses.

True, the Greek and Roman philosophers were understood not only as writers but as men of action—models of right thinking— and Jesus' actions are portrayed in similar measure. Yet the model for his life was closer to that of a Jewish sage. There were many biographies of Jewish sages at the time, and many of these found their way into the Talmud, yet few were as focused upon the biographical details as we find in the Gospels. Not as many details as we would expect in a modern biography, of course, but the hints are there. For instance, Jesus instructed his disciples to leave their families behind them, and his own relations with his family in Nazareth were probably strained. His several brothers and sisters, along with his mother, joined the nascent Jewish-Christian sect in Jerusalem—but only after Jesus' death. During his life they remained in Nazareth, basically out of touch. Jesus' father Joseph, who may have been a carpenter, would also have been known as a wise man. Carpenters were looked up to and often were acquainted with Jewish Wisdom literature, both Hellenistic and Hebraic.

Joseph probably died before Jesus was a teen, and Jesus would have been sent to study with a rabbi outside of Nazareth. He was, after all, the firstborn in his family. Being "the son of a carpenter" was quite an honorable title for him to bear in his rabbinic circle, and his swift mind would have drawn him closer into the sphere of rabbis and sages—and further away from his family in Nazareth. Now we are entering the realm of a Jewish biography, like that of Moses, who was also separated from his family and whose later relations were troubled. But aside from these details, such a Jewish biography is unique in dramatizing the inner life and the thinking life of Moses and Jesus. Plutarch, for instance, adumbrated the accomplishments of his biographical subjects, and while he often focused upon their influences, we do not sense how the inner lives of his nobles were roiled and fecund. What was missing in Plutarch was the intense presence of a cosmic theater that is never far from any situation involving Moses or Jesus.

. . .

Today, we speak figuratively of writers as wearing a mask, and what we mean in general is that the actual person doing the writing is protected from being confused with the narration or the narrator of his or her text. The actual person, hidden in this way, remains free to tell us whatever he or she may wish—even on the book jacket's biography or anywhere else outside the text. There are other ways the figure of a mask distinguishes between inner and outer lives, but they all go back to the usage of masks in preliterate societies, where inner states of being are acted out in ritual drama and dance, rather than narrated.

We have seen such masks in museums and art galleries; the ones most familiar, however, come from ancient Greek origin and were transferred from religious ritual into the Greek theater of tragedy and comedy. Simply the common motif of a sad face and a happy one, represented on intertwining masks, also comes from this era.

Actors on the Greek stage as well as the narrating Chorus wore the masks of the mythological or legendary characters they played. Since many of these characters were gods, the Greek cosmic theater allowed for their safe interaction with humans by masking them equally with human characters.

So it is no great surprise to find Moses wearing a mask when he confronts YHWH in the Tent of Meeting, as even a primordial priest would in the presence of the divine, and neither is it that unusual when Moses wears his mask as he walks among the Israelites. However, it is fairly strange to think he would be wearing this mask for most of the forty years in the wilderness—concealed from the Israelites, but removing it only within the privacy of facing his God.

> *And when Moses had finished speaking with them, he put a covering on his face. And when Moses came before YHWH to speak with him, he took the covering off each time, until he came out again; then he went out and spoke to the children of Israel what he was commanded. Then the children of Israel saw the face of Moses that it was radiant, and Moses again put the covering on his face until he went in to speak with him.*
> *(Exodus 34:33)*

The tale about Moses acquiring some radiance from his intimacy with YHWH seems arbitrary: a kind of sunburn in need of masking? And yet, in his dealings with people for many years there is no mention of this awkward situation. Even today, a recent translation of the Five Books of Moses explains away this anomaly by comparing it with the "divine halo" of pagan priests and kings (enveloping them, rather than suspended decorously over their heads, as in the much later depictions of Christian saints). Moses, however, is neither priest nor king, or anything resembling such a figure. Rather than bear the "radiance" either proudly or humbly before humans, Moses hides it behind the mask. A primordial priest, on the other hand, would have put on his mask during the divine rituals of his cosmic theater, and taken it off after.

What most likely happened in Moses' day was that he did use a "cultic mask," as scholars refer to it, just as many other cultic props were described in the Book of Exodus as essential to the priesthood, such as the "Urim and Thummim," or oracular breastplate, worn by the early Israelite priest. Yet these props have become exotic gestures within the real cosmic theater that Moses and the Israelites take part in: the writing of the narrative itself. The detail about the mask lends an authenticity to the text, rendering it historical, as we witness the transformative stages of the journey in the wilderness.

At the same time, we see the development of the Jewish religion in how the descriptions of ark and tabernacle later evolve into the Temple appurtenances, eventually to be built in Jerusalem. These details about elements of the cosmic theater—already being worked out in the wilderness by a generation of slaves—similarly render the journey historical. Just as Moses has transformed his Egyptian education, Exodus among other books is witness to the process of transformation. Most crucially, it's a process that requires the time and discipline to wait, as more is revealed, and to persevere during forty years of a cosmic journey.

Whether it took Moses four months or forty years to write the Torah, figuratively speaking, it also took more than four centuries to have it written in its nearly final form. The Israelites had to establish not only cities and governments in ancient Israel but also a Hebraic culture that could develop over time. So the key to the Torah is the ability to enter its cosmic narrative in a wholly historical manner. That is, it recounts not a mythical time but a reasonably historical reconstruction of what took place at the origin of the Covenant. Certainly some things are representative rather than exact.

Moses may have carried a mask for forty years, yet this potential fact is only representative of the deeper historical situation. Some translations call it a "veil," so as not to suggest an image could have been upon it. But the way in which the detail of a mask is recorded more likely suggests that Moses had to separate his role as leader from that of his role as writer, for the latter requires the protecting or masking of the author's inner life.

A writer does not need a pen or a computer with which to write; these are aides, but a writer can also simply dictate his words. The same is true of the mask of Moses (which most likely he did not literally wear among the people; it may not even have existed as more than a personal artifact, imaginatively written). Nevertheless, the mask was still a historical artifact, even if turned into a narrative aide for the Torah Moses must write. Such small aides to historical veracity—to a witness of the actual evolution of history as it is happening—are rendered in greater detail when the building of the sanctuary in the desert comes to be described.

Some modern Bibles include a simple blueprint of the tabernacle that Moses describes being built in the desert. The blueprint includes such structures as the Ark, the Altar of Incense, the Menorah, the Altar of Burnt Offering, and the Holy of Holies, all laid out like props on a monumental stage. The sizes and distances between the structures are exactly designated in biblical "cubits" and the furniture and drapery are precisely described. All this renders the religious institution historical by its similarity to Egyptian structures of much earlier date. Almost two thousand years earlier, a tomb at Giza reveals a structure of hanging curtains to form a canopy, along with gold-cased furniture. Many other such structures convey a sense of portability by the shape of their canopies, so that the tabernacle of the Israelites fits into a certain history.

And this history is really brought home today by the traveling exhibit from Egypt of Tutankhamen's tomb and its contents, which originated close to the Exodus in time. Yet these bits of historical veracity are but the mask, as it were, of what is held within: not the mummy of a dead king, but the narrative of a period in our history that was transformed into a cosmic drama by Moses. We may enter into it today, by reading, without having to wait for the exhibition to arrive. In fact, the reading of the Torah is a religious requirement, and what is required is precisely that we enter into history.

Further, the ark and tabernacle in the wilderness of Sinai put all that has come before in Jewish history on a stage. Like "I am that I am," these are truly separate objects, numinous and yet rooted in history. What happens when God becomes real?—that is, becomes real on the stage of human history? The ark and tabernacle allow the Israelites to make God's quest for intimacy with history an integral part of their journey. YHWH wants to dwell among the people, not merely be represented there.

. . .

Much later in history, in the time of Jesus, we encountered the rabbinic circle based on a sage and his disciples. Yet long before the sages, and before Plato and Aristotle, the Hebrew prophets formed their own schools. The school of Isaiah continued down the generations from the eighth to sixth centuries BCE: there were several who wrote in the name of Isaiah, and many more who were disciples. Isaiah, while he critiqued the lawful establishment, was not against the law itself but rather its misinterpretation. Like most prophets, Isaiah wrote in the tradition of Moses and a Covenant which included "all of Israel." Thus, the voice of YHWH could still be dramatized: "I will make you a light of nations that my salvation may reach the ends of the earth . . . to the honor of YHWH, who elected you" (Isaiah 49:6). Since Israel was "elected" or chosen to bring the nations of the world to its own revelation, something greater than Israel's own uniqueness was hoped for.

It was the same "when Moses went into the Tent of Meeting to hear the Voice addressing him from above the cover that was on top of the Ark of the Covenant, between the two cherubim . . ." (Numbers 7:89). This is how it happened in the writer's mind of Moses: YHWH's throne rests above the Ark, "Enthroned on the Cherubim." Can we still verify this history? YHWH's divine throne had for its footstool the Ark of the Covenant; that is, the footstool was the visible Ark but the throne of God was invisible above it. If this seems strange, it's only because of the history we lack. And some of it now comes back, as in the Egyptian tombs reopened in our own time: there the mummy of the Pharaoh rests, entombed together with his throne and footstool of gold. In Moses' Torah, there was no *actual* throne, and the Ark contained written tablets of the Torah— it was a historical text, even then.

But the Ark was made numinous (remember, a footstool!) and contained the seed of the Torah and of all the texts that flow from it. It was thus prepared to become a numinous narrative from the beginning, so that several centuries later, Isaiah could write: "YHWH, God of Israel, enthroned on the cherubs, you alone are God of all the kingdoms of the earth, you have made heaven and earth" (Isaiah 37:16). And a century after that, the Hebrew prophet Jeremiah will write: "One day, no one will ever say again, Where is the Ark of the Covenant? There will be no thought of it, no memory of it, no regret for it, no making of another. It will be a time when Jerusalem shall be called, The Throne of YHWH; all the nations will gather there in the name of YHWH" (Jeremiah 3:16). What Jeremiah envisions is that the invisible "Throne of YHWH" will become visible in historical time and space: it will be the city of Jerusalem, since YHWH's words—and thus the writing of Moses—will be visible there.

Will anything look like an Ark? A golden footstool? No, they will be the words of Moses' Torah only, in which YHWH remains invisible in his numinous text. Why is it that these words should be stronger than any visible or material manifestation of the Divine? They hold within them two things: one is the historical fact of their writing, whether by Moses or later Jeremiah, and the other is the voice of YHWH, that is only known to Moses and other Hebrew prophets because the Covenant is sealed in their mind.

Today, there are all kinds of synagogues, mosques, and churches in Jerusalem, and even the outer remnant of the Holy Temple's Western Wall. There are also museums that hold Egyptian mummies and ancient golden artifacts. But it would be a mistake for anyone to look for the "Throne of YHWH." Jeremiah made it clear that the throne "shall be called . . ."—in other words, "The Throne of YHWH" is a *saying*, an artifact of words that is historically rooted in Moses' description of the invisible Throne, sitting above the footstool of the tablets. We have the words of the tablets, the Ten Commandments, but the stones themselves are lost.

Yet we have the image of them bound in the Mosaic narrative

and lending personality to this history. One verse in Exodus, for instance, by having us imagine "the Finger of God" etching the words, gives the scene even more personality while at the same time rendering it invisible. No one asks us to imagine God's Finger literally, any more than his Throne. But it is crucial that YHWH's personality be present in the human world and not only in the writerly mind of Moses. The impact of the writing, however, echoes down twelve centuries to the rabbis and sages of Jesus' day, who write of God as a social being. Among other representations, God is a teacher:

> *He sits and teaches school children, as it is said: "Whom shall one teach knowledge, and whom shall one make to understand the message? Those who are weaned from milk." (Isaiah 28:9)*

Isaiah wrote this many centuries before it is now being quoted by a Jewish sage teaching his disciples in the first century AD, but we know of it because it is recorded in the Talmud many further centuries later. Here God is a teacher, and in other places he may be a warrior, a young man, and a father. The sage himself could be an incarnation, if not of God then of the Torah. The Talmud describes a process where a sage could be the embodiment of the Torah—the Torah made flesh, in order to render it a source of salvation. And further, the sage and the Torah were equal. It was not a metaphor; it was a legal point: "He who sees a disciple of a sage who has died is as if he sees a scroll of the Torah that has been burned."

. . .

Like any sage, when we consider Jesus to be a writer as well as one conversant with his Creator, it's not surprising that his writer's authority personifies YHWH. The twentieth-century philosopher Karl Jaspers wrote that Jesus' "reality is courage, above all in the fulfillment of his divine mission to tell the truth, to be the truth. That is the courage of the Jewish Prophets: not a courage to be mirrored in the fame of great deeds and a brave death for posterity, but before God alone." When Jaspers writes, "to tell the truth, to be the truth," he means the telling is the writing, the truth is the embodiment of the Torah—and all this is not uncommon to the rabbis whom Jesus knew.

And when a writer of our time or any other writes, "before God alone," he embodies the authority for the numinous text of Moses. It is the Covenant that brings God's writing hand into the picture, signing it, as it were. But from then on, the personality of YHWH becomes essential. It is what animates the life of Moses and that of Jesus. Without the power of YHWH's supernatural presence, given a stage in the cosmic theater of the Covenant, Moses and Jesus could not write or be quoted. And in the same way that Moses' wonder-working was intended to cement his credibility as well as YHWH's, the healing powers of Jesus are not represented as those of a magician but rather invocations of YHWH: the initiative comes from the Creator.

The Gospels suggest that Jesus' theological journey in the world is intended to "defeat" death, and then "return home" to the original Kingdom of Heaven. Yet this journey is already well-known in his day as the Pharisaic concept of resurrection. In the writings of many sages and rabbis, the Creator-father's judgment of each life is what makes our lives credible on the soul's journey to the Last Day—but meanwhile, as we live, we read Moses' Torah, as Jesus did, quoting from all of its books. More than that, however, Jesus embodied Moses the writer: he transformed the words into speech again, re-creating the numinous stage of YHWH's cosmic theater— but Jesus himself was alone with YHWH.

It's not easy to dramatize the life of a writer, who sits alone with his or her words, but what Moses and Jesus have done is to turn their lives into a journey and we must become aware of it if we're to give new meaning to the term *Judeo-Christianity*. There's no question that meaning is long overdue. The notion of Judeo-Christianity that prevails is confined to ethics, emphasizing the Hebrew prophets as the forerunners. But the relation of Jesus to Moses is not simply about ethics, nor is it a story of founding prophets. Focusing upon their lives, we've now seen that it is their *thinking*, in relation to Jewish history, that has been the missing part of their biography. It is the relationship of their ways of thinking that can now amplify the term *Judeo-Christianity*.

I've insisted upon exploring their educations because the similarity is astounding: I've imposed the concept of their authorship— of both Jesus and Moses as writers—in order to bring this out. They're not ordinary writers, of course, and that is why it is essential to create a cultural context for their cosmic dimension. They are not mythical figures and yet they are always conscious of their cosmic theater and its mythic precedents. We tend to think of writers as both self-conscious and aware of unknown possibilities—but we do not expect them to be conscious of what is *unknowable* to the human species.

Moses and Jesus were writers of a kind we rarely see (perhaps Sophocles and Freud are others) because they are conscious of the unknowable in the only realistic aspect man has been able to devise: a constant vigilance over where the border lies that guards our human limitations. This border has never been more convincingly dramatized than in the biblical Covenant, which represents the physical time and space in which a negotiation of human limits (and thus, human nature) was begun. It began and continues with a Creator on the other side of the negotiation—one who only becomes knowable to us in the form of a personality. This personality might not be necessary—it is not needed, perhaps, by metaphysicians—if it were not essential that we explore our nature culturally as well, in a theater of interaction.

And since this theater includes the supernatural Creator, we have called it a cosmic theater, where both human and supernatural may act upon each other without purely mythic consequences. It is only on this stage that the personalities of Moses and Jesus are enlarged by their thinking process. They are both thinking, and acting out their thinking, in relation to their education—and for both of them, that education was cosmic as well as rational. For Moses, it was rooted in the Egyptian cosmic theater but also the development of Egyptian Wisdom, a tradition of rational thinking about human

nature that would influence, in turn, Greek and Roman thinking. And Moses was also exposed to the original Hebraic cosmic
theater, going back to the ancient conversation between Abraham
and his God, and for this Moses had forty years to educate himself
in Canaanite Midian, expanding upon all he'd already learned in
Egypt. For Jesus, on the other hand, it was all rooted in the Hebraic
cosmic theater that began with Moses and continued through all
the Jewish prophets as well as the multitude of Jewish writers of
additional books in the Hebrew Bible.

The scholars of the historical Jesus (and those few who have
explored the background of Moses) have limited themselves to the
academic definition of human history: as if Jesus or Moses were
like any other person. But great writers are not like any other, nor
will it explain the majesty of their works to describe their ordinary
lives. Because so much is happening in the minds of these writers,
the biographer must also be a literary critic and devise a theater
in which aspects of the writer's life are in imagined conversation
with the characters or the narrators of the author's work. Shakespeare's Hamlet and his own family drama in Stratford-upon-Avon,
for instance. But we need not devise such a theater for Moses and
Jesus because the Covenant that was central to both of their lives
is already a cosmic theater—and it has been reinterpreted and
restated among countless other writers down through the history
of Judeo-Christianity.

The problem is most pronounced when comparing academic
and religious scholars. Most Jewish scholars who study the time of
Jesus in Israel are academics limited to a rational tradition of history
that excludes the cosmic theater. They are trying to describe a Jesus
or a Moses who is not utterly changed by his conversation with the
Creator. Thus, it is always a surprise to read the work of Christian
scholars who bring their belief into play. Consider the crucial issue
of Jesus' literacy. Catherine Hezser has written the most extensive
study yet on Jewish literacy at the time of Jesus, attempting to apply
current academic methods. She finds that probably not more than
10 percent of Judean Jews could read and write, and therefore she

concludes that Jesus and his disciples may indeed have been illiterate, in line with the common impression. Yet even 10 percent means half a million literate souls, of which there is no special reason to exclude Jesus and his disciples.

Nevertheless, Christian scholars, such as Paul Eddy and Gregory Boyd, sense the blinding limitations that Hezser's academicism imposes. They are equal to her in scholarly credentials, yet they are willing to bring the Hebraic cosmic theater to bear. First, they emphasize that Hezser's statistics are based upon the general population of the Roman empire and do not take into account the unique literacy standards of the Jewish population, which would suggest a literacy rate well over 20 percent. When Hezser proposes that there was no public education system in Jewish Judea, Eddy and Boyd contradict her by reminding us that every town had its synagogue and every synagogue had its teachers and students. Yet more important is the evidence of literacy we already know: the Dead Sea Scrolls of the Essene sect of Jews represent a complex library and high rate of literacy. They were written and read by all.

While Hezser does not argue with this, she claims that this community "cannot be considered representative of Palestinian (Judean) Judaism as a whole." Eddy and Boyd take issue with what Hezser judges as "representative." All we have to do, they suggest, is to not arbitrarily assume that the Essenes were more intellectual than other Judean Jews, whether they be Pharisees or Sadducees. They conclude, therefore, that "a fair portion of Palestinian (Judean) Jews around the time of Jesus were, in fact, quite literate." It is precisely their willingness to sense that the Jews are exceptional that brings Eddy and Boyd to assert that Jesus himself, as well as his disciples, were literate. They do not need absolute proof of it. They are just as comfortable closely reading the Gospel tradition as the tradition of modern academic methodology. Thus they find Jesus debating scribes and Pharisees on interpretation of the Hebrew Bible, and can elaborate from this the assumption that these debates require knowledge of "rather technical interpretive points of the Law and tradition."

Nor do our Christian scholars, Eddy and Boyd, find any friction from Jesus' original Jewish audiences about his level of literacy. These Jewish contemporaries of Jesus assumed that a Jew from Nazareth would naturally be an educated man. Those whom Jesus encounters recognize him as a rabbi and teacher. Eddy and Boyd go on to quote the Christian scholar John Meier, that Jesus "is not an ordinary peasant" but actually possessed "scribal literacy." We must also realize that few Jewish scholars attest to Jesus' literary powers, partly because of their lack of empathy—not with Jesus but with the rabbinic tradition at the time. Like their academic colleagues who may be Christian but not serious believers, the Jewish scholars have trouble envisioning either Jesus or Moses as exceptional—especially as great writers, though that is how we are able to place them in a context that is both historical and at the same time cosmic. In other words, we owe to them the Testaments we are reading, thanks to their uniqueness as well as their unity in interpreting the Covenant.

So if we take cues from evangelical Christian scholars like Eddy and Boyd, who represent a new direction by putting the Hebraic cosmic theater on the same level as academic acumen, we begin to see how a new conception of Judeo-Christianity is being born. We find the same tendency to bridge religion and culture among young scholars in Israel today. And we must also reconsider those who have explored the psychological dimensions of Moses, such as Sigmund Freud and Jan Assmann, our foremost living Egyptologist. In cultural terms, their elucidation of a "psychic theater" brings together personal and social history in a cosmic theater of its own, inasmuch as religion is found inseparable from the building of civilization.

A new Judeo-Christianity places an emphasis on history that leads to the footsteps of Moses and Jesus—but now, these are very real footsteps that have walked in the Sinai and the streets of Jerusalem. For Jesus, these are not the footsteps of the Stations of the Cross, the Passion; nor are they the supernatural footsteps of the resurrected Jesus. Yet we do not need to deny the afterlife of Jesus or the belief of the Jewish Pharisees in the resurrection of the dead. When we mark Jesus' footsteps historically, they are following in those of Moses. True, Moses did not live to see Jerusalem, but the Hebraic culture that he inspired produced the writers in ancient Jerusalem who completed the Torah and the rest of the Hebrew Bible. As well, the writers of the Gospels may not all have written in Jerusalem, but all that they wrote was inspired by how Jesus spoke: in a manner of provocation that inspired his audience and disciples to become more educated in the Hebrew Bible, and to produce more writers.

Just as "All Israel" is included in the Mosaic Covenant—all must read and all must teach—we can describe the Covenant in itself as a theater for making one literate. Thus, when one walks in the streets of Jerusalem today, one is walking in the footsteps of the many writers of the Bible, an entire culture, and this new awareness makes concrete our need to go further into the past. The old idea of a Hebraic "religious genius" can now be expanded to a Hebraic culture of down-to-earth writers and scholars, editors and translators.

Let us start by going back halfway to Moses, to the fertile renaissance of Jewish culture in the first century AD. Soon, however, we will be forced to leave Jerusalem in desperation, in the year 70 AD. That is, if we are still alive after the Roman massacre. But Judaism continues in other parts of Israel, where the sages meet and write a new Torah: the "Oral Torah." In place of the lost Temple and its sacrificial rites, we will receive the forerunners of the text that becomes the Talmud. But already the taste for animal sacrifice had been discounted in both the Jewish and the Roman world. Jews could trace their dissatisfaction back many centuries to the Hebrew prophets, and in more recent times the Pharisees had substituted prayer for obligation to the Temple rites.

Now just as the Jews were developing a new interpretive and numinous text in the "Oral Torah," rooted in Moses' historical example and thus written down as well, the Jewish Christians also substituted a written text of prayer for sacrificial rites. It was the ancient Hebrew Book of Psalms, and it remained in common between Jews and Christians, even as the Temple was lost—the same Temple in which many of the Psalms were written by priests who had descended from Aaron and Moses. And yet Christians to this day do not read the Hebrew Bible in full awareness, because these aspects of Jewish authorship and Hebraic culture are lost to them. Instead, the New Testament provides its own continuity in the form of disciples of a sacrificial rabbi named Jesus, and who, in their flight from Jerusalem, eventually find themselves talking to Jews as well as Gentiles in foreign lands.

Many Jews also left Israel (or were pushed out) who will find it unnecessary to even consider the New Testament because the Oral Torah provides their continuity with the ancient Temple. All the old rites become integrated into a new narrative—or, to be more accurate, a narrative of multitudinous conversation among rabbis and sages across the centuries, now known as the Talmud. We would not ask Christians today to immerse themselves in the Talmud, nor would we require a Jew to become fluent in the New Testament; nevertheless, each has its common origin in the Hebraic cosmic theater of Moses and YHWH, and it is important that the distinction between these post-Temple Jews becomes clear.

Jewish Christians in the late first century AD developed the Hebraic cosmic theater into one of theology and salvation; they accepted a new path to survival. For them, it is the soul's survival that becomes crucial and, not to mince words, the soul is illiterate and innocent. Why? It is the soul's innocence of the struggle between good and evil that puts it in jeopardy and that asks for a path to salvation. Yet the Jewish Covenant is not mainly about the survival of the soul; rather, it is about survival in history. Its insistence on exploring the moral law is propelled by the need to explore human nature. And of course, this is an intellectual and literate pursuit, knowledge-hungry for the origins of Creation and civilization. "All Israel"—rather than the individual soul—must be involved in this pursuit for it to survive. The Jews were still writing boldly in the tradition of Moses.

Even so, the words of Jesus do not revolt against the Jewish

Covenant or Law, as is often assumed. His words came from a critical attitude established many generations earlier. It was later recorded in the Talmud but it was first written in the early part of the second century BCE by a Jewish writer using the Greek name Antigonos of Socho: "Be not like slaves who serve their master for the sake of reward, but like slaves who serve their master with no eye on any reward; and may the fear of heaven be among you." Such thinking was prevalent in rabbinical circles because it was interpretive, for instance, of the Book of Job, a book of the Hebrew Bible written at least a century earlier. The Book of Job focused upon the disappointment of the righteous person. Why must a righteous person suffer when an evil one can enjoy his life? The line between sinners and saints was questioned, as well as the limits of God's love for his people. And as we also see in Antigonos, the moral act bears no connection to the reward at first scrutiny.

In Roman civil life, quite familiar in Jewish Judea, it was evident that loving good people and hating evil ones was no longer recognizable. The good could act badly and vice versa. The way forward was love and mercy toward all, as if one were imitating God himself. And thus the Gospel of Matthew records: "You must be perfect, as your heavenly Father is perfect" (Matthew 5:48). Here, Matthew is paraphrasing an old saying from the Midrash, and there were many rabbis thinking this way. It is no surprise that Jesus declared, "Love your enemies" (Matthew 5:44). All of it went back to the Torah of Moses and its statement of the Golden Rule.

Nowhere else in the New Testament does anyone refer to the commandment in Moses' Torah to love one's enemies—no one, that is, except for Jesus. In the Gospel of Matthew (22:35), Jesus explicitly teaches the Law of Moses by quoting what he describes as the two primary commandments:

You shall love the Lord your God with all your heart, and with all your soul, and with all your mind. This is the great rule in the law. And the second is similar to it. You shall love your neighbor as yourself. On these two commandments depends all the law.

It is plain to see that Jesus taught the Golden Rule as he found it in the writing of Moses (Leviticus 19:18) like no other, but he uses Moses' words here in the way that many rabbis had, of his day and earlier. Certainly we see Jesus in a foul mood among many of his neighbors, from the citizens of Nazareth—who in fact were his real neighbors while he grew up there—to some of the Pharisees he encounters in Jerusalem. If Jesus took the Golden Rule literally, he might have kissed his onetime neighbors and the Pharisees, or at least responded to them with respect. This doesn't happen because Jesus in fact considers the first of these two commandments more important; that is, he teaches that the love of God is the crucial love, and in this he remains the stereotypical Jewish thinker. And more than that, the unconditional love of God was at the heart of contemporary Pharisaism.

The Talmud describes seven different kinds of Pharisees—five of them are negative types, so it is quite certain Jesus was not alone in his criticism of fellow Jews. The two good types of Pharisees are the ones who emphasize the fear of God and those who emphasize the love of God. But of numerous references to the fear of God and love of God in rabbinical writings, unconditional love was emphasized far more than the fear of punishment. So not only did the commandment to love God and neighbor exist before Jesus, it also was common in the time that he lived and was probably rooted in his education.

. . .

As a typical Jew, Jesus came to Jerusalem during the Passover festival to offer a paschal lamb at the Temple. The remains of this roasted lamb had to be eaten within Jerusalem's walls. So the Last Supper was a paschal meal, as the Gospels intended, because it takes place within Jerusalem. Jesus and his twelve disciples, being pilgrims to Jerusalem during this Passover festival, would have been generously hosted for their Seder meal, the Last Supper. And when he is reclining along with his disciples at the Seder table, he foretells his death and the "hand of him who hands me over." But the telling of the betrayal and the motive of Judas Iscariot, and even the death of Judas, is never clear. After such a betrayal, Judas would naturally disappear, since not only Jesus' followers but almost any Jew would have been against him for handing over another Jew to the Romans. The only attempt at a universal justification in the depiction of Judas is that he betrayed his fellows for silver coins—in which case, he is hardly a Jew at all since Jewish fellowship is primary. No, there is something missing in this history.

Moreover, among devoted Jews like Jesus and his disciples, a Jew can think like a Jew and come to the aid of his fellows, and in that way he is a universal type; but a Jew cannot be a sinner because then he is really just like everyone else—and not really a Jew at all. That was the thinking. But what comes later in the New Testament is that the world requires that a Jew *be* a Jew, and therefore necessarily *different* rather than universal. So how was Jesus naturally Jewish in that he was different? In fact, he was perfectly a Jew—except that he was without sin. So we cannot say he was like everyone else; rather, we can only say that he was different from all others inasmuch as he was supernatural.

We seem to encounter trouble here, because the historical and supernatural Jesus appear at odds. But this is exactly the kind of "trouble" that Jewish rabbis and Jesus himself, especially Jesus, relished. The paradox in the parables of Jesus is usually meant to expose the hypocrisy of a person who claims to be righteous, or merely right. These people are always Jews in the Gospels, because it is only the Jews to whom Jesus speaks. Even the "Good Samaritan" is a type of Jew, or was. The hypocrisy of those among us today who think that Jesus spoke to Gentiles, or even preferred Gentiles, is very similar to the falsely righteous persons that Jesus must expose.

When Jesus wants to depict the hypocrisy of some Pharisees, his comment is beautifully wrought and the paradox stinging:

Woe to you, scribes and Pharisees, hypocrites! For you build the tombs of the prophets and adorn the monuments of the righteous, saying, "If we had lived in the days of our fathers, we would not have taken part

with them in shedding the blood of prophets." Thus you witness against
yourselves, that you are the sons of those who murdered the prophets.
(Matthew 23:29)

. . .

In other words, these Pharisaic Jews are as if claiming to be Christians by separating themselves from their "fathers" who on some
occasions found a prophet, false or true, to be an outlaw. But now,
it is as if Jesus is telling them no, they are not as Christians, because
just by claiming to be the sons of "those who murdered the prophets" testifies that they are not separate—that there is no way for
them to claim to be anything but Jews. And of course, while pointing out the depths of hypocrisy here, Jesus is not condemning his
fellow Jews to any punishment.

What Jesus is doing, like many rabbis in the Midrash and Talmud,
is critiquing his companion Jews, just as had the Jewish prophets in
earlier centuries. So it would be quite ironic for a Christian today
to falsely assume that Jesus separated himself in any way from his
fellow Jews, nor in any way spoke, taught, and figuratively wrote
to anyone other than Jews. In fact, the Pharisees themselves were
ashamed of much of the criticism they had directed against fellow
Jews who attacked them in earlier decades—especially the Essenes,
and even the Sadducees, who may have been the first to persecute
them. Nevertheless, even as we explore how much like any other
human being is a Jew, the contrary impression remains that Jews
are different, and we can see why even from the brief quotes from
the Gospels we have made.

But Jesus does not separate himself as a Jew from the Pharisees
when he criticizes them—so why do the Christians who follow, even
up to our own day? The answer lies in the absence of a serious idea
of Judeo-Christianity, going beyond the commonality of texts and
ethics to acknowledge a common commitment to history, to the
historical truth. It took forty years of human history for the Jews
to accept Moses' Torah and the necessity to continue the journey—
not only into the land of Israel but also to continue interpreting

the Hebrew Bible and the Covenant on up to our own day. So it is merely a further advance of the journey to come together now, Jews and Christians, to study our past more closely.

We have just left Jesus and his disciples at their Passover Seder meal in Jerusalem, and we note that Jesus, like all Jews, would have reclined in emulation of a Hellenistic banquet, as is customary at the Passover Seder meal. But more importantly, Jesus was observing the already ancient custom of the Passover meal that Moses first described in the wilderness of Sinai, when it was a commemoration of the escape from Egypt. Underneath was another meal, however, a truly numinous sharing of bread with YHWH—this was the crucial Mosaic significance. It was the original meal of the Covenant, in which YHWH had invited his guests to come up his mountain and eat with him, and to share his hospitality.

YHWH provides the food, and he provides the context for a communion with the unknowable realm of heaven, the Covenant meal. It is only later that the humans will bring the food for the meal: it becomes the sacrifice of food to the Creator, as if it were an offering in thanksgiving for the original Covenantal meal that YHWH himself provided. There,

> . . . *they saw the God of Israel. Under his feet a pavement of sapphire was created, a likeness pure as the substance of the sky. He did not lay a hand on them, the noble pillars of Israel. They beheld God; they ate and drank. (Exodus)*

It is this numinous meal of creating a Covenant that was a subtext for the Passover tradition in Jesus' day. And it is what Jesus no doubt referred to when he offered the unleavened bread (matzot) to his disciples at the Last Supper, describing it as a part of his body. For once again, a numinous Jesus is providing the food for the Covenantal meal—even though his disciples do not yet realize that they are in the presence of the Kingdom of Heaven. Yet this communion meal will become the basis for remembering the original Covenant with YHWH, just as the Passover Seder records the original journey.

Jesus has expanded the communion meal between the Jews and
YHWH into the Covenantal concept of the Kingdom of Heaven,
as he found it in the Jewish Prophets. It is YHWH's Kingdom, of
course, and it is understood as such by all those who hear Jesus during his lifetime. And since it is an ancient Jewish concept, it does
not beg a question of the afterlife, for the Jewish Covenant had
created a space in which God and man could meet without caus-
ing death. Yet the Kingdom of Heaven, as elaborated by the later
Hebrew Prophets and the Pharisees in the century before Jesus'
birth, was now suggestive of the afterlife—and thus we must conclude that Jesus' emphasis was historical. He specifically reminds
his disciples, and us, his readers, of the numinous Covenant with
YHWH, because the Kingdom of Heaven he describes was about
to become present on earth, and thus in history.

Like YHWH, then, Jesus taught that one must inhabit the image
of a God that can so come into contact with humans that a meal
can be shared. He taught by acting it out in such a way that the
Covenant would no longer have to be studied and interpreted; it
could be replaced by the ritual of Holy Communion. It is "holy"
because it suggests the numinous presence of the flesh and blood
of Jesus' historical body, just as the original Covenant brought
down the numinous YHWH for a shared meal. Yet the Passover
Seder is not a numinous event; it is a reimagining of the historical
journey through time—the time of slavery in Egypt and the time of
deliverance—plus the difficult and complex forty years of sojourn
in the desert.

It may be said that for Christians today the life of Jesus completes
the Passover journey and that the Kingdom of Heaven is imminent,
beyond the death of each of us. Still, it will take on vital new meaning if it is placed in the Jewish context of Jesus' life as a Jew in Israel.
Because there, in Judea under the Romans, it was physical survival
that was the critical issue, even as the life of the nation and Temple
was in jeopardy (and indeed, would soon be destroyed). Survival of
the soul, on the other hand, could be worried about later—there had
to be living Jews first, to do the worrying. This may seem obvious,

but from a Christian perspective today, it is not at all clear that it was necessary for the Jews to survive as Jews.

After all, even without the Jews, the Torah of Moses and the entire Hebrew Bible could still be saved in the form of the Christian "Old Testament." So is it only from a Jewish perspective that one says that the text is meaningless or ultimately impenetrable without living Jews to read it? It would seem so at first, because the Church and the Christian world can take the place of the Jews as the "New Israel." Yet the fact remains today that there actually *is* a new Israel—in the Middle East and in history—and it is full of Jews who read the original Covenant as a cosmic theater in which we continue to study and learn. The laws of living for the religious Jew are the same as the laws of reading—there need be no great separation. And for the secular Jews, in Israel and the Diaspora, the reading of Moses' words still requires a setting in history: one is there in the historical past as one reads, and the reader is present today in the act of continuing to interpret the words anew.

Yet survival is always a historical issue, because it is not a question of who will read the Torah but rather of who will enter into its interpretation with their own lives on the line. This is what Jews can still offer to a new Judeo-Christianity. It was always a mistake to blame the Jews for being the Chosen People. As the Hebrew Bible makes clear, the Jews were a Chosen Nation in order to read, to weigh the burden of history, and perhaps to become ready to teach. Still, it's another load, an obligation of "homework" when others are playing "outside," oblivious to history. This emphasis on study, on reading and writing, continued to hold open the meaning of what constitutes an educated man.

I will make you a light of nations that my salvation may reach the ends of the earth . . . It is the holy one of Israel who elected you. (Isaiah 49:6)

What, then, were the elected to do? If this had been a Christian text rather than a Jewish one, we might interpret it to mean that we've been elected to become missionaries, traveling to "the ends of the earth." But for Isaiah, the ancient Hebrew prophet, no traveling was involved; instead, the representatives of the nations would be traveling to Israel. This is also echoed in the story of Jesus' birth, as representatives from afar are guided by a light in the sky to witness the child in the manger. Yet the more obvious interpretation of Isaiah's parsing of the words of YHWH is that the words themselves will do the traveling—in the form of the books of the Hebrew Bible.

The first question a Jewish reader might ask of these words is, how do they change the Covenant? And, what happens when Israel wishes to renegotiate their obligations—after all, being such a light means studying the light, and is there already not enough to study? These questions, standing in for a myriad of other questionings, are not refusals; and in the sense that they lead to further interpretations, they are what makes the reading and writing of the Covenant a uniquely Jewish thing. They are questions that can lead to an additional one: What are the obligations of a universal religion still represented by a small nation?

The answer was still being articulated several centuries later and even as Jesus was a child in Nazareth. We find it in the first book of the Mishnah, "The Sayings of the Fathers":

> *Joshua, the son of Perachya, said, "Provide thyself a teacher; get thee a study companion; and judge all men charitably."*

· · ·

This "Joshua," a rabbi in Israel, bears the same name as Jesus, and indeed may have lived at the same time or not much earlier. And Jesus follows exactly what he says: In his adulthood, he himself is the teacher; he gets himself a following of disciples; and he judges all men charitably. Or does he? The word goes back to Moses' Torah: "In lovingkindness shalt thou judge thy neighbor" (Leviticus 19:15).

Once again, we see that Jesus' emphasis on love and charity is a form of learning, interpretive and illustrative of the Mosaic text. Thus, the "teacher"; and thus, the writer—for like Moses, Jesus teaches by his words interpreting other words, and all the words go back to two places. The Sinai wilderness is one, and the second is the royal court in Jerusalem where most of the writing of the Torah was done by educated men, and perhaps women. Jesus establishes his own court, one can say, so that his words will be written down by the evangelists setting out for "the ends of the earth." Many of the Greek philosophers also spoke to their disciples, who wrote down their words or kept notes; the same held true for Jewish rabbis and their circles, so that the "Sayings of the Fathers" in the Mishnah may not have been originally written down by them. There can be little doubt that there was note-keeping among the evangelists, leading to a first Gospel, now lost but referred to by scholars as the Q text or the Ur-Gospel, upon which the later Gospels in the New Testament drew.

. . .

In the Torah's Book of Deuteronomy, Moses describes the human obligation of the Covenant to be an observing of the Law in order that "you will display your wisdom and understanding to other peoples." But how will this be displayed, except through learning? Jesus and his disciples, learned in the Torah, would display this learning as they brought the words with them. As we see from the exchanges between Jesus and his disciples, their questions are not about how to act with lovingkindness but rather about how to interpret the words. Even the displays of healing by Jesus are not intended to teach his disciples how to do the same.

So the question remains: is the "Kingdom of Heaven" to be imagined and acted out as if already real, or is it a text to be interpreted? When YHWH spoke and Moses recorded, it was already apparent that YHWH anticipated his audience's response and emphasized—in fact, taught—that his part of the bargain in the Covenant was fundamentally about thinking.

The commandment that I lay on you this day is not too difficult for you,
it is not too remote. It is not in heaven, that you should say, "Who will
go to heaven for us to fetch it and tell it to us, so that we can keep it?"
(Deuteronomy 30:11)

. . .

In this way, using YHWH's words, Moses emphasizes that all falls
upon interpretation, even of the word "heaven." The understanding that is required is not so much a display but rather the work of
thinking and interpreting. That is why we can say, as the centuries
pass and as Israel's history becomes further text and commentary
for the Hebrew Bible, there was always the misguided hope that
YHWH would return and intervene supernaturally—a hope that
no doubt still exists.

But when we turn from hoping to reading we can always find
YHWH's presence in the words of Moses' Torah. There he is-
there's no need for any further reassurance. After YHWH attends
his Covenantal meal on Sinai with the Israelites, there is no need
to ask why he has not attended another one. The words display, but
it is how we interpret them in the moment of reading, in the present, that educates us in the crucial text. Jesus taught the same: the
words, being numinous as we read them, bring us into the presence
of the Kingdom of Heaven—without "going to heaven to fetch it,"
as YHWH had made clear in Moses' Book of Deuteronomy.

Now if one doesn't "believe" in God, how are we supposed to
read this? The answer: you can only read it by believing that the
Bible's emphasis is not upon *what to believe* but upon entering into
a history where educated men and women are thinking about what
must be done to keep this text alive. Only if it lives can they live as
educated men and women, for the survival of the "eternal text,"
paradoxically, is always in doubt, just like the survival of the Jews
and the nation of Israel. The text exists within the cosmic theater
of the Covenant, and to the extent that the reader is aware of that,
his education brings him to the boundary of what is unknowable

but can be dramatized. It is staged in the drama of Israel's history, and in the Kingdom of Heaven—so long as we do not go there, but rather envision it.

Jesus would now bring this vision of the Kingdom of Heaven to Earth, and what makes it different from any prophet's or poet's vision is that it is in the mouth of the Messiah. We have seen that the Jews for a long time had not expected any divine intervention from YHWH, yet they had developed the exceedingly complex idea of a man who would represent YHWH, being in relation to him as the kings and prophets that came before. Indeed, he would be a son of Moses and David, in the sense of genealogical descent from the first king of Israel.

After Jesus has met John the Baptist and learned from him that the Kingdom of Heaven may be interpreted further—to be within you—he began to internalize the mission of the Jewish Messiah that he had studied since early youth among the rabbis. On occasion, he now spoke *as if* he embodied the words. Many other rabbis have done the same, but at a certain point the "as if" is removed in Jesus' words. For his audiences, it is as if YHWH really could return. But why wouldn't YHWH tell us so? Why would it be up to us to discern the truth for ourselves?

The nub is in the discerning, for in Jewish terms "to discern" means to study, to learn, to interpret. And that is why Jesus must be tested by Jewish scholars when he is brought into Roman custody. Jesus responds as the teacher himself—in a way that only Moses would have, in such circumstances.

. . .

How does Moses teach? Moses interprets places and events on the journey as proofs of God's presence. From the crossing of the Reed Sea to the manna seeming to fall from heaven, YHWH's presence is interpreted by Moses to be one of nourishment, ensuring survival. But Moses also teaches that the ultimate nourishment comes from the words taught in such a way that any time or place in the future can take the place of Sinai. In the Book of Deuteronomy, where we find Moses actually writing his own teaching, we see that his method is still alive in the words of the rabbis of Jesus' day. It is what we call midrash (or the Midrash, for the texts that collect them). In place of the actual events that Moses described in Sinai, the rabbis substitute the textuality of the Torah for the events themselves. Not to read literally but to read deeper. Yet Moses was already doing this himself when Deuteronomy describes him as "expounding" the Law rather than "commanding" it.

> But if you search there for YHWH your God, you will find him, if only you seek him with all your heart and soul. (Deuteronomy 4:29)

These are no longer the words of the Commandments; they are the words of a teacher and writer.

> Moses had put down in writing the words of this Teaching to the very end . . . "Take this book of teaching and place it beside the Ark of the Covenant of YHWH your God and let it remain there as a witness." (Deuteronomy 31:34)

· · ·

These are the very words that were discovered in the Book of Deuteronomy in the sixth century BCE at the court of King Josiah. The King and his court writers read that Moses' Torah was to be public knowledge, not the possession of priests and kings alone. It was to be read aloud to everyone and taught to one's children. Each individual was encouraged to "seek him with all your heart and soul," as if study was just as important as sacrifice. And centuries later, Jesus will find Moses' emphasis on the heart and soul still expounded by the Pharisaic rabbis who taught him.

All these rabbis, when they read the words of Moses in Deuteronomy, were primarily reading the educated writers who existed at the time of Josiah's royal court. They recast the Mosaic core, and presented it as a lost book suddenly rediscovered. Where did the writers of Josiah's day come from? They were probably attached to the royal court of the northern kingdom of Israel, which had just been overrun by the Assyrians. These writers escaped to Josiah's Jerusalem with their Mosaic text: it was their kingdom's interpretation of the Covenantal journey in Sinai.

Since Josiah and his own writers accepted this text of Deuteronomy as a lost Book of Moses, its words of instruction were to be proclaimed in both ancient and contemporary context:

> *You shall read this teaching aloud in the presence of all Israel. Gather the people—men, women, children, and the strangers in your communities— that they may hear and so learn to revere YHWH your God . . . Their children, too, who have not had the experience, shall hear and learn. (Deuteronomy 31:12)*

King Josiah and his court used this text to inaugurate sweeping biblical reforms, and the most significant of them was to democratize the *reading* of it. By Jesus' time, the Pharisaic rabbis had made it a life's mission to make the reading of the text (and acting out of the social beliefs of the Prophets) available to everyone. Jesus, no less educated in Moses' Torah than the writers of Deuteronomy (who arrived in Jerusalem after fleeing the Assyrians), returned to the same Jerusalem in his last days, now in the hands of the Romans. But remember that before he came to Jerusalem Jesus studied and taught in synagogues throughout Galilee—the same region that once belonged to the northern kingdom of Israel. There is no escaping the coherent dimension of Jesus' life when it is placed in the context of Israel's history.

There were no other institutions like the synagogue in the Greco-Roman world, where the public reading and teaching of Moses' Torah were already part of an ancient civilization. In the words of the rabbis of the day, later collected in the Midrash, Jesus would have read this voicing of YHWH:

> *Take upon you the yoke of my kingdom and emulate one another in the love of God and practice kindness to one another.*

. . .

We can see that already there were those who were living as if they were in the Kingdom of Heaven. Thus, nothing that Jesus would say when confronted by representatives of the Sadducees and Pharisees would be strange to them.

From creating the context for the following scene to the scene itself, as we read the Gospel we can now overhear what happens when Jesus speaks with educated rabbis and priests, after he has been taken into Roman custody. A Pharisaic lawyer asks him the question that the rabbis had long debated: "What is the greatest commandment in the law?" (Matthew 22:36). Jesus answers by quoting back two commandments, one about loving God and the other about loving thy neighbor, the source of the Golden Rule. It was quite common for these two commandments to stand in for all of the Torah of Moses, and even the writers and prophets who followed. However, the Gospels depict this scene as if Jesus had actually refused to accept all of the Torah as integral to his own words.

> *You shall love YHWH your God with all your heart, with all your soul, with all your strength. Let these words . . . be written on your heart. You shall repeat them to your children . . . (Deuteronomy 6:5)*

Can we really assume that Jesus would have refused these words of Torah—that he would have stood above or outside them? The words are a reflection of how rank and class among the Jews were abolished by the Torah text they held in common. The same words are also echoed by the Prophet Jeremiah, as if it is a new Covenant:

> *Deep within them I will plant my Teaching, writing it on their hearts . . . There will be no further need for neighbor to teach neighbor, or brother to say to brother, "Learn to know YHWH!" No, they will all know me, the least no less than the greatest. (Jeremiah 31:34)*

Jeremiah, centuries before, had already envisioned a new Covenant; Jesus was not the first. Jeremiah's words were also echoed among other Hebrew prophets, and the Prophet Zechariah could write of himself in the fifth century BCE as a shepherd of Israel, with the people his flock. Zechariah wrote further, after the destruction of the First Temple and the Exile to Babylon, that his words will "gather the lost sheep of Israel." However, the shepherd is then attacked and killed: "one they have pierced." We can hardly doubt that Jesus knew these words, part of any synagogue study-house education.

In fact, the shepherd that Zechariah was describing was the captured Jewish king taken into Babylonian exile and killed. A more accurate translation of the word might be "impaled" rather than "pierced." Nevertheless, it is common for Christian interpreters to read these words as applying centuries later to the death of Jesus. For certainly it is recorded, and quite poignantly, that Jesus says to his disciples, "I have come to gather the lost sheep of Israel." Jesus quotes these words from the Jewish Prophets knowingly. He knows that they refer to the remnants in Babylonian exile, who will soon return to Israel in their day—to a "New Jerusalem," though that was long ago.

It would also be appropriate to cite these words after Jesus' death and after the destruction of the Second Temple by the Romans, when the Jews are once again scattered like lost sheep. But the Temple did not fall until approximately forty years after Jesus was crucified by the Romans, and even if Jesus had spoken clairvoyantly, those apostles and Gospel writers who spoke in his name were no longer concerned about the "lost sheep of Israel"—only the new sheep that they would gather around them on their missions out of Israel.

When Jesus quoted Zechariah in his own day as if a Messiah were speaking, if his audience was ignorant of the Torah, then it would be natural to remove the "as if"—because they would not know the words' origin. But in fact, even the Gospel writers, long after Jesus' death, were writing for a largely Jewish audience. The apostles and Paul had been received and spoke in the synagogues of the Roman Empire wherever they went. Jesus spoke as an educated man to others also educated, and the "lost sheep" he gathered were the same as Zechariah's: those who needed to be reminded that the words of the Torah—as Moses wrote and the Pharisees continued to teach in Jesus' day—must be interpreted for the children of each generation.

. . .

The death of Moses would have been a model for Jesus' thinking in his own final days, seeing and struggling with his own death. A model of complexity, as we consider the historical Moses today, but a rabbi like Jesus would have discerned it as well. Having rejected literal mummification, Moses had made of himself a figurative mummy: the Torah, based on a core of his words, contains him into the future. More than that, the future, as it does for the mummy, stretches into an eternity whenever the Covenant is reinterpreted, from generation to generation. Jesus, too, leaves a core of a text, the New Testament, and thus has learned from Moses. But that text must be made to come alive, as was the final expectation of the mummy—it becomes a numinous text, so that the reader takes part in the ongoing journey.

Like his fellow Jews, Jesus read of the death of Moses in the Book of Deuteronomy. That death is foretold in Sinai when Moses and his people arrive at Meribhat-Kadesh. Kadesh was a huge oasis, and Meribha its primary spring. But first, we wander in the wilderness with the Israelites and don't yet know we will find the oasis of Kadesh. We only know that we're about to die in a mass catastrophe unless we find water quickly, and plenty of it. The people "strove with Moses," as they had at an earlier stop in Sinai when there was no drinkable water. Did they cry and tear out their hair? Did they revert to Egyptian prayers for rain? Did they seek to kill Moses, as Sigmund Freud suggests? All that we know is that they say to Moses:

Would that we had perished when our brethren perished before YHWH! Why bring this assembly of YHWH into the wilderness to die here, along

with our cattle? Why bring us out of Egypt into this evil place? It is no
place of seed or of figs or of vines or of pomegranates; neither is there any
water to drink! (Numbers 20:1–13)

These people appear angry enough to kill, if we pay attention to
their words. The "brethren" to which they refer were those who had
worshiped the golden calf and were killed subsequently on Moses'
orders. Now these survivors are saying they would have been better off dead already—better off having worshiped the calf. It is a
suicide mission, they cry. We were better off in Egypt than where
we are now: an *evil* place. These do not sound like people waiting to
hear an explanation or even expecting divine intervention. There
is no argument that Moses could bring to counter their insinua-
tions about his death-dealing—the death he already had dealt to
the calf-worshipers and the death facing them now, along with their
cattle. There is more sting in this threat than Jesus faced among his
accusers—with the possible exception of Satan, who is somewhat
more subtle, as we shall see.

Now what happens is that Moses retreats to the Tent of Meeting
and "falls on his face"; then YHWH appears, to instruct him on
how to provide the necessary water. YHWH says: "Speak unto the
rock before their eyes that it give forth its water." So Moses goes
back to the people and says, "Here now, you rebels! Are we to bring
you forth water out of this rock?" Perhaps Moses is almost as mad
at the people as they are at him, for his words are high sarcasm.
And perhaps it is in this mood that Moses forgets to *speak* to the
rock, as YHWH instructed, and instead "smote the rock with his
rod twice," suggesting an Egyptian with a mythic wand. The result
was water for all and for the cattle. But later, YHWH speaks can-
didly to Moses, accusing him of changing words into acts: instead
of speaking to the rock, he beat on it as if the power was in his rod,
rather than in the words themselves.

Commentators have long split hairs about just what Moses did
to merit his own death. For that is what YHWH now tells him: "You
shall not bring this assembly into the land which I have given them."

Moses learns that he will die in the wilderness for not "speaking" to the rock. Does this not seem vastly disproportionate to the deed of smiting rather than speaking? Yet perhaps not, when we remember that Moses is a writer, responsible for both recording and interpreting the events along the journey in Sinai. YHWH has spoken to him also as a writer, placing the deepest emphasis upon the words—first spoken, then to be written. The drama we have just witnessed has not depended on the physical act but on the words. That the waters of the spring in the oasis of Kadesh "saved" the people and their cattle was really not the point. In fact, myriad peoples had been saved by the oasis of Kadesh for millenniums before the Israelites ever arrived. That's what oases are for.

But now let us consider the punishment. Moses has recorded YHWH's words, so his fate was known. The question that remains is how would he interpret the punishment? Was it simply disobedience, as many commentators have believed? I believe the issue of authorship was at stake here, an issue at the core of what makes the words of Torah numinous. Most commentators, until modern times, did not have the critical tools and historical record to deal with authorship of the Torah, and so they did not focus on it. Yet even modern scholars fail to use their knowledge of authorship, as if it's not a matter of importance. But without it, and without a sense of the writer—even as Moses himself would have conceived it and all those in Jerusalem who wrote after him—we lose the cosmic theater of the narrative Covenant. After all, the Covenant assumes a coauthorship, and if we and scholars today do not think authorship matters, then it dilutes the Covenant and the Hebraic cosmic theater.

If we don't try to know our authors, then what God said, what Moses said, what the people said—and, when it comes to Jesus, what the devil said—all becomes mixed up and confused. The wrong questions appear. Why did God do this and not that? Why did Moses do that and not this? We can refocus, however, by asking how the passage in question was written and why. It was the Priestly author, known as P, who supplied the story of Moses'

punishment in the style that J, the main author of the narrative, had
used centuries earlier in Jerusalem. It is not usual for P to bring
such irony to bear as imagining the sarcasm of Moses' accusers—
as well as Moses' sarcasm in response. J was a master of irony, and
her focus in this story was on the root of the names for Meribha and
Kadesh, as if these ancient roots from an earlier language foretold
what would happen there. P, on the other hand, is not concerned
with that, but here he has added his own original insight. Or more
likely, that insight about Moses' punishment had also belonged to
J and was now merely rephrased by P. If so, the sarcasm was even
stronger, for J was quite conscious of her own authorship at the
royal court of Solomon's son, Rehoboam, as well as of her sources
in Moses.

Moses will die, of that we already know, since he is human. Now
we are simply being told when, and even at this point Moses has
lived a very long and fruitful life. Further, as we read in the Book of
Deuteronomy, YHWH will meet Moses on Mount Nebo, in what
was then Moab and is now Jordan, and will show him the entire
vista of the land of Israel, stretching north to south, just as it was
promised to Abraham. "But you shall not cross into it." And then,
YHWH "buried him in the valley." It does not look like such a punishment now. Moses has seen the Promised Land, and has been
assured that his descendants will make it theirs.

Some have asked how Moses could have written his own death,
and some have asked, who saw the burial? Let's answer by returning
to the common interpretation of the "punishment." Most critics
reiterate the idea that Moses was punished for appearing to take
credit for delivering the water in the wilderness—as if in acting
like a sorcerer with his rod, he had committed the sin of pride and
ignored YHWH's desire to have the credit reflect on the Creator.
Again, such views will be reductive so long as it remains acceptable
for scholars to avoid authorship—and especially in a passage such
as this, which is about the written word itself. The word is spoken,
written, and read, yet without the sense of physical intervention.
Still, Moses has envisioned his death as only a writer can, and he

sums up his life by the flaw no human creator-out-of-words can avoid: at one point or another, he has ignored the very words and taken the action too literally. YHWH's words, on the other hand, are the source of all life and action—they can be interpreted and reinterpreted in words themselves, but their origin in the Creator is not to be ignored. To put it in modern terms that a Darwinist, a biblical writer, and a rabbi can all agree upon: language was not created by humans, though we often forget the fact. Disregarding it, we can also fail to remember that life was not created by us, either.

. . .

Before his impending death, Moses already knows that his words and Hebraic culture will live on in Israel—and this is precisely what Jesus will also know, when he offers no physical resistance to his own death. Instead of acting against his impending death, Jesus continues to speak and to figuratively write for his disciples the words that will live on. Most of these words that Jesus spoke come from the Hebrew Bible, and no doubt as he contemplated the death of Moses, Jesus understood that the writer's words, Moses' words, are the essence of YHWH's desire. For they are not mere literature or history; they record a journey in time, the harshness and the difficulty of it, but also the revelation of the Covenant in the midst of the story. The life of Jesus was also a hard journey in the end, and it too carried the revelation that the Covenant must be lived. Right up to the end, Jesus struggles with death, struggles with interpreting it, until it is clear to him that offering no physical resistance will result in triumph: the words will win, as the Gospels travel the world to their readers.

There are no words without the journey itself, no Covenant without the land of Israel. It is, in fact, a fierce resistance that Jesus offers in defense of Moses' Torah and the Jews. By remaining a teacher, a rabbi, a Jewish writer to the end, Jesus adopts Moses' wisdom about not asking for too much: Moses will not set foot in the land and Jesus will not see his words come true. The victory is in not having to see it but having to know that there will always be Jews surviving in Israel to read the words as if God spoke to them. For two thousand years after the death of Jesus, Jews all over the world read the Torah in the certainty that they would return to Israel one day to join the remnant that remained. After Roman times, there was no program or crusade to accomplish this with physical force; on the contrary, the hatred of war was ingrained.

In the Jewish journey through time and history, their survival has depended on not asking for too much. Divine intervention is not an option, and neither is death. Neither did Jesus himself "die." He did not leave his fate up to God; he took it in his own hands; and in the claim to be one with God himself, the responsibility was all his. He does not call upon his Father for help or expect the Covenant to save him.

In the same way, Israel does not argue with God about the journey. We are coauthors of that journey when we enter into the cosmic theater of the Covenant and thus we are entitled to certain rights. Such as the right to life, the right to our own land, and the right to live in history. History is no small thing. If we can live in the present moment as if it is already historical, then we can see our own lives as if an artifact of Moses' Torah. But the "as if" is crucial: the writing must continue, our responsibility as the coauthors requires new translation in every generation. In this awareness of the writing, we might also say that the New Testament was a continuation and thus an artifact of the Hebrew Bible.

The consciousness of being written suffuses the New Testament, as it draws upon the books of the Hebrew Bible in almost every passage. The awareness of authorship, including the gospel authors who wrote in the name of the apostles or those who came a bit later, makes it unavoidable that educated writers are fundamental to the text. In the past, the writers have been treated as mere recorders of words, especially of those of Jesus—not so unlike the mythic idea of Moses as God's secretary. Recently, with scholarly emphasis on the history of Israel and the historical Jesus, all this has been changing. And the best evidence is a new tome of well more than twelve hundred pages, entitled *Commentary on the New Testament Use of the Old Testament*. This is not the first study to exhaustively track the quotations from the Hebrew Bible that underlie the New Testament, but the exhaustive detail and the joy with which it is delivered are something new.

The authors, G. K. Beale and D. A. Carson, are not only biblical scholars but evangelical Christians. One would expect them to privilege the Gospels over any Hebraic sources; indeed, one would expect any Christian to easily wave aside studies of Jewish authorship and prefer to immerse themselves purely in the words of the Gospels. Thus we would have expected such a volume about biblical authorship to be written by Jewish scholars, devoted first to the Hebrew Bible. Yet now, once again, we must face a redefining of the meaning of Judeo-Christianity. Whether they are discussing the Jewish authorship of the Torah, or referring confidently to Jewish scholarship upon the writers J, E, P, and D (for Deuteronomy), or quoting the scholarship upon the Q Gospel (the fragmentary first writing of a Gospel for the surviving Jewish followers of Jesus after his death). Beale and Carson find strength in the cultural origins of the Jews. This Hebraic culture, in which the Bible was written over centuries, is far from something to be swept under the carpet for these new Christian scholars; rather, it is to be embraced as evidence of an educated man in the Jewish definition of it.

Why is it surprising that evangelical Christian scholars would accept the writers—the historical Jewish culture—rather than dismiss them? Traces of such a dismissal are still evident in their book's title itself, where "Old Testament" is rendered without a flinch. But instead of amplifying the old idea of the New Testament superseding the Old, the term is given fresh meaning, so that the emphasis falls upon the richness of the historical—"old," in other words, becomes precious. It was the same when the writers of the Blues almost a hundred years ago changed the meaning of "the blues" by attacking its negative connotation and revivifying it, lifting it almost to the level of Gospel singing. The scholars Beale and Carson have uplifted the meaning of "Old Testament" so that even Jews and even Jesus might have recognized the honor. This is hardly a small irony, because the Torah of Moses, the Books of the Prophets, and all the other Hebrew Writings comprising the Old Testament would not have been considered "old" in Jesus' day—except as an honorific. In fact, the words of Moses were as near and fresh to Jesus as would have been those of Rabbi Hillel, a near-contemporary.

Although Jesus used the term "Kingdom of Heaven" in the common rabbinical style of his day, he did add an innovation that was critical: his time was the messianic age that the Hebrew Prophets had envisioned. He first stated this to his Jewish cousin, John the Baptist, quoting Psalm 1:

> . . . *the dead are raised to life and the good news is proclaimed to the poor:*
> *happy is the man who does not lose faith in me. (Matthew 11:4)*

Of course, in speaking as if he was proclaiming the time of salvation, Jesus was aware that many believed that John embodied the ancient Hebrew Prophet Elijah. It had long been expected that a returning Elijah would proclaim the coming of the Messiah. The belief began with the description of Elijah's death: he did not die, he was assumed into Heaven on a wondrous chariot. This vision, as recorded in the Hebrew Bible, was not meant to be confused with the historical record. The emphasis is not upon Jesus "believing" that John was Elijah, but rather that John, like Jesus himself, was deeply educated in the Hebrew Bible. Thus Jesus could speak to John in the prophetic words of the Hebrew Prophets, and could join these to the rabbinical thinking that the Kingdom of Heaven, an eternal and supernatural idea, had now become a historical reality on earth.

So the words of the Hebrew Bible that Jesus continues to quote serve to extend the Hebraic cosmic theater. Now, not only is the land of Israel the cosmic stage but the negotiation between God and man that has taken place on this stage—the working out of the Covenant—has been blurred. God and man could now be imagined as interchangeable, not in some visionary hallucination but rather in the textual sense that Jesus makes clear: "The Kingdom of Heaven is within you." The rabbis had also said that, yet Jesus has extended it into the historical dimension. As his words to John the Baptist confirm, Jesus understood that his prophetic signs, as in healings, represented a new era.

The words of Jesus are entirely governed by a consciousness of this new kingdom: one in which Satan will be overthrown and the world order destroyed—and therefore hardly to be given a thought. More significantly, Jesus' words were imbued with the teaching that one's enemies, including the enemies of Israel, would only be strengthened and multiplied when they were physically opposed. Instead, one must love one's enemy, and those who do evil should not be resisted physically but spiritually. Not even the Roman Empire should be provoked, since the Kingdom of Heaven is imminent. Nevertheless, it still lay in the future, just as the rabbis believed. What Jesus changed was that now one must live *as if* it is already here. That is why the author of the Gospel of Matthew can relate a scene in which Jesus speaks to Satan.

"Speaks" is already a misnomer—Jesus' words are entirely quotations from the Hebrew Bible. Even Satan quotes chapter and verse, and when he says, "I will give you all these"—referring to all the kingdoms of the world that "the devil showed him"—we cannot fail to remember the scene on Mount Nebo when YHWH showed to Moses all the Promised Land before his death. (Satan, too, speaks to Jesus after "taking him to a very high mountain.") And as we think of Moses, we recall that the land of Israel, which might have represented a future of worldly power, was something he had already refused by accepting the sovereignty of God. Jesus, too, refuses by quoting from the "Shema"—the essence of Moses' writing in the Torah—to Satan in rejection: "You must worship the Lord your God, and serve him alone" (Matthew 4:8; Deuteronomy 6:13).

On the other hand, Moses could not quote the Hebrew Bible when speaking with YHWH because he was writing the text in the moment. Nor was there a supernatural Satan for him to converse with. But there was the Shema, which describes a relationship with God in which "the Lord will be king over all the earth." Furthermore,

"You shall love the Lord your God with all your heart and with all your soul and with all your might." The emphasis on the word "love" by Moses is still reverberating in rabbinic thought at the time of Jesus. They interpreted this commandment to love as being superior to the "fear of God," to which Moses had also referred. And Moses speaks here as himself also: a writer, a teacher. The very next words are "Take to heart these instructions"—and when we find similar expressions in the Hebrew Bible, it is always in reference to a father teaching his son to internalize the words. Jesus, too, speaks as a son who has more than internalized his father's words; he acts as if he embodied them.

The Prophet Jeremiah, long before Jesus, had written a "new covenant" by embodying YHWH and speaking as a Father:

Deep within them I will plant my Law, writing it on their hearts.
(Jeremiah 31:33)

. . .

And to drive this message home, Jeremiah writes in YHWH's name that "Were this established order ever to pass away from my presence, only then would Israel also cease to be a nation" (31:36). Jesus too embodied these words; he could no more imagine a world without Israel than he could imagine that his father was not speaking through Jeremiah. Thus, the Kingdom of Heaven was not imagined to replace Israel, for Jesus does not intend the destruction of "the established order"—only the changing of the "old order" into one that is "different."

Different, rather than "new," because Jeremiah also wrote that the "new covenant," applying in his day to those returning from Babylonian Exile to the ruins of the First Temple in Jerusalem, will be changed at heart. YHWH, the God of Israel, says, "I will give them a different heart and different behavior" (Jeremiah 32:39). It is this difference of behavior that cues the sayings of Jesus, which are designed to surprise his audience with an unconventional idea of behavior. A sense of alarm would hold especially true for the Sadducees, the priestly caste who ruled the Jewish polity in the name of Rome. For the Sadducees, who were attacked on just this point by the Pharisees, denied the possibility of resurrection, which went hand in hand with the Kingdom of Heaven. These Greek-minded men whose sense of the Torah was that not only did YHWH write it himself but also it was cast in stone: there was no writer named Moses, and thus no interpretation and elaboration, either in Moses' day or later in Jerusalem, when the Hebraic writers completed the Torah.

And since, in Jesus' day, there was no historical method with which to analyze the writing of the Bible, the Sadducees were further empowered to resist "new ideas," including those of the Hebrew Prophets themselves and later books of the Hebrew Bible. So when Jesus quotes to them from a Prophet like Jeremiah, or a psalm from the Book of Psalms, the Sadducees react as if they never heard of it. In their own minds, they are too smart and sensible to believe in an afterlife or in a Hebraic cosmic theater that is still alive. To them, the Torah is ancient history; it can be accepted on its own word as such, but it cannot intervene in contemporary history, which is "rational," as elaborated in Hellenistic education.

The educated Greeks themselves had by this time long given up any serious belief in their gods or anyone else's. So here comes this Jewish Jesus quoting Pharisaic ideas about the afterlife as well as a messianic interpretation of the Kingdom of Heaven. In Psalm 2, YHWH says to the messianic figure: "Thou art my son, this day have I begotten thee." Written many centuries earlier, this Hebraic quotation makes clear that speaking of sonhood in relation to God is an established idiom. Further, this psalm envisions the messianic figure as an inheritor of the Covenant:

Ask of me, and I will give the nations for thine inheritance,
And the ends of the earth for thy possession.

. . .

These are almost the exact words of Satan, when he impersonated God in the Gospels by offering to "show the ends of the earth" to Jesus (as God had done for Moses—showing him the Promised Land from a mountain before his death).

It is different when Jesus speaks to the officious Pharisees who, for political reasons, are aligned with the Sadducees at the Temple. Jesus knows that they understand the messianic resonance of sonhood, and so he asks them about the Messiah, "Whose son is he?" They answer: "David's." Jesus prods further, asking why YHWH spoke to David as if he was also a god: "The Lord said to my Lord: Sit at my right hand." Jesus has here quoted back to them a line from Psalm 110, and he is asking how the Messiah could be David's son when he has just been called "Lord" by David. "Not one could think of anything to say in reply." Perhaps they understood that Jesus was speaking to them as a rabbi, even more educated in the text than themselves. However, the Gospel writers, depicting this scene many decades later, go on to infer that the Pharisees were insulted. But it's not very likely, since such argumentative interpretation of the Hebrew Bible was their love; it is easier to believe that the Gospel writers misunderstood the education that Jesus shared with the Pharisees.

And when Jesus is interrogated by the "chief priests," namely the Sadducees, he again quotes from Psalm 110. They ask if he is "the Messiah, the Son of God." Jesus answers: "The words are your own," referring them back to the biblical text, and then he adds a new "difference." He tells them that from now on they will see "the Son of Man seated at the right hand of the Lord." But these Sadducees, unlike the Pharisees, appear ignorant of Psalm 110, which Jesus is quoting to them, and thus "they struck him, saying 'Play the prophet, Messiah! Who hit you then?'" They are so "smart and sensible" that not only do they ignore Jesus' education, they expect him to supernaturally deflect the attack, as if it made sense that the Messiah would be some kind of Magician.

This was not something an educated Pharisee would have said, and once again it is likely that the later Gospel writer has misunderstood the scene, in order to depict Jesus being denied the role of Messiah. In fact, the role that Jesus is really being denied in this Gospel's depiction is that of rabbi. It is possible that the Gospel already has lost touch with the essentials of an educated man, a Jew, though there is no reason to believe that Jesus himself would have tolerated such disregard for Torah learning. We have by now seen him dismiss the grandiose Sadducees for their ignorance of the full Hebrew Bible and its ongoing interpretive tradition.

The Passion narrative that ends the Gospels, especially that of Matthew, makes full use of the Hebrew Bible, so that everything that happens on the journey to the cross seems to have been envisioned before by Jewish writers, from Jesus' being beaten (Isaiah 50:6) to the Psalms, from which the mockery of Jesus is extracted—just as were the mockery and insulting of King David by his enemies. But the Jews would never use the Psalms for mockery, and to depict them so is not credible. Is it an attempt to deflect attention from the actual murderers, the Roman authorities? And perhaps more crucially, isn't the disappointment in their former fellow Jews by the Jewish-Christian Gospel writers based upon their loss of the centrality of the Torah?

Jesus himself, however, was a teacher of Moses' Torah, a rabbi, and thus the final narrative could not avoid being steeped in it and the Hebraic cosmic theater. Jesus' life ends as it has been lived, based on the model of a journey toward receiving, writing, and teaching the Torah: it is the journey of Moses reinterpreted in Hebraic fashion. Without the life of Moses, the historical life of Jesus is impossible to consider.

VI

· JUDEO-CHRISTIANITY·AND·
· AN·EDUCATED·MAN·TODAY·

I used to think of an educated man or woman as a very fast reader. He had to be fast to get through so many books that were tied to the meaning of Western civilization. He even had to have read the books of other civilizations. Some of us, however, are slow readers. It was only later I would discover that there was much merit in this: the slowest reading was optimistically called "Talmudic." The Talmudic scholar read all day, every day; he even engaged in dialogue while he read. But was he an educated man?

What the university taught was that he was only half an educated man, missing many of the great books of Western Civilization. But we must also realize that the "Great Books" reader is half an educated person as well. The fast readers not only did not read slowly enough, like the Talmudist, but were innocent of the Talmud itself and even its core text, the Torah.

We cannot expect to find both halves—Talmudist and Great Books product—put together in the same person, but we can imagine a reasonable facsimile: the Great Books reader who is also a sacred reader of the Bible, not one who simply lumps it with the other books. What is, then, a sacred reader? That all books are sacred is a feeling of callow youth that most of us outgrow, but now we must imagine that *readers* can be sacred. As such, we must read as if we were angels.

And if we were angels reading, then the space that enfolds book and ourselves is a sacred *space*. Religions create such sacred spaces for reading in synagogue and church, so that the book being read becomes *liturgy*. But how would such a reading space be possible for the private reader? I most recently rediscovered it for myself as I was translating the passage in the Book of Genesis known as the *Akedah*, or the Binding of Isaac. In this passage God is speaking to Abraham, but very slowly. Of course YHWH usually speaks slowly because he is giving instructions, but here it is especially slow because it is a dream.

How do we know this? In my historical research into the biblical author of the Akedah story, known to scholars as E or the Elohist, I found that the only conventional context in which God could speak was a dream or vision. Most of the history of Abraham was written by a different author, known as J or the Jahwist (pronounced Yahwist), and this great Hebraic writer, living a century earlier than E, had no qualms about YHWH speaking in broad daylight. But in E's day, it was considered very modern to render God in a dream—and in the case of Abraham's binding of his son Isaac, in a nightmare.

Although E will adopt the convention of "dream-talk," which comes from Canaanite literature, he overlays it upon J's earlier narrative standards. And so it was that the dreams and angels of Canaanite convention were absorbed into the cosmic theater of Abraham's God. When we reach the climax of the life of Abraham, Elohim (God) not only speaks in a dream but the dream has become all-enveloping. God will appear capable of saying and asking *anything* ("Please take your son/ whom you love . . .") and Abraham will say *nothing*. It is the God of a nightmare, who can say anything, abolishing the boundaries of the Covenant. This dream we are about to enter is not the theater of Abraham's God but instead the drama of its *absence*.

> *And some time later*
> *after these things had happened*
> *God tested Abraham*
> *speaking to him*
> *"Abraham"*
> *"I am listening," he answered.*
>
> *And God said*
> *please take your son*

whom you love
dear as an only son
that is, Isaac
and go out to the land of Moriah

There you will make of him a burnt offering
on a mountain of which I will tell you
when you approach

There is no mention of the Covenant here, and no negotiation or elaboration of it. The testing of humans by the gods was a venerable tradition in many cultures of the Near East, and we see it most dramatically in the Book of Job, where God seems to be absent from the terrible suffering of his righteous believer—as if it were a test of Satan's power. The Hebrew Prophets too were tested, although their ultimate model was Moses and the elaboration of the Covenant: a negotiation rather than test. That is why the testing of Jesus, whether by Temple guardians, Romans, or Satan, raises the drama to the uncanny level of Moses writing the Tablets, the creative result of Covenant-making.

Jesus is the veritable writer of his own drama since he has the power to turn the test inside out: he, as messianic figure speaking for God, is testing the men who are deaf to the drama. And that drama is a new version of the negotiation of Moses' Covenant—one in which the words are made new:

> *Then he took a cup, gave thanks, and gave it to them, and they all drank*
> *   from it.*
> *He said to them, "This is my blood of the Covenant, which will be shed*
> *   for many." (Mark 14:23–24)*

· · ·

Since this testing takes place at the Passover Seder of the Last Supper, the ritual wine refers back to the original paschal blood that was smeared on the door lintels of Hebrew homes in Egypt so that

the angel of death would pass over them during the final plague. At
that time too, the blood was a sign of YHWH's Covenant, as first
made with Abraham.

Meanwhile, in the Akedah passage we have been reading, Abraham is being tested without a word of negotiation on his own
behalf. No wonder God speaks slowly, certain that the man cannot
respond—as if there were no words, no Covenant! It is a nightmare
of nightmares.

But now, something equally wild will wake Abraham from his
nightmare.

> *But a voice was calling to him*
> *an angel of the Lord, calling*
> *from out of heaven*
> *Abraham, Abraham*
> *I am listening, he answered*
>
> *Do not lay your hand upon the youth*
> *you will not do anything to him*

If we are reading as if we were angelic witnesses, we already know
that God prefers an animal sacrifice, the custom of the age. And the
required ram is waiting to be found right then—not in a dream but
in a real-world thicket.

God himself usually sticks to aspects of the Covenant when he
speaks, which is why an angel spoke about the ram to Abraham.
I'm reminded of an indelible conversation about the speech of
God with the French writer and director Claude Lanzmann; it may
help explain the necessity of reading like an angel when the cosmic
theater is invoked. Lanzmann and I came to the conclusion that
writing in its highest form is a quotation or paraphrasing of God's
Covenantal words—whether it is the Prophet Isaiah quoting God,
or Moses recording the elaboration of the Covenant in moral law,
or when Jesus quotes both Isaiah and Moses in the Gospels.

In the early 1980s, when Lanzmann came to New York to raise

money to finish his classic film on the Holocaust, the eight-hour documentary *Shoah*, I was invited to a screening as the potential editor for a book edition of the film's dialogue. I find this portion of our post-movie conversation in my journal: "You opened the film with a quote from Isaiah: 'I will give them an everlasting name.' Yet there is no mention of the Bible in the film. So what is the biblical context for you? Or is it meant to be ironic?"

"It is not meant to *mean*," said Lanzmann. "It is simply a voice, a Jewish voice quoted from the past, another voice among the many voices in the film that speak of the past."

I was moved and perplexed. "But it's the voice of God!"

"It is the voice of a Jew, the Prophet Isaiah," Lanzmann corrected me, "not strictly God. He is a writer making a quotation, as writers do. Many of the voices in the film also make quotations, such as the historian Raul Hilberg."

"Quotation or not," I protested, "the power that God claims in naming the Jews 'eternal,' or His 'People,' can also be infamous for us—the worst sort of fame—when connected with the Holocaust." It was a theme that dominated Holocaust thinking at the time, the world's obsession with the Chosen People. "It's as if this 'everlasting name' is the first cause of anti-Semitism. It's as if the belief that God is dead, which overtook European culture, meant that His People had it coming."

"Yes," Lanzmann conceded, "perhaps that and more. But I'm asking you something else. You have just watched a part of my film. I presented it as a new text for you. And yet it is little more than quotations. Different sorts of people are quoting their memories. They are like writers of their own history, quoting from memory. When Isaiah quotes God, or even when Moses or Jesus quotes Him, this is what writing is, in its highest form. So this is what I make of the documentary film now: a text of quotations."

Lanzmann was suggesting that the access Moses and Jesus had to God was far more than as spokesmen. It was, in fact, parallel to the art of a writer, who creates the dramatic space for quotation in the Hebraic cosmic narrative. How else to hear what happened? If we enter this space as sacred readers we needn't fear or tremble, for we're being educated in negotiating the Covenant by listening for civilized origins without conditions. Put differently, it is learning of the origin of civilization through sacred words.

> *And YHWH said to Moses, "Come up to me, to the mountain, and be there, and I'll give you stone tablets and the instructions and the commandments that I've written to instruct them." (Exodus 24:12)*

. . .

In essence, YHWH has provided the original words, but Moses will quote them as he *writes*. This scene unfolds a sacred origin to "the history of writing" the Bible. We are still learning that history today, and how the telling of it was sacred to Hebraic culture, and most especially, how the writing of it was the crucial cultural art.

Yet we do not learn enough about the Bible's writing and reading at its origins, which renders our educations incomplete. For instance, we're often limited to short-term memory in this regard. We may identify who was first in our immediate family "to graduate college" or first to collect a home library—relatives who embody for us an "educated person." An older cousin of mine was first to get a Ph.D.; he became a professor of sociology and in my own college years he was esteemed the family's nonpareil. Once, in a conversation with me, he disavowed the honor: "We're sure to have some ancestors whose Talmudic knowledge was more breathtaking. Not to mention having a house full of books."

Suddenly the buried memory of my own pious grandfather, my *Zaydeh*, who was my closest confidant until he died when I was seven, came flooding back. We had an Encyclopædia Britannica and some Book-of-the-Month selections in the den, but only *his* room was actually permeated with the smell of books, from old leather-bound tracts and commentaries to stiff-boarded manuals and pungent, unbound journals. These came in at least three different languages—Hebrew, Yiddish, and Aramaic—and he taught me to read their titles and authors out loud while he translated. However, the family considered him its least educated member because he "only read old books from the old country." So much for the authority of history.

But as I grew older myself, it was hard to disagree; science and the humanities were what represented progress at mid-century, and what epitomized worldliness. Only now do I realize that Zaydeh was reading such worldly thinkers as Maimonides, who had absorbed Aristotle, and also neo-Platonic rabbinic thinkers. Back then, when I could barely reach the matzos in the center of the dining table at Passover, Zaydeh had an honored place when he led the Seders—but only during this yearly meal. Yet by the obligatory fourth cup of wine, when the American family could barely sing children's songs, Zaydeh was still holding forth with complex meanings and memories.

Was it so different at the Passover Seders of the millions of Jews in Jesus' day? Was it any different at the Last Supper—except that no children were present (or perhaps they went unmentioned)? Were not many tables covered in books, and were not the leaders of Seders educated men? But by the time I went away to college, with my grandfather and his world long buried, the books I considered legitimate were taught by modern literary critics for whom Greco-Roman mythology (but no longer the Greek or Latin language) and Freudian psychology were the key to a liberal education. James Joyce's *Ulysses* and Freud's *Civilization and Its Discontents* dominated what we might call the secular Passover Haggadah of that day: it was as if we could part any sea with our improvement on the classics.

Northrop Frye was an exception among literary critics back then, devoted to writing about the Bible as cosmic theater when hardly anybody was reading it through. Yet he hadn't developed a way to confront the original Jewish authors. He was, however, Canada's leading thinker at the time, when I was a fledgling literature professor in Toronto, in 1968. One evening, he gave a public lecture on the English poet William Blake and the Bible. However, it turned out to be mainly about the Bible, not Blake, and Frye's emphasis on reading it as a *sacred* text was disconcerting, since he was known for writing about the Bible strictly as literature.

There are many who think of Blake as a kind of Biblical poet, and yet Frye was not interested in the many actual "Biblical poets" to be found in the Bible itself. In fact, he claimed in his lecture that it was futile to try to distinguish an "original" poet in the Bible, because "all sense of individuality has been stamped out of it by the later editors." I couldn't fathom why Frye would dispense with the facts and take a conventionally religious attitude so readily.

In the brief conversation that ensued, I find the sparks that first propelled me into Biblical scholarship. My journal notes that there were wine and cheese for faculty members after the lecture, just outside the chapel. The picture window overlooking the parking lot now revealed a thick snowfall that had continued all evening, topping our cars in oversized white hats. The lecture in the chapel of St. Michael's College had been complete with a crucifix at Frye's back. Yet there was no shortage of women faculty in leather mini-skirts. I waited my turn to speak with our lecturer.

"You created the image of a Jewish people and their sacred book as if they were not individual poets and authors, not Blakes and Miltons, and as if they didn't actively create it," I said, embarrassed to sound contentious. Frye had shaken my hand graciously, as if he remembered me. "They might as well be any people who stumbled upon the book in Sinai or in Galilee," I continued.

"But would you not agree that that is the way we are intended to *read* it?" he replied softly. "The Jewish culture you're speaking of is more accurately described as a nation of readers rather than a nation of writers. Isn't that wondrous enough—to have such a nation of inspired readers?"

I was in fact wondering; it did sound like a new kind of compliment to the Jews. But I hadn't finished my own thought. "You still attribute the book to religious editors rather than the original authors, and yet in English literature you teach Blake, Yeats, and Joyce while watching out for anyone who might deny or even slightly edit their individuality."

"I'm not sure I follow," he offered. "We live in different times. I'm thinking especially of readers today. We are the readers and we must consider how to read the Bible in *our* time—like a momentous Hollywood movie. Nobody can be sure who wrote the movie, even the names in the credits are pseudonyms—or the real writers aren't named at all. Furthermore, the directors and producers have changed and edited the script numerous times without attribution. The important thing, then, is that we suspend our disbelief and accept the movie as if God created it."

Three decades later, I'm still defining that way of reading the Bible that welcomes consciousness of authorship without desacralizing it. This is what Frye suggested in his late work on the Bible, *The Great Code*, but he was wrong to expect that individual Jewish authors of either Old or New Testament should remain repressed. He was also indifferent to the early Germanic and anti-Semitic Biblical scholarship that assumed the Hebrews were "primitive" and had to be "inspired" by God—to the point that their literary culture was insignificant in and of itself.

What we can still learn is that history and the telling of it were sacred to Hebraic culture, but the writing of it was nevertheless a great cultural art. It only came to seem sacred in itself a few centuries later, in King Josiah's day of reformation, when the Torah was "rediscovered" and the primary art became the "reading" of it rather than the writing. Yet today, with some of the individual sensibilities of the Biblical authors becoming better known to us, it's the *history of the writing* that can become sacred again, in keeping with the Biblical love of history. We recover that sacral experience in the reading if we suspend our disbelief as we enter this narrative cosmic theater and its dramatic confrontations with an unknowable eternity. Whether the episodes at Pharaoh's court in imperial Egypt, or at the crossing of the Reed Sea; whether the scenes at Mount Sinai and Kadesh, or the drawn-out wandering in the wilderness—these were historical moments when the enormity of our human aloneness in the cosmos was faced. The peril of extinction and emptiness was somehow filled. We may have lost the *experience* of those moments but the historical writing of Hebraic culture preserved the losses and transformed them into biblical text.

But how could I better emphasize the original culture in which Biblical writers thrived? Perhaps a symbolic connection between writers then and now would reveal some possibilities. So two decades ago, I asked some of my writing colleagues to read the Bible from the perspective of the writer; it led to the publication of several anthologies, in which each writer described one of the books of the Bible as a *reading* experience. In one of these anthologies, *Communion* (1996), I wrote: "The Old Testament, as Christianity calls the Hebrew Bible, may make sense as a foundation for the New Testament, but the sense it makes avoids facing the loss of the Hebraic culture that produced both. Yet the culture that wrote the Hebrew Bible is one with a long history of facing loss and remembering it." All of it—the *sense* of experience and the *losses* of history as well— was dramatized in the Hebraic cosmic theater, which underlies the Hebrew Bible. Many of my contributing writers helped make it plain that, without reading as if in the audience of this theater— and without reading in the daring presence of the unknowable—we remain uneducated in the supernatural.

Some would say that the supernatural is irrelevant to an education because they confuse the term with "superstition." But is it superstitious to fear the unknowable, such as death? Is it superstitious to desire moral transcendence? Does superstition have anything to do with making the love of life sacred? Of course all of these goals are open to corruption—but what isn't? And this last question is to the point: all life decays, but is there nothing else outside of the natural world worth thinking about? When we can ask these questions, we're speaking of the unknowable; and although we may not like the answers that Judeo-Christianity offers, our education remains incomplete if we're unfamiliar with how deeply the questions have been explored. For instance, where is the boundary beyond which we can't ask questions? Wherever that boundary lies, the supernatural lies on the other side.

When humans cross over into the supernatural they are represented in narrative and poetry upon a numinous stage, be it Moses on the mountain or Jesus walking upon water. It took Kant in the

Age of Enlightenment to determine philosophically that what he called the "noumenal" sphere is unapproachable rationally. But the concept of cosmic theater, as we have seen, provides a bridge between rational and supernatural: it brings together the suppressed culture that wrote the numinous text with the religion that provides the audience. Just as a student ignorant of Kant would not be considered fully educated, so would a student unable to conceive of the cosmic theater today. Referring to his Ivy League students, Philip Rieff, in *The Jew of Culture* (2008), designates them "the educated but religiously illiterate of our time."

To put it more kindly, we may have lost our place in the greater cosmos of meaning, as if it were a book we no longer know how to read. We hardly notice, because the material universe, with its lower-case "unknown" expanse, continues to be explored, from theory to rocket ship. In this lower-case universe, we may be content to simply read as if all can become known one day, even if we must cross to the other side of outer space to discover it. Yet the space created by conceiving of the "unknowable" is of a different order: a numinous space in which natural and supernatural can interact, as in the negotiation of the Hebraic Covenant and the Christian reinterpretation of it. In this Covenantal space human creatures, although limited to Homo sapiens bodies, can read— and contend and quarrel with—their origin and destiny.

The Bible provides the model: things happen, things are remembered and forgotten, but it is all a journey toward recovering a greater drama than any other—a pushing back at the boundary of the supernatural in the form of Covenant-making. Civilization is negotiated in terms of what it means to be human and not-human. It began with Abraham's argument with YHWH over the meaning of justice at Sodom and Gomorrah, and continued with Moses' elaboration of the Ten Commandments. There is always more to be uncovered, because once the meaning of YHWH's truth has entered history and unfolds in time, it's as if a sacred intimacy of communication is always possible in human language, one day. Today it takes the form of inspired rereading.

"Contract or covenant, in short, works only when an accompanying sense of promise and blessing is felt," wrote Yale critic Geoffrey Hartman in my first anthology on reading the Bible, *Congregation* (1987); furthermore, negotiation of the Covenant is "a balm that mitigates what must be endured." This was no calm covenant negotiation in a court or country estate, and what is "endured" required forty years' wandering in the wilderness. On that journey, the Israelites came up against every human limitation and weakness, from not being able to feed themselves to loss of faith in life itself. Yet, "even when the fulfillment of a promise is delayed," continues Hartman, quoting *Midrash Rabbah*, "it is not 'late.'" And for this to hold true, a renewed depth of reading and interpretation becomes that balm. Hartman concludes, "Whenever good exegesis takes place, there is a renewal of joy in the reception of the Torah."

But the emphasis falls on the context: the "reading space" that is created where the drama of the Covenant can take place on earth. It reflects a journey through history for both Jew and Christian that remains indeterminate—a border that we continue to probe the dimensions of, from our side of the natural realm. Does that sound like we're obsessed with surrendering to the supernatural and uniting with God? According to Leon Wieseltier, who also writes in *Congregation*, the Jewish reader is focused not on the outcome but squarely on the cosmic theater itself. "Does he long for union?" Wieseltier asks of this Jew. "Not even when God spoke was there union. There was only—only!—communication. And that is what he dares to dream of." That dream of communication was and remains the negotiation of the Covenant. Negotiating in itself—negotiating our way—is the drama, whether it is a contract or a journey through history. Contributing to *Congregation* as well, Harold Bloom posed the term *contingency* to describe the writing of the Torah's core—with the outcome always in doubt, as in most ongoing negotiations.

Yet when we do look at the Bible through an intimate, numinous reading, we can at least claim to be fully educated, as the poet Alfred

Corn asserts in his contribution to *Communion*. Just like Moses, who was allowed to see the Land of Israel but not to enter, Jewish "readers exiled from the Land could also 'see' it . . . but their bodies could not go there." Instead, by entering the text of Moses, they joined an ongoing drama: learning where we can and cannot go, and what we can and cannot know. We can find the same example of the educated-man-as-deep-reader in the New Testament's Gospel of Matthew, when Jesus interprets the Hebrew prophet Jonah:

> *For as Jonas was three days and three nights in the whale's belly; so shall the Son of man be three days and three nights in the heart of the earth.*

. . .

Jesus expected his original Jewish audience to know the Book of Jonah without his having to remind them of the whole story. They would also know that while in the belly of the whale, Jonah authored this passage within his desperate psalm:

> *I cried out within my despair*
> *I called to YHWH and he answered me*
> *I implored him within the belly of death itself*
> *Yet he heard my voice . . .*

It is the communication between Jonah and his God that reminds us that Jonah himself (or a Hebrew disciple of his, a writer) had to have written this psalm we are reading.

> *From destruction you brought me to life*
> *Up from the pit*
> *YHWH my God . . .*

. . .

And thus, Jesus is telling his disciples—in Jonah's words—that after three days he will rise from the pit of Hell. Jesus uses Jonah's communication with God to magnify his own: When Jesus will return from the pit of Hell, he will have triumphed over death as the Son of more-than-man.

Hearing these biblical words now, in our day, the poet Robert Polito (also writing in *Communion*) describes how powerful they seemed when read out by his high school Latin teacher—in conjunction with Virgil's classic epic, the *Aeneid*. It "had the effect of transforming the Bible into literature—not 'literature' like at home, extrinsic and negligible, or purified and safe like the catechism, but Virgil, Dante, Milton—strange, wondrous, necessary, terrifying." Supernatural beings speak in those great epic poems, creating a form of cosmic theater, yet they do not reecho and *embody* the words of a Jonah the way that Jesus' utterance does. Just as Jonah could speak to God in his psalm, Jesus could speak to Satan. And only as we hear the echo of Jonah do we realize this Judeo-Christian cosmic theater demands knowledge of a deeper history along with a more educated reading.

When I was in college in the 1960s, the old order of reading had broken down: no longer was anyone concerned about the original classics, or in learning Latin and Greek. Certainly not Hebrew. The agenda of ancient history was consigned to specialists, and with it went Homer, Virgil, and the Bible. The problem with specialists is that they are rarely creative writers themselves, so that both their translations and their interpretations lack the practiced ear or sharpened eye of a poet. Yet poets too have become specialists today, with few of them devoted to knowledge in other fields.

When the supereducated literary specialist approaches the Bible in our day, a crucial component of his or her education is missing: an empathy with the biblical author's poetic engagement of the Hebraic cosmic theater. The critic Jack Miles, for instance, writes in *Christ: A Crisis in the Life of God* (2001) that "there are very few Psalms that do not, at some point, allude to a fight in progress and ask God's assistance in winning it." For his example, Miles offers Psalm 139:

Do I not hate them that hate thee, O Lord?
And do I not loathe them that rise up against thee?
I hate them with perfect hatred . . .
. . . lead me on the path everlasting!

. . .

Miles describes this passage as "virulent hatred . . . almost conventional when the Psalms were written." The problem is that he reads exclusively for meaning rather than poetic depth, and without awareness that the biblical writer is a poet. The Psalmist uses "hate" not to hate but to cancel out hatred—he wishes his hatred to erase the hatred of God. Within the Hebraic cosmic theater, the poet-psalmist speaks like a son identifying with his father. He doesn't wish that all his father's enemies be killed; his wish is to cancel out their hatred. No loving child wishes to see his father hated, nor is he drawn to murder in response. But literary critics like Miles, lacking an established practice of poetry, miss this when they ignore the sublime drama of the Hebraic cosmic theater—one in which man and God are on intimate terms—and treat the text as if primitive.

The Hebrew poet's sense of drama, however, is mature and most often concerns the Covenant. Thus, the "path everlasting" he aspires to in Psalm 139 is the negotiation and interpretation of the Covenant (he would wish to go on interpreting forever!). It's not a Covenant of wars and victories as Miles describes it, but one in which history can be dramatized: it becomes a stage upon which whatever happens must continue to be negotiated and interpreted. When Israel is defeated and God's Temple is destroyed, neither history nor the story ends. The ancient losses to the Assyrians and the Babylonians are faced up to, and history goes on. Israel survives and the mighty Babylonian Empire turns to dust, yet no victory is celebrated—other than the continual and life-renewing interpretation of the Covenant, upon which Jewish literature of all genres is usually based.

So when critics claim, as Miles has, that "God's historic mission [is] as military warrior for Israel," it is a tragic misapprehension of even Joshua's mission to inhabit the land of Israel. This critic is fond of reminding us that Jesus was both the "second Joshua" and, in Christian opposition, a "pacifist warrior." However, this paradox reflects a determination to replace the poetic interpretation of midrash with a sledgehammer of meaning. It is hardly different when another literary critic, Robert Alter, in his recent translation of Psalm 139, renders God as a slayer whose enemies deserve "utter hatred."

> *Would you but slay the wicked, God—/ O men of blood, turn away from me! . . . Why, those who hate you, Lord, I hate/ and those against you I despise./ With utter hatred I do hate them.*

In the lines preceding this passage, the poet-psalmist has fallen asleep trying to count the "weighty" thoughts of God: "Should I count them, they would be more than the sand./ I awake, and am still with you." Thus the lines above that follow seem to wish slaying and hatred. What is lacking, however, is the poet-psalmist's sense of drama, moving from the breathtaking thought of Creation to the awareness that, since the Maker gives breath, he can also withdraw it. And thus the translations above obscure the Psalmist's poetry; he sounds merely vengeful.

It's not the hatred of men but rather the hatred of lies that the poet-psalmist evokes. To account for this in my own translation, I began with the same counting of thoughts and then called to mind—with the use of "breath" and "face"—the inadequacy of human language in itself:

> *. . . like grains of sand I try to count*
> *I fall asleep and awake*
> *on the beach of your making*

> *My Lord—stop the breath*
> *of men who live by blood*
> *alone and lie to your face . . .*

If we turn to another Psalm we may further understand how easy it is to confuse primitive emotion with poetic complexity. A fully educated person needs both a cultural and a religious sensitivity, combining the two in a single sensibility. Consider the famous Psalm 137 ("By the waters of Babylon . . ."), in which critic Miles finds an agenda of simple vengeance and that critic Alter then bears out in his own translation. In this Psalm the Hebrew poet-psalmist is literally quoting an ancient enemy of Israel, the Edomites, when they encouraged the Babylonians to destroy Jerusalem: "Raze it, raze it,/ to its foundation!" It seems for a moment that the poet-psalmist encourages similar vengeance in response to the Babylonians, when he adopts a conventional curse-usage: "Happy who seizes and smashes/ your infants against the rock."

But the Hebraic cosmic theater is deflated if the poet-psalmist is portrayed as craving this literal revenge. Miles reads it as payback, pure and simple, though Alter accounts for its hatred differently. He views the passage as a curse in contrast to a song—such as the one the Babylonians had earlier requested from their Israelite captives: "Sing us from Zion's songs." Yet even here, the poet-psalmist has been brushed aside in the specialist's lunge for literal meaning. What is missing is a crucial "as if"—the psalmist does not wish to murder infants but rather to cancel out Babylon's hatred.

If we translate it as it was written—within the Hebraic cosmic theater—the original drama is reinforced by a personified Babylon: first, by emphasizing the personification of Jerusalem as a woman also, and then by holding up "Babylon's babies" *as if* to dash them.

> *. . . you who screamed to strip her*
> *strip her naked*
> *to the ground . . .*

> *. . . who holds up your crying babies*
> *as if to stun them*
> *against solid rock.*

. . .

What we are forced to imagine is the paralysis of the mother—not the murdering of infants—as it cancels out the helpless Jewish witnesses of Jerusalem (as it was being raped and destroyed, leading to the captivity in Babylon). Without the crucial "as if," inherent in the ancient psalm, we lose touch with the Hebraic cosmic theater, in which Jerusalem (representing all of Israel as "Zion") is the site of God's intimacy with man.

But a cosmic theater requires an audience and a narrative cosmic theater needs a community of readers. Reading is a necessary reflection of a person freed from the death obsessions of Egypt and pagan civilizations; it provides the story of an Exodus of the mind as well as the body. Moses' God untangles contradictions that begin in Egypt's history, and Moses resolves the Egyptian afterlife into the redemptive power of facing up to history, the good with the bad. Instead of simply leaving Egypt behind, Moses internalized and transformed it into an ongoing journey.

Like a great writer, we need to realize how Moses, out of the knowledge of classical Egypt, fashioned a new way to see the world. It depends on an "inner life" that resonates in a reader, as it did for the original hearers in the desert. It's a shared inner life in Judeo-Christianity: as if we're made in the image of God *as we read* the Covenant-making of the Torah. The parting of the Reed Sea for the Hebrews to escape Egypt may have seemed a shocking rescue in the past, yet it pales in drama when compared to what we must understand now: the ancient world's long-held ideas of time, nature, and the afterlife were shattered by Moses. Now, history takes over, as if the Covenant makes of our inner life a book, subject to the laws of form and content. The complex Egyptian idea of the body's supernatural journey after death, played out in an eternity of time, has been transformed into the Hebraic journey through physical time and human history. Although Moses framed the new history of the Hebrews with seeming miracles, from plagues to the pillars of fire and smoke, they were based on Egyptian forms. It all comes down to his Egyptian education in sacred mysteries. But Moses would convert these into historical events, as the Israelites made their journey out of Egypt.

How was such a small remnant, the ancient Hebrews, able to outlast the empires of Egypt and Babylonia, Persia and Assyria, Greece and Rome? Every Israelite revival was rooted in the power of transformation, but it was Moses who set the monotheistic and ethical reformation in motion. Before Moses, ancient civilizations embraced time as constant, exclusive of an evolving idea of the future—especially a future that would end in something like a new species of human being. In short, our Western idea of a world with a creation, a salvation story, and a messianic resolution was created with the hand of Moses. Without an understanding of intellectual history and how this transpired, can one be considered educated today? The nut of the problem was then, and still is now, the meaning of our deaths.

Although the Egyptians envisioned a life after death, they never expected to reawaken on earth. Instead, they looked to a heavenly Egypt, a kind of bigger and better Egypt in the sky. A human future on earth that *evolves in history* was not to be expected. Yet that is what Moses and the Torah promise, based in the Covenant: an evolving humanity in *this* life.

Unlike an Egyptian, Moses did not prepare his body to be memorialized, nor has a description of his face survived; what he left behind was a more precious definition of individual character, the uniqueness of his *voice* in the core of the Bible. When Moses sees the golden cow and smashes his tablets in anger, he asks Aaron, who had crafted the holy Egyptian cow: "What could this people have done to you?"

Aaron replies, "You know this people, their memory quickly melts away . . . 'This man Moses,' they say, 'who led us up from the land of Egypt—who knows what has happened to him?'" So the Israelites returned to traditional Egyptian ways, just as the princes of Pharaoh Akhenaten rejected his monotheistic sun-worship a generation or two before Moses. No sooner was Akhenaten in his tomb than the Heavenly Cow of old Egyptian mythology was worshiped again—and now we see a reprise of this situation when the Hebrews dance around the cow. Yet there is a huge difference. For Moses' voice—and the voice of the God he translated into writing—are what will survive this time. Neither the Heavenly Cow nor the mute face of the mummy will be seen again among the Israelites.

Nevertheless, we are left with a mistranslation of the Egyptian cow into a "golden calf" by the early Hebraic authors after Moses, who were writing in Israel, surrounded by Canaanite cultures, and no longer up-to-date on Egypt. The calf was a Canaanite deity, and the Israelites, newly freed from Egypt, would not have worshiped it as the fond incarnation of Egypt that the cow represented. And yet even as we recognize the fact, we are once again exposed to the nuances of history that the Hebrew Bible offers us. So much of the ancient world is absorbed in it—and reabsorbed in the New Testament—that it constitutes an education in how the world was transformed.

One of the more unusual Commandments Moses records in Sinai concerns the Sabbath Day. After the Golden Cow episode is past, the time to create the Tabernacle and its accoutrements arrives, with this warning from YHWH: "But my Sabbaths you shall observe." On one level, Moses is reminding his People that the physical sanctuary was not intended to be worshiped in itself; it was not as sacred as a day in time, the Sabbath. Sabbath was a forethought of a messianic future, when all days would be like the Seventh: instead of work and material cares, the joy of education prevails. It's easy enough to see the transference to Christian Sunday School.

In our terms today, and in the event the Sabbath was tedious for us as children, it was largely because we were not yet convinced that study was a splendid thing. Jesus not only gave his sermons and lessons on the Sabbath, he taught his disciples to live the writer's life on it—but without the "work" of physically writing. The originality of Jesus as a religious leader can be viewed through his life in the drama of creating character. He instills it in his disciples by forcing them to think through his parables and allegories, with the underlying allegory pointing toward God's Creation internalized.

Similarly, Moses had to internalize YHWH. Beyond the images of a bearded prophet leading the Jews out of Egypt, the truly startling life he led was at a table—in a tent, in the desert. This is where he wrote the bedrock of the books of Moses, the basis for what later biblical writers would turn into the Torah. It is the Jerusalemite author of the last of the Torah's five books, Deuteronomy, who actually pictures Moses writing in his Sinai tent. If we can see Moses there now, as our primal author, we can regain a cosmology upon which our confidence in the future has always been founded. That view of the world requires our focus on the boundary between life and death—and the confidence to push it back with knowledge of the world, with history, science, and art: that public side of an educated person. But the sacred boundary is crucial, or we would be pushing against air. After Moses, the *art* of writing is what the biblical authors enlarge by continuing to interpret the life of Moses, and that is why we must concentrate on him as their inspired progenitor. He is the author in spirit of our civilization today: he can be read in secondary school even by secular Jews in Israel (thanks to Modern Hebrew's conformity to the ancient language) as if they were reading the newspaper.

When Moses first began to write, on the mountain, history replaced mythology: all that would happen to Moses and the Israelites thereafter would be written into the Hebrew Bible. But as the biblical tradition of commentary has continued, through all the intellectual fashions from Plato to Freud, we ourselves are those who have survived into a Judeo-Christian future. It was there, in the wilderness of Sinai, that the Egyptian education of Moses inspired a new tradition of reinterpretation that could actually *change* the future. It displaced Egypt's static myth.

Today, we can contemplate such history-specific questions as how the forty years of wandering and Torah-writing of Moses derived from the specified forty days of royal mummy preparation. Similarly, Moses spends forty days with God upon Mount Sinai, but what he returns with—in place of mummified innards—is an inner life in writing. In place of a sarcophagus inscribed with classical

Egyptian texts, Moses bears the commandments of life—rather than rules for an afterlife.

But our contemporary culture no longer comprehends the historical Moses, nor the later Jewish writers in Israel. They understood the necessity for historical sources, and they shaped Moses' life and words by using the Egyptian stage trappings of the supernatural: a magician's wand (Moses' staff), hovering clouds, fire, natural wonders. The supernatural drama of Moses and the escaping Jews in Sinai is rooted in the Egyptian drama of personal immortality. It was an eternity of the mummified body extending into the future, surrounded by supernatural texts.

In the same way, if we're to comprehend the historical Jesus of Nazareth and his disciples' messianic resistance to Rome, we find it in the strength of his transformative reading and writing within the Mosaic tradition. In Jesus' day, the Hellenized and Romanized Jews were the equivalent of Egyptians to Moses: they absorbed worldly knowledge into Judaism that Jesus and other rabbis in Israel transformed. In their readings, the stage of the cosmic theater turns from Israel's earthly landscape into the cosmic landscape of "the Kingdom of Heaven." As we read the Gospels, it is as if we are reading over the shoulder of God. This is not new to Judaism, since it was already reading in God's presence—but it brings a new urgency to our self-consciousness today as readers in the Hebraic cosmic theater.

What we are still learning is that history and the reading of it (or reading out loud) were sacred to Hebraic culture, but the *writing* of it was a great cultural art. The Torah did not come to seem sacred in itself until a few centuries had passed, when it was "rediscovered" in the seventh century BCE and a primary art became the "reading" of it rather than the writing. Now, with some of the individual sensibilities of the Biblical authors becoming familiar to us, it is the history of the *writing* that can be sacred to us again, true to the Biblical love of history.

We can recover this sacral experience in the reading if we suspend disbelief and enter this narrative cosmic theater: it is not only a record of human history that is found there, but the moments of confrontation with an unknowable eternity. Episodes at Pharaoh's court in imperial Egypt and at the Reed Sea, at Mount Sinai, and at Kadesh, or wandering in the wilderness—these were historical moments when the enormity of human aloneness in the cosmos was faced. A great peril of extinction and emptiness was filled, and though we have lost those moments, the historical writing of Hebraic culture preserved the losses.

And later, a brief ancient Greek mention:

When the Egyptian Sesostris, being on his way homewards and bringing many men of the nations whose countries he had subdued . . . It was these men who dragged the great and long blocks of stone. (Herodotus, on the historical enslaving of the Jews in the previous millennium [450 BCE])

"These men" included the captive Hebrews. Moses learned Egyptian history at Pharaoh's court, but the enslavement of the Hebrews was also part of his education. How was their slavery accomplished? We get an idea of what the Egyptians thought about their captive peoples by comparing cultural records. The monumental inscription of the Pharaoh Merneptah records the history of Israel by the Egyptians themselves. But it is also the most ancient echo of the threat to wipe out the Jews:

The princes are prostrate, saying: "Shalom"
Not one of the Nine Bows lifts his head:
Tjehenu is vanquished, Khatti at peace,
Canaan is captive with all woe.
Ashkelon is conquered, Gezer seized,
Yanoam made nonexistent;
Israel is wasted, bare of seed . . .

The Egyptians more often *avoided* chronicling history— whenever it came to recording their own losses, failures, and defeats. But in Moses' eyes, study itself is the new norm, rather than the Egyptian wish for immortality. The latter was represented by the preserved, mummified body—too literal a wish. Until Moses transformed it, we might say that the human face preserved in a mummy represented a personal consciousness—yet it was a person *asleep*. Egyptian texts do preserve the drama: "The Book of the Dead" navigates the dangers of arriving in the afterlife. But the mummy itself, and the person it preserves, can no longer grow in understanding and moral insight because it remains as if asleep. Moses woke this sleeping fantasy of Egyptian immortality.

Today, the sleeping faces of Moses' ancestors are turning up in Egypt's tombs and sands, for even the enslaved Hebrews in Egypt had adopted mummification. Preserved for these many millenniums, the bodies have become astonishing natural phenomena rather than signs of the supernatural. But when the physical artifact of the Biblical text is in our hands, and we are reading, we all need to be believers in the supernatural. Closing the book, we're free to believe what we wish. As we read, however, we must see ourselves as the spirit does, whether manifested as God or an angel, and what *it* sees is a human creature that must die. Is there any power that humans can muster to challenge eternal life? Not very likely. Prior to the Hebrew Bible being written in Jerusalem, ancient myth and even the Epic of Gilgamesh presented a quest for eternal life— missions that must end in failure. But the Bible presents something new: coming face to face with eternal life. That is, not merely eternal beings but relationships in which the spirit of eternal life can be grasped and internalized in human form. And we, as we read, become capable of reading over an angel's shoulder—that is, the sense of our own mortality blends into the larger journey of Israel's history and Judeo-Christian civilization.

But how to read over an angel's shoulder has not become part of our public educations. In *The Closing of the American Mind* (1988), his best-selling study of higher education, the late Allan Bloom lamented our secular ignorance of the Bible. He wrote further that the teaching of the Bible in the humanities is counterproductive: "The Bible is subjected to modern 'scientific' analysis, called the

Higher Criticism, where it is dismantled, to show how 'sacred' books are put together, and that they are not what they claim to be" (374). In reaction to Bloom, some sentimental scholars claim the original authors are real enough yet unimportant. But I've intended here to show the opposite of both claims, Bloomian and sentimentalist. Rather than dismiss the revelation of the Bible, I've worked to illuminate it as a revelation of culture as well, one concerned more with truth than the contemporary cultures we live in.

It's never easy to show this because our cultural factions are often intractable. In 1984, for instance, while editor of the Jewish Publication Society, I organized a conference in Philadelphia that brought together prominent contemporary poets, including Robert Pinsky, Allen Ginsberg, and Louise Glück, with Judaic scholars such as Susannah Heschel and Arthur Green. Each side saw their role as educator of the other: the poets lectured the scholars on modern poetry and aesthetics, which represented for them contemporary culture as a whole, and the scholars lectured the poets on the need for historical knowledge, discipline, and insight. Once each side recognized the ignorance of the other—the Jewish poets knew little of Judaism and the Jewish scholars knew little of literary postmodernism—they refused to see themselves in the equal roles of student and teacher. They became increasingly belligerent pedagogues and the conference ended in acrimony.

And in 2007, at a conference in Jerusalem billed as "the first world conference of Jewish writers," I found the same dynamic still at play. Half of the writers considered the term "Jewish writer" an anachronism improved upon by their radical "individuality"—they preferred, in other words, to be considered "world" writers—while the other half believed that only by engaging Jewish historical knowledge could there be a contemporary Jewish culture of significant writers. After twenty years nothing had changed. Can it be any different among conferences of Christian writers, if they are open enough to include mainstream postmodernists, who were brought up as Christians yet who find the term "Christian writer" objectionable?

However, the tendency for religion and culture to be at odds is overcome in a Judeo-Christianity that is foremost a community of readers. In his psychological reading of cultural history, *Moses and Monotheism* (1938), Freud describes the God of Moses that Jesus knew: "as all-loving as he was all-powerful; who, averse to all ceremony and magic, set humanity as its highest aim a life of truth and justice." How did this happen? Out of a culture of writing, reading, and interpreting a cosmic narrative was established—and may be reestablished once again.

Freud also conceived of Moses as a model for Jesus, yet as a scientist he viewed both as representatives of social upheaval, bound into the natural history of human evolution. As a result, unfortunately, we don't feel Moses' and Jesus' Jewish love of learning, which permeates the biblical text. Neither do we grasp their love for YHWH's "truth and justice."

While Freud's insights come from outside the text, it has been my intention from the beginning to read the Bible from inside, to live and breathe within the audience of the Hebraic cosmic theater. It was there that the Covenant was conceived, negotiated, dramatized, elucidated, historicized, and reinterpreted. Freud understood the power of the monotheistic God, but like most historians of religion he focused on the conception of a Creator, as well as on the Biblical characters, rather than on the Jewish culture which produced them. As a result, he neglected the negotiating process of the Covenant.

So I have described the Covenant in cultural terms to make up for this neglect and to aid the secular reader. In a nutshell, I've described the Covenant as the crucial negotiation of the Hebraic cosmic theater: a border space where natural and supernatural can meet without intruding. It's certainly true, however, that there are some among the religious for whom superstition rules everything and who wish to intrude on secular life. It's the same on the other side: many atheists and others would like to intrude upon religion and push it offstage. But my contention is that the more the Covenant is understood by Jew, Christian, and atheist, the less that superstition can hold sway.

From a Judeo-Christian perspective, the boundary or "border space" is a point of origin, where the negotiation between natural and supernatural first becomes written, and then takes the shape of a journey in history and toward self-knowledge. In our up-to-date lives, that journey can take the form of reading. But it also took this form in ancient Jerusalem, especially in the time of Jesus: a *reading* of Mosaic history that began with Creation and absorbed all of known human history up until the lives of King David, the prophets, and the writers of ancient Hebraic literature, as well as Judeo-Greek and Judeo-Roman authors, whose non-canonical books played upon the others. The Bible became a multifaceted library.

Ingrained in the ancient history of Jerusalem is also a memory of loss. Long before Jesus, Jews had died there by blessing its memory. The desire to redeem memory by reinterpreting it in the present reality is another shared aspect of the Jewish and Christian testaments; it becomes not simply the religious history of Jews and Christians but the common reality of humanity. This common history is given new meaning by the Judeo-Christian awareness of loss and redemption—of transforming loss. Yet there was a time in the Middle Ages when Christians thought themselves freed from the complexities of history as written in the Jewish testament. It was as if Christianity stood for forgetting.

What Judeo-Christianity returns to our consciousness is not only the Jewish history that Jesus himself studied, but the Jewish emphasis on recording history back to its root in a single Creation for all humanity. Judeo-Christianity represents an exception to the universalism of the old Christian belief in forgetting the origin of human history and neglecting all that came before Jesus of Nazareth. In place of one revelation, Judeo-Christianity provides one origin.

Moses' story is an Exodus of the mind as well as the body. We encounter a text obsessed with defining the boundaries between life and death, between secular and sacred, for these are the boundaries that became most confused in Egypt. Even today, this drive toward an objective view of our situation defines an educated person.

And not only a material view, but a cosmic one that seeks to dramatize and make objective the question that can't be successfully repressed: the "Why?" of why we are here.

We are in Moses' presence as we read through the question, as Moses was in the numinous presence of God. The same holds true for Jesus: as we read his words interpreting the Covenant as a cosmic boundary to be made new, we become cosmic readers in a line of history going back to Moses. Thereby acquainted with both sides of the boundary between natural and supernatural, we're prepared to be fully educated.

VII

·A COMMUNITY·OF·READERS: ·A·LETTER·TO·THE·POPE·

In November 2007, the *New York Times* invited favored authors to establish a "reading group" blog. As in a secular Bible study class, they would all reread and comment upon the consensus summit of modern literature, Tolstoy's *War and Peace*. Several of the themes one might expect from a Bible group turned up, from killing and the nature of hell to the meaning of it all. But the most startling result was the obsession with secular prophecy, as if Tolstoy were a substitute Isaiah.

"I only wish that the battles Tolstoy describes sounded less like the war in Iraq," wrote one novelist, who can't be blamed for our contemporary neglect of history—until it's confronted in a work of fiction from the nineteenth century. With less irony, another contributor wrote, "Is General Petraeus Kutuzov? Or Napoleon?" Finally, several authors came to a similar conclusion: "How little we appear to have learned in almost two centuries." Perhaps if the Bible were to be the book under discussion, we might find "two centuries" replaced with "three millenniums."

To be fair to both the Bible and Tolstoy, we must note that we are still reading and still edified by each book. And yet, as the *Times* blog amply proves, there is a fundamental difference in how they are discussed. The author of *War and Peace* is profoundly admired for the artistry of his authorship; the writers of the Hebrew Bible, on the other hand, usually go unmentioned. Their devotion to history is often in question—as if they could not discern the difference between legend and fact, the hallmark of any great author. However, the Jewish people's "reading group" throughout history makes up for this in a creative engagement of the text called *midrash*. In a dual act of reading and retelling, midrash probes the authenticity of Hebraic authorship.

During the period of the European Inquisition, Jewish midrash could be denounced as Satan's work, since its interpretive nature seemed to play with—and thus call into question—what the Church determined as the text's dogmatic, Christological meaning. In other words, the rabbinic authors of midrash (and they are usually known by name) were damned as "fiction writers." Much of this attitude has been eradicated by enlightened Biblical scholarship; nevertheless, it comes as a surprise to discover that the current Pope Benedict holds midrash in high esteem. And beyond that, the Pope has written a best-selling historical biography, *Jesus of Nazareth* (2007), in which he honors the term *midrash* by using it himself.

If we think back to the original Biblical audience for Moses or David or Isaiah, these hearers or readers wanted first to know who they, the readers, were. The question of how to live would follow, but first came knowledge of historical origin: who, why, and where we are. And that is the origin of midrashic creativity: the need to peel back our current self-involvement and reestablish our history. The original Biblical audiences were devoted to history, both human and Covenantal (the negotiation of what is beyond us); and the later Biblical audiences reestablished this devotion with midrash in its many forms, including the Kabbalah.

Today, the esteem of reading is in decline. Although barely a century ago reading was considered a mark of intelligence, now it has become politicized: we tend to read for "relevance"—for immediate application to self-centered lives—rather than to deepen our education. As an audience, therefore, we resemble a political caucus: we already know who we are, so we want to know the fitting way to think. Our idea of midrash would be social midrash, making the Bible relevant to our local headlines, and this indeed is what we most often hear in our pulpits.

In its most universal sense, a midrash is a reading of a part of the Hebrew Bible that interprets and retells the text as a story. It makes a new story out of the interpretation. Originally, it was history that was the story; later, the story could be built around Biblical characters and prophets all the way to contemporaneous rabbinical teachers; still later, the story could be derived from nature, linguistics, or supernatural legend—a range of storytelling equal to any modern culture. By retelling the life of Jesus of Nazareth as a prophetic rabbi, the Pope interprets Hebrew sources to tell the story of a being whose provenance as a man or divinity is a compelling mystery to be solved.

Most crucially, however, Pope Benedict allows us to see the historical Jesus as a Jewish maker of midrash himself. Jesus' Jewish education becomes palpable, allowing a new intimacy between Judaism and Christianity. As Benedict quotes Psalm 22—"Why have You forsaken me?"—we are now thoroughly aware that it was known to the original readers of the Gospels, many of them students of Jewish law. Since it was one among hundreds of quotations and allusions made by Jesus from the Hebrew Bible, his education as a rabbi is confirmed. Thus we now can realize that the early Christians, no less than the ancient Hebrews, were *readers*—and readers in the Mosaic (and later, Christian) textual tradition.

The writers of midrash who are collected in the canonical volumes referred to as The Midrash are largely named authors. Their sayings are prefaced with "Rabbi so-and-so said . . . ," so that if the sayings of Jesus were recorded there (rather than in the Gospels) they would begin, "Rabbi Joshua ben Joseph of Nazareth said . . ." Thus being named, their invocations of Moses and other Biblical authors force us to recall them as writers also, along with those whose names have been lost to history. In other words, a writer of midrash engages the history of Hebraic culture, and not only the Hebrew Bible. We become far more conscious of the significance of the Biblical writer as part of a cultural community.

Benedict's recent book helps suggest how Jews and Christians can read together by forming a "contemporaneous bond across the ages." It probes the Jewish knowledge of Jesus, and it leads to my own starting point, exploring the similarly deep education displayed by Moses:

If we can consider Moses a core writer of the Torah and Jesus a core writer of the Gospels, then we are now proposing a "community" not simply of believers but of readers . . . How does the love of Torah by a Jewish reader differ from what Jesus loved? It is here that I would answer: it does not differ. Jesus' love is one and the same as his interpretive power of the Torah; he reads Moses as a writer, and it is as thus that he reveals himself.

Even today, however, a serious Jew knows the Hebrew Bible, but one need not know it or even the New Testament to be a serious Christian. The reason for the difference is a certain disregard for the historical—a neglect that Benedict now remedies so forcefully. The Jesus whose gospel makes reading unnecessary is an ahistorical Jesus, the supernatural Messiah. As one identifies with him, it is his *love*, like a father's, that is spiritual sustenance; one doesn't normally think of one's father's *books* first. So it is from this identification and displacement from the historical that the life of Jesus can seem that of an illiterate peasant, and even a Gentile with no knowledge of Torah. Yet the text belies it. Every word and action of Jesus' life is an echo of the Hebrew Bible—and not least, the concept of Messiah.

Scholars have long recognized these points, but only now is the full extent of Jesus' Jewish education being understood. A scholar himself, Benedict has entered this conversation, suggesting a new community of readers can reinvigorate Judeo-Christianity. He shows how Jesus' education as a Jew is integral to his teaching, but also how his personae as a teaching father and a loving father were originally merged in the conversation between Moses and his God. The conversation of Jesus with his Jewish contemporaries flourished within the historical culture of Israel. And with the exile of the Jews forced by the Romans, coming not long after the death of Jesus, Judaism, like early Christianity, will become more deeply indebted to its Diaspora community of writers and readers.

Letter to the Pope

My Dear Benedict XVI:

No doubt many Jewish scholars have written to you about the publication of your recent book, *Jesus of Nazareth*. I am particularly disarmed as you take up within it *A Rabbi Talks with Jesus*, by Jacob Neusner, an American colleague of mine. As you enter into dialogue with Rabbi Neusner's book, you are also speaking to me. And thus, I too become engaged in a creative historical midrash with you on Biblical subjects—precisely the kind of dialogue you call for, between Jews and Christians.

I once proposed a book of creative midrash that would compare Moses and Jesus in terms of how their lives are told in the Bible. I expected that Moses' life would equal or overshadow that of a Jewish Jesus. The Torah's commitment to the dialogue between God and Moses is only part of it; the dialogue between Moses and the people of Israel is another part, and yet another is that between Moses and Egypt's Pharaoh. Without exception, however, my colleagues at the Jewish Publication Society thought that Jesus would appear the more rounded figure when only historical understanding is allowed, even if just because his era is closer to our own. The book idea was moved to the back burner.

Now you have swept away such demurrals with your concept of "a contemporaneous bond across the ages"—putting Moses and Jesus on equal footing. Nevertheless, you write "Jesus was a 'true Israelite,'" as echoed in the Gospel of John, and that even as he embodied "the inner dynamic of the promises made to Israel, he transcended Judaism." Curiously, your description of that transcendence parallels what is called Hasidism. You describe the Christian as always "being-in-relation" to God, and how "God is always at the center of the discussion." These depictions are not only applicable to Hasidic Jews, for the influence of Hasidic thought has spread throughout Judaism. The modern Jewish philosopher Martin Buber founded his ideas upon them. And we can trace the seventeenth-century rise of Hasidism to similar Jewish movements that formed the background of Jesus' life in Judea, from John the Baptist to the Essenes. We can also look back even further to origins in the Hebrew Prophets and ultimately to Moses.

So I now ask you, my dear Benedict, to think again about Moses: What happens when we engage him in a contemporaneous bond? His biography in the Torah is vivid; there is a *story* of a man who was born and died, and also a *historical* context that renders his life plausible. When it comes to the story and history of Jesus of Nazareth, however, you claim something almost ahistorical: "Jesus was God." But I would contrast this with "Moses was *with* God"—in a conversation and relationship that is greatly detailed. Though Moses is human, the Torah's words themselves are numinous, and thus the Jewish and Christian testaments are on equal ground. If we dig deeper to consider the roles of Moses and Jesus in numinous relation to God, both are revealed as writers—that is, creators of numinous texts in relation to their Creator.

Historicists shy away from this striking bond; they prefer to call each man a "teacher." Even the terms *rabbi* and *prophet* are more comfortable for us than *writer*. Authorship has long been a repressed subject in Biblical scholarship, and when the written sources of the Torah are distinguished from each other they are not even imagined in terms of flesh-and-blood authors. True, the Gospel authors are named and given brief biographies but they are bereft of education and writing prowess. The latest scholarship identifies them as Jewish, with differing approaches that lend each a distinct character and sensibility, as you note. Yet little is made of the writers' sensibilities, so that as Jewish men, even when called evangelists, they do not come alive as living writers with unique Jewish educations.

Since writing is a cultural issue, it complicates the universal layer of the text, which seeks to erase historical distinctions. A common demeaning of writers in the past was to label them "scribes," so that the issue of imagination would not come up. Now just here, my dear Benedict, is a painful issue between us: I believe you cannot help but diminish the numinous text of Moses by avoiding his authorship. Yes, God was involved, so that the Torah is numinous, but the writer Moses is more than a servant or scribe here. He is the interpreter to the people, and the later authors in Israel continue in this role. And since the Torah is an interpreted text, it also contains a midrash upon the truth and justice that is God's intent. In other words, "the Law" *unfolds*—and brings along within it the history of human cultural endeavor, all the way back to the insights of Sumer and Akkad, of Egypt and Canaan, as they are transformed in a Hebraic context.

Indeed, this unfolding of time, as represented by the desert years of Moses and the Hebrews in Sinai, provides many dramatic episodes for interpretation. In other words, the recounting of history becomes numinous text itself because, as Moses writes within or beside the holy tent, he also elucidates the text as if God looks over his shoulder. And this writer's consciousness is what the later Gospel authors tend to lose sight of, I believe, when they disguise *their* midrash—based upon their quotation of the Torah and Prophets—as if it were original. But that too may be our own cultural misreading; at the time of actual writing, each Gospel's extensive quotation from Hebrew sources was certainly known. The original audience of the Gospels, many of them with Jewish educations, must have understood the midrashic nature of the text: it was culturally normative that the gospel genre be written to include the Jewish interpretive tradition.

And you, my dear Benedict, describe the Gospels yourself as often a form of midrash upon the Hebrew Bible. Jesus creates midrash as he quotes the Twenty-second Psalm in a context that changes its meaning from terror—"My God, my God, why have you forsaken me?"—to tenderness, since he cannot be abandoned by God, simply by definition. We have also listened as Jesus delivered a midrash upon the Ten Commandments within the Sermon on the Mount. Today, we know that most of the books of Jewish midrash from this period were made up of sermons by rabbis. So the basic text for rabbis and Gospel writers, the Torah, being numinous in itself, is what allowed the words of Jesus to take on the character of divine authorship. Still, both the original Jewish Psalmist—and Jesus, who is depicted as quoting it—knew the Hebrew psalm was created by a human hand. In the same way, we must also presume that Jesus had written out at least a portion of his sermon, if not before then after delivering it, and no differently than other rabbis.

Consider the authorship of Jesus compared with Moses. You describe the word of Jesus as "the Torah of the Messiah" (itself a midrash based upon a Hebrew prophecy) added to the Torah of Moses. Wonderfully, you make it clear that Jesus does not wish to replace the Torah, not by a single jot, but that he insists he is merely its fulfillment. Nevertheless, whatever Jesus says or does is authored, and we know it today not just because of the Gospel writers but because Jesus was presenting to us *a text to know him by*, a beginning of a Testament; just so, the Torah of Moses only begins the Hebrew Bible.

Philo of Alexandria, a Jewish writer and contemporary of Jesus, defined a prophet's perfection by Moses; others have described traits of the prophetic personality in the Gospel writers. But today, I believe that the theologically encrusted concept of the "prophetic personality" can be elaborated by the concept of a numinous writer—a new form of midrash. As you do for Moses, my dear Benedict, you place Jesus within the historical Jewish family by insisting that his "intention is not to abolish either the family or the Sabbath-as-celebration-of-creation, but he has to create a new and broader context for both." So, as an interpreter of creation, Jesus for you takes on the authority of writing midrash. I would go even further: I find the intention of Jesus rooted in a traditional Jewish education, which he has interpreted as an *education* in creation.

Of course, the authority of such an education transcends mere schooling and scholarship: it is the writer himself who dramatizes authority by disarming us with speech and action. It is not unusual in the Jewish tradition of Prophets that we see them more in action than in study. Still, as we see Moses in terms of his experience, we also have descriptions of him sitting and writing the Law (and his life) into Torah. If we do not witness Jesus writing, it is because his disciples prefer the authority of "hearing"— just as it was at various points in Jewish history, right down to when Ezra "proclaimed the Law" (read out the Torah) in the Second Temple period (a time that long preceded but also included Jesus). And when it comes to the Torah, as you put it, Jesus "can be understood only in the context of 'the Law and the Prophets.'"

Some of the Hebrew Prophets embodied oracles for their writing identity; they were not "writers" of oracles, but rather "speakers" of their own writing. And these prophets, among them Isaiah, Zechariah, and Ezekiel, included additional writers—we have to say "included" because more than one writer in different eras took on the identity of Isaiah and other prophets. So surely Jesus' audience would have expected that the Sermon on the Mount, for instance, was written by him—that it did not come out whole in an oracle-like trance. For as you make plain, this lecture or sermon (even as modern scholars deem it a composite text) is filled with learned and sublime references to Torah, and embedded in a Jewish education.

It's not without reason that I will insist upon the education of Jesus as a primary link to Moses. The Hebraic culture in which they were educated, separated by more than a millennium, is based upon the authority of text. And yet Judaism continues to be marginalized by theologians who, by attributing a genius for "religion" to the early kingdoms of Israel, deny its culture and education, which are held to be "primitive." However, what you have now done so astonishingly, my dear Benedict, is to implicitly recognize that Jewish and Hebraic culture today remains tied to the same inspiration in which the Bible was written.

A few years ago, I refocused my Biblical study further back in time, to the history of the patriarchal age and the life of Abraham. I averred that the young Abraham would have been trained as a scribe in his cultural capital of Ur, and thus he would have been familiar with classical Sumerian and Akkadian texts (accounting for the many references to them in his story). And so I began a book on Abraham by building upon the model of contemporary historical scholarship surrounding Jesus of Nazareth. It's impossible to imagine that Abraham wrote (or spoke) just for his family, or that Jesus did for his disciples and followers alone. In the same way, Philo of Alexandria wrote several books exclusively for a universal audience throughout the Roman Empire, seeking to persuade others of the Torah's universal relevance.

Numinous means a scene in the Bible where the natural and supernatural can interact. Often it may be in disguise, as when only a part of God's being is present, as his hand or his voice, or when angels appear as humans. Most crucially, it may concern the writer of the text itself, as when God is described as author, or when a Prophet quotes God's words. And there are also scenes in which the supernatural is an unseen observer, watching over the proceedings, as in the nativity of Jesus or his crucifixion.

But the most significant usage is when a force outside the text itself is brought into play, as when the Torah is said to be written by God, with

Moses his interpreter into human language. Thus the entire text can be said to be numinous, just as the Gospels of the New Testament are said to be numinous whenever Jesus is present, since as God he himself is supernatural.

Yet unlike either a Hebrew Prophet or Jesus, Philo's own words did not strive for the numinous or for midrashic interpretation. He most resembles a modern writer whose lack of historical scholarship limits him to logic and tradition on the one hand, imagination on the other. Bereft of deep history, one may also lose the ability to read a numinous text as shot through with drama and excitement, in addition to wisdom and truth. And drastically marginalizing the Bible as a "sacred text" can further intimidate the reader. I know, I was once such a reader myself. But what you have demonstrated in your book, my dear Benedict, is that we can become numinous readers, entering fully into the Bible's historical drama—and with the confidence that the historical authors, creative as they were, rarely lost sight of having been created themselves.

My personal project continues to shore up belief in the *written* Bible by providing a new revelation in private, individual reading: a sudden awareness of the human presence of the writer as he serves the creation of a numinous text. This awareness can't be accomplished by either sacralizing or ignoring the writer. A skeptical mind in a modern culture needs a new depth of cultural history in which to freely suspend his or her disbelief. When I began translating the Hebrew Psalms and Prophets into contemporary verse almost forty years ago, one of my first scholarly supporters was the same Rabbi Jacob Neusner you embrace in your new book. He wrote unselfishly about my work: "The full power and majesty of the prophecies, stories and psalms here come to full and final revelation in our own language." This generous spirit is what engaged you also, and it allowed for Neusner's unabashed conversation with Jesus—in other words, the reflected creation of numinous text in the book of his own that you cherish. And this is the kind of midrash that you describe as integral to the Gospels: it includes the writer as a midrashic *imago dei*—a creator in the image of the Creator, as Moses confirms when he exclaims to God in the Torah (Exodus 32:31), "Blot me out of your book!" (Equally, without Moses there could have been no written Torah.)

The later Hebraic writers in Jerusalem and Samaria who completed the life of Moses entered into the numinous text by creating the context in which God and Moses spoke. You emphasize that "Moses spoke face to face with God, as a man speaks to his friend. It was only because he spoke with God himself that Moses could bring God's word to men." A further interpretation of these words is created by the Hebraic writers who enter into a cosmic theater of narrative and dialogue. And you describe the ambition of these Biblical writers yourself, my dear Benedict, when you write that "Any 'self-knowledge' that restricts man to the empirical and the tangible fails to engage with man's true depth. Man knows himself only when he learns to understand himself in light of God."

These Biblical writers erase the demeaning idea of the "scribe" that is a traditional way of denying the intellect of Hebraic culture. In its place, we encounter a writer whose education includes the *unknowable*, and who therefore must always be aware of the boundary between Creator and man. That boundary is delineated by the Covenant, a moral pact elaborated in the Torah—and also represented as the Torah itself, a numinous text. Jesus too confirms the text, and when he embodies it we also must see him as the figurative writer whose New Testament will be completed by Jewish writers who come after.

The Hebraic writer's stance I have been describing is fleshed out when you portray us today as numinous *readers*: "The highest things, the things that really matter, we cannot achieve on our own; we have to accept them as gifts and enter into the dynamic of the gift, so to speak." That "so to speak" you use is telling, my dear Benedict, for it's an interpretive disclaimer of your own role as writer. It describes, in other words, how you yourself are writing midrash by "entering into the dynamic of the gift." But allow me to more fully clarify what this gift is: it is the gift of the writing itself. Without it, there is no interpretative life.

For instance, the conversation into which Rabbi Neusner enters with Jesus, as you describe it, is also about written text, especially the Sermon on the Mount, and the midrash Neusner makes of it is at your disposal to comment upon, in order to create further midrash, as you do in your own book. Directly pertaining to this, I recall a conversation between Rabbi Neusner and the renowned Hebrew poet Yehuda Amichai. It took place in

1980, at the launching party for my *Chosen Days*, a book that interprets the
Hebrew Bible's poetry. My publisher's penthouse apartment in New York
provided the setting, with two fireplaces blazing on a bitter winter evening.
Yehuda, whose poetry I had translated into English and whom I'd known
for years, was visiting from Israel. He held the opinion that religion was
a beautiful dream for children, and that as adults we must enter into it by
reimagining ourselves as children; in other words, Yehuda took the Biblical term *Children of Israel* quite literally, if not midrashically.

Neither was Yehuda patient with what he took to be the pomposity
of grown-ups—especially rabbis—whose academic degrees in the Bible
seemed to entitle them to drone. Neusner too could be a prickly character
when confronted with pretentious authority. So as I introduced them, I
feared tension between the rabbi-professor and the anti-clerical poet, and
even though Yehuda's opening remark appeared jovial—"we need more
professors who read poetry"—there was a barb hidden in it, for I was
afraid that Neusner had not yet read *Yehuda Amichai's* poetry. I intervened
by advising Yehuda that Professor Neusner "knew where your words come
from," by which I meant Hebraic culture, ancient and modern.

"That's better than a rabbi," Yehuda quickly responded, "who imagines
them as pure!"

"I *am* a rabbi," Neusner said. "I can assure you the living ears of our time
are not pure, whether you refer to the Bible or to your own poetry. In addition to new poetry, we need new ways of reading, too, don't you think?"

And to my amazement, they hit it off. As I recall this encounter of
many years ago, I'm reminded of Rabbi Neusner's recent "conversation"
with Jesus—as well as one I can imagine he might have had with Moses.
"Moses, I'm comfortable with disputing the text, as rabbis always have
done. Yet for you there was no text, no Torah yet to interpret. So I can only
ask: How was it, based on your education, to have interpreted the texts
of Egypt? You have allowed thousands of years of culture to be replaced
without protest by a voice—the voice of the Lord that interprets nothing
but its own words."

As Moses begins his response, Rabbi Neusner pulls a pen from his suit
pocket, as if ready to take down notes. "Rabbi Neusner, I am not even a
'prophet,' for that word has not yet been spoken in God's language, that of

the Torah. True, I was educated by Egyptian priests to mediate between gods and men, a matter of deep meditation. Yet it was done as if without words. The universe our texts reflected was a theater in which nothing changed: history recorded good and bad times, empire and occupation, explorations and arts of all kinds, but Egypt was timeless—and therefore, all was literal, just as it was. The object of mediating between the gods, of meditating, was to read their minds. We did not form questions in words but rather assumed a questioning frame of mind. And thus it was, as you might say, that I was prepared to be a reader without a text."

"So there could be no such thing as a midrash or a sermon?" asked Rabbi Neusner. "No *art* of creation to reflect the universe of creation?"

"Not exactly," answered Moses, almost professorially. "Egypt was not thought of as created. As I said, it was timeless. Had I not left, I too could have remained forever in Egypt—Upper Egypt, above."

Moses looked sympathetically at the perplexed Rabbi Neusner. "And so, rabbi, you may put down your pen. For what you need is already written down in the Torah. In place of a sermon, there is a song, a *poem* to creation. The world yielded to human memory in timeless words":

Listen, heavens, while I speak;
Earth, hear the words that I am saying.
May my teachings fall like the rain,
may my word drop down like the dew,
like showers on fresh grass . . .

As Moses had recited these words, his arms spread out in an embrace, as if involuntarily. Then they dropped to his sides. "However you wish to interpret this, rabbi, you must start by realizing that the text you are reading reenacts creation. And here the reader is the Creator himself, the one who hears and has created":

. . . he gives him honey from the rock to taste,
and oil from the flinty crag;
curds from the cattle, milk from the flock,
with rich food of the pastures . . .

As I leave off this imagining and return to the text itself, the history of Creator and of human creator has come into agreement, a history the Jews have elaborated in time by studying the Covenant. And that is how we became Moses' readers, my dear Benedict, for "Moses committed this Law to writing and gave it to the priests . . . and to all the elders of Israel" (Exodus 31:9). As readers of Moses, we become for the first time the readers of our future. Unlike most books—where we read to know what is going to happen and why—we instead *encounter* the text of Moses' Torah and then ask of ourselves: What does each word and event mean, about the future and about the past? I am allowed to do this because, as a numinous text, the Bible includes our lives as well as eternity (nothing can happen outside of it). Even our ignorance, and even our refusal to read (such as began with the celebration of a golden cow) is included within it!

As I read it over the shoulder of Moses, its first among many writers, the Torah seems to come to me from the future, just as it did to Moses. As he was made closer to his Creator, today I am drawn closer to Moses, the writer. The proof is in the writer's very sense of himself as a created being—a character in a greater book of life in which he may even demand eternal revision:

> *And Moses returned to Yahweh. "I am grieved," he cried. "This people has committed a grave sin, making themselves a god of gold. And yet, if it please you to forgive this sin of theirs . . . But if not, then blot me out from the book that you have written!" (Exodus: 32:31)*

So is not Moses' "written book of creation" the source that ultimately allows Jesus to step into the text and speak also as the writer (or, as you expound it, my dear Benedict, as God himself)? When we dig deeper into the Hebraic culture that produced the writers of the Bible, do we not come closer to Jesus as well?—since he, in his historical time, and ourselves in our time, are equally the readers of Moses' numinous text?

But why, you may ask, do I deem this to be crucial historical knowledge for Christian readers of your *Jesus of Nazareth*? Because, I would say, in the largeness of your learning, you suggest a new Judeo-Christianity that is enriched by origins and that needs the full history of the Torah and Israel.

Even the new Israel among the nations today shows us that writers and thinkers, religious as well as secular, derive from a Hebraic culture about which we still can learn more. You also wrote that "a *literal* application of Israel's social order to the people of all nations would have been tantamount to a denial of the universality of the growing 'community' of God." I find this less critical than you may have imagined, in particular because the word "literal" remains creatively open to interpretation among Jews as well. Is it not fair to say that Israel itself was less inspired by its social order than its cultural one, including authorship? It was the *interpretive* embrace of the text that blossomed out into Torah and the numinous majesty of Hebrew Bible and Midrash. It could happen because the cultural air that Israel breathed was a rich education: the study and interpretation of both moral and historical context, rare in the world and far deeper than the letter of the law.

It's for precisely this reason that Jesus could command an audience for his Sermon on the Mount. Long before, the text of Torah had commanded by its poetry: "Put [this poem] into their mouths that it may be a witness on my behalf . . ." (Exodus 31:19). Thus began the Torah's "Song of Moses" that dramatizes creation and textuality—the spirit over the letter of the Law. This is also the spirit of interpretation that Rabbi Neusner brings to his imaginary dialogue with Jesus: "Let's dispute the text as rabbis always have."

So let's pose a "community" not simply of believers but of readers. The "we" that makes us readers today is perhaps more complex than what you have called "the obedience intended by the Torah." You have written that Jesus "has brought the God of Israel to the nations," but to this must be added a cultural knowledge: he did it by writing the core of a new text or testament that I can read today as midrash—and remain discrete as a Jew. In so doing, I look toward a new definition of Judeo-Christianity that embraces us all as educated readers, including Moses and Jesus.

You write, however, that "Jesus sits on the cathedra of Moses . . . as the greater Moses." I think by now you have understood, my dear Benedict, that I will dispute your judgment of this. Once we consider both Moses and Jesus as foundational writers, the notion of supersession recedes. Just because God embodies the writer in Jesus, rather than speaking to him as with Moses, you note that "God now speaks intimately, as one man to another." On the other hand, the Jewish interpretive tradition has already made the numinous text of Torah *intimate*: it has become an intimate dialogue between text and reader, even before the great Hebrew Psalmists and Prophets. The God whose First Temple in Jerusalem has been destroyed is lamented by the Hebrew Prophets in exile in the most intimate of terms— precisely the messianic terms of suffering that ameliorate the intimacy. Yet by continuing to assert the supersession of Jesus, you note that a *lesser* Moses could deliver his Torah only by "entering into the divine darkness on the mountain." But is this a deliberate misreading?

The writing of the Torah comes *after* this mountain encounter and takes place over many years in and by the Tent of Meeting and wherever Moses sets up his writing table in the wilderness. These written texts of Moses will be the basis for Jesus' education more than a millennium later, and you verify this as you write that it is a "new version of the Torah that Jesus offers us. Jesus stands here in dialogue with Moses." But now I ask you: What of the education of *Moses*?

I began my own book on Moses and Jesus in order to answer this question and to understand how Moses became our civilization's first great writer, regardless of what else he may have been. There was, in other words, a dialogue between Moses and Egyptian cosmology and history. Without it, and thus without the maturing of Moses into the great writer he became, the numinous text of Torah could not have been written.

You imply as much, my dear Benedict, and you have made an exciting new emphasis on the historical human being and the Bible. Among those reading the Biblical text during a thousand years before Jesus was born were Jews of many races from all parts of the globe, in Egypt, Ethiopia, India, Greece, Persia, and Rome. Hebraic culture unites these readers: a figurative, not a literal descent from Abraham. So when you argue that "it is the *spirit*" that matters now through Jesus Christ, rather than the flesh, you may unwittingly suggest a false dialectic. While it appears that Jesus "spiritualizes" the Law, it is already represented by a numinous text. Nevertheless, you boldly imagine that Jesus embodies God as if he was the writer of a messianic Torah—so that now, if we can open our minds to consider both Moses and Jesus as writers of Torah, you have helped create the basis for a new understanding of Judeo-Christianity.

After all, you quote the prologue of John's Gospel as a wonderful proof of the "historical" Jesus, and a further confirmation of authorship: "In the beginning was the Word, and the Word was with God, and the Word was God." Whether Moses was "with God" or Jesus "was God," it is still true that both brought to us a numinous text. And if Jesus did not wish to change the Torah of Moses "by one jot" but rather "came to fulfill it," as you say, then his brotherhood with Moses is undeniable.

Although the Torah is also known as "The Five Books of Moses," scholarship now reveals to us several authors writing later. So why do I emphasize the figure of Moses as writer? First, it signifies his deep education; then, it roots Moses in a Hebraic culture that is still intertextual today—that is, a modern Hebrew writer in Israel today will echo and reiterate Biblical Hebrew. Finally, we need constant reminder of the variety of Biblical writers who came after Moses and sprang from Hebraic culture, whether in Jerusalem, Samaria, Babylon, or Alexandria. It is precisely the variousness of writing that underscores how the written Torah is miraculous—both in its quality of writing and in its genius for engendering interpretation and renewal.

You might still ask, my dear Benedict, what this change of emphasis to Moses and Jesus as *writers* will accomplish for a new Judeo-Christianity. By studying their lives in their historical cultures, we have a new chance to change our own lives. We don't live in a time of prophets; rather, it's a time of readers—and of interpreters like yourself and Rabbi Neusner. Do you not limit yourself when you write of a "'we' formed of those who are united with Jesus and, by listening to him, united with the will of the Father, thereby attaining to the heart of the obedience intended by the Torah"? For this is also a "we" of readers, both Jewish and Christian, who are united by our *education*—I would change your word "obedience" to "education."

And when you write, "Jesus insists that he can be understood only in the *context* of 'the Law and the Prophets' and that his community can live only in this properly understood context," you are posing a historical education by paying attention to context. When you refer to Jesus as the "new Moses," how can we help but think of Moses' service to the Biblical text—and of the two as writers of history and midrashic imagination? Yet how, you might ask in turn, can God himself be a writer of history and imagination? This is precisely the question that midrash addresses in the twelfth century when it evolved into the *Zohar*, a major text of the Kabbalah. And now, you have provided a contemporary answer with historical context, implying that the God of both Moses and Jesus entered history and enabled our texts, at different times. For the "image" on which the word *imagination* is based is the Biblical God's creation, the image of man, and it was the Biblical origin upon which written images became poignant re-creations.

Thus it is that the imagination thrives in a self-consciously written culture. Since Hebraic culture provides the education of Moses and Jesus, it also allows you, my dear Benedict, to enlarge our awareness of midrashic writing in your *Jesus of Nazareth*. We can no longer assume that Moses and Jesus were rooted in "primitive" cultures but rather in the complexity of their Hebraic education.

We might call the life of Moses, in all its extremities of experience and education, "soul-making." In other words, his education in Egypt and later in Midian trained Moses' mind to read between the lines and reinterpret this ancient pagan knowledge he studied. And then, the education—or "soul-making"—of his heart began as the Bible recounts: from the killing of an Egyptian to the colloquy with Pharaoh, from the narrow escape with the Israelites into the desert to the smashing of the Ten Commandments in despair, from the writing in the years of wilderness to the unknown burial by God's hand. The same can be said for the life of Jesus: the soul-making of his death came after a mature Jewish education. But I wonder, my dear Benedict, if you are aware of how crucial "soul-making" is to modern poetry?

The English poet John Keats asked: "Do you not see how necessary a world of pains and troubles is to school an intelligence and make it a soul?" What Keats described as soul-making has recently been brought to new attention in the posthumous publications of Philip Rieff, who was widely regarded as the eminent sociologist of our time. In *Charisma* (2007), Rieff describes the charismatic person as one who understands that our origin is bound up with creation and is unknowable—that the context of history and memory is all that we have of our own. In Professor Rieff's mind, Jesus stood for both: for Jewish history, which encompasses creation of the world as well as creation of the Torah's numinous text; and for Jewish memory, which commands each individual to negotiate his or her life by internalizing knowledge of the Covenant.

But this could hold true as well for our most ancient Judeo-Christian ancestor today, the Ethiopian Jew. During the summer of 1991, Professor Rieff and I were residents of Mishkenot Sha'ananim, the Jerusalem guest house for writers. One afternoon we shared a taxi to the four-star hotel that had been converted into a hostel for bare-footed Ethiopian Jews arriving in Israel—those whose ancestors had left for Africa in the times of the early Israelite kings. Today, they were untutored in bathrooms and telephones, and they also preferred to sit on the hotel's marble lobby floor and take their meals there. Rieff and I sat down with a group of rabbis and interpreters of Amharic, their ancient African language. Instead of cameras, they held in their laps their very old leather-bound volumes of the Torah. When they heard that Professor Rieff was a world-renowned sociologist, they smiled and introduced one of their elder statesmen as "a professor of the Torah" and another as "a professor of Moses' genealogy and of Israel's history in Africa," and yet another as "a professor of the science of translating the Torah." Rieff grew uncharacteristically silent as he listened to these primeval professors (who had barely spoken a word to their first Israeli interviewers).

The next day, Rieff was the keynote speaker at the conference marking the 100th anniversary of the birth of the Jewish philosopher Martin Buber. After placing his notes on the podium, Rieff stepped down from it and walked around to face it. There he examined the small shrine to Buber the organizers had set up, complete with flower-wreathed photo and a table of books with memorial candles beside them. Returning to the podium, Rieff began his lecture on the dangers of false charisma, suggesting that if Buber had been present he would have overturned the table like Jesus amongst the Temple moneychangers. Buber, argued Rieff, believed in the soul-making education of reading the Torah as a disciplining encounter with the inexperienced mysticism of the heart. In other words, each individual's education requires a direct dialogue, unmediated by pretentious shrines.

It is this familiarity with dialogue—you find it fully formed already in the most ancient Hebrew psalms—that also made it easy for Rabbi Neusner to imagine the dialogue with Jesus that enriches his own book as well as your own. You hold Rabbi Neusner in similar regard as you have him showing "that faith in the word of God in the Holy Scriptures creates a contemporaneous bond across the ages." In other words, the reader's timeless soul is allowed to read the Torah as numinous, unencumbered by current fashion. Buber has shown this in the Torah's text: the soul-making of the reader requires the assumption of love and goodness, because the soul is always innocent of the world. So how does this love of Torah by a Jewish reader differ from what Jesus loved? It is here that I would answer: it does not differ. Jesus' love is one and the same as his interpretive power of the Torah; he reads Moses as a writer, and it is as thus that he reveals himself.

Because Rabbi Neusner has an exchange with Jesus as a writer, he can be seen to disagree with Jesus without demeaning him. I would call this "disagreement in love" the new Judeo-Christianity, and it is Israel's renewed existence that has allowed it. The blessing of Israel in the world today is a midrash on the nations, in particular the United Nations and its bloc of members who resent Israel's crucial existence. We can counter the resentment with a new "disagreement in love"—a dialogue about the world's creation and civilized origins. All our secular history and science can be reanalyzed into a poetry of ideas about creation and our cultural origin in writing. And *that* is the Judeo-Christian education that Moses and Jesus represent, the Torah's story of revelation and its interpretive elaboration.

I experienced a variation on Neusner's "disagreement" when I received a phone call several years ago from *U.S. News & World Report*. The reporter had just spoken with Professor Neusner about a new portion of my translation of the Torah, *The Book of J*, which had emphasized authorship. This reporter was eager to hear my reaction, after first having asked Neusner: "Is this the revelation of the Torah you had hoped for in English?"

"No, it is not!" thundered Neusner, according to the reporter. "The wish to reincarnate an original writer of the Torah reminds me of an early Christian sect."

But the reporter made the mistake (as I did too, initially) of thinking this comment was a condemnation of my new work. After feeling sorry for myself, I read again Rabbi Neusner's magnificent historical re-creations of Jewish-Christian writing. Now I could see that Neusner was holding my translation in the same regard as he held the interpretive Jewish movements of Hellenistic Judea: he "disagreed—but in love!" For Neusner had shown that radical interpretations of even the Torah's commandments were loving disagreements.

You, my dear Benedict, offer several examples of such disagreement, including Rabbi Neusner's description of the Torah's "metaphor of genealogy" (rather than its literalism). None is more telling than when you show Rabbi Neusner reminding "his reader that students of the Torah were called by their teachers to leave home and family and to turn their backs on wife and children for long periods in order to devote themselves to the study of Torah." Here the *reader* of Torah is direct descendant of the *writer*: "The Torah then takes the place of genealogy," you quote Neusner as saying, "and the master of Torah gains a new lineage." And thus you come to agree with Rabbi Neusner that Jesus was of his historical time, a typical loving critic of Jewish family life. "It seems that Jesus' claim to be founding a new family does remain after all in the framework of what the school of the Torah—the 'eternal Israel'—allows."

In sketching a new biography of Jesus, you have breathed new life into his youth and early maturity in Nazareth, and you join me in focusing upon his education and how he learned to read and write midrash. But the picture of Nazareth as an uneventful town in the half-Jewish province of Galilee may misrepresent your thinking. You write that Jesus was not born in Jerusalem or another center of Jewish learning, and that this foretells the mission to the Gentiles. Yet most of the Hebrew Prophets over many centuries also came from the provinces. In the centuries before Jesus, the family of Maccabean Jewish priests began a revolt against the Greco-Roman world in a small town and among a host of followers that might be deemed peasants. These peasants were educated Jews nonetheless, just as were the disciples of Jesus from Galilee, and that is the reason they could respond to the Jewish core of his learning. To ignore the power of a Jewish education can only obscure the actual history.

You wrote further that you were "greatly helped by Jacob Neusner's *A Rabbi Talks with Jesus*," but now I wish to remind you of a similar book by a renowned Jewish writer, Sholem Asch, that appeared in English when you and I were young, in 1945; it was subtitled, "An Epistle to the Christians." This little best-selling book, *One Destiny*, which led to a final chapter, "The Judeo-Christian Idea," in which the unity of the Torah and a midrashic New Testament is delineated, was a harbinger of a new understanding between Jews and Christians after the Holocaust. It would be a reconciliation rather than a conversion, according to Asch, and it bears quoting on the very issue of historical Nazareth, my dear Benedict, that is central to your own book.

"Let us pretend for a moment that the miracle of the Maccabean triumph did not come to pass, but that, as might have been expected, the Greek army together with the strong Jewish assimilationist party won out. Jerusalem is transformed into a Greek metropolis . . . But then what would have become of the promise, made to the prophets in God's name, to bring forth the Messiah? Such a contingency would have upset the life, civilization, psychology, and conditions that were necessary for the birth of a Jesus. For this reason, many people have learned to reckon the Christian era from the birth of the society which made possible the development of the Messianic idea."

Asch goes on to make a midrash of the historical period of the first three hundred years of Christianity, in which Christian persecution at the hands of the Romans is made of a piece with Roman destruction of Jewish Jerusalem. What we can learn from such historical midrash is how to deepen our own education in Jewish and Christian sources by an imaginative engagement. The shared history is critical. Nevertheless, Jewish studies will remain basic for Jews; it is a great treasure, as is the life of Jesus for Christians, but as we begin to share a *Judeo-Christian* education in historical study, Moses and Jesus can meet in imaginative dialogue.

And thus have we, my dear Benedict, met on this common printed page, furthering a journey back in time and forward in self-awareness of the author. To read and to write, read and respond, inspires engagement of the word: *inspirare, spirare*, to breathe. Does the word play with the breath, or the breath with the word? That is what all human authors must help each other with.

Most sincerely,
David Rosenberg

· NOTE ON CAPITAL LETTERS ·

Several terms are sometimes capitalized, sometimes not. For instance, bar mitzvah, covenant, and others. It all depends on context and usage. To take one example, Bible is capitalized when it infers the text in some way, and it goes uncapitalized when referring to things generally biblical.

· BIBLIOGRAPHY ·

Allen, James P., *The Art of Medicine in Ancient Egypt*, New York: Metropolitan Museum of Art, 2005.

Amichai, Yehuda, *Poems of Jerusalem and Love Poems*, (2nd Ed.), Riverdale-on-Hudson: Sheep Meadow, 1992.

Anchor Bible, vols.1—ff., New York: Anchor; New Haven: Yale, 1962-2009.

Assmann, Jan, *Moses the Egyptian*, Cambridge: Harvard, 1998.

——. *The Mind of Egypt*, New York: Metropolitan, 2002.

——. *Of God and Gods*, Madison: U. Wisconsin, 2008.

Assmann, Jan, and Lorton, David, *The Search for God in Ancient Egypt*, Ithaca: Cornell, 2001.

——. *Death and Salvation in Ancient Egypt*, Ithaca: Cornell, 2006.

Auerbach, Elias, *Moses*, Detroit: Wayne State University Press, 1975.

Beale, G.K., and Carson, D.A., *Commentary on the New Testament Use of the Old Testament*, Grand Rapids: Baker Academic, 2007.

Benedict XVI, (Pope), *Jesus of Nazareth*, New York: Knopf, 2007.

Bloom, Allan, *The Closing of the American Mind* (2nd ed.), New York: Simon & Schuster, 1987.

Bloom, Harold, and Rosenberg, David, *The Book of J*, New York: Grove Weidenfeld, 1990.

Boyd, Gregory, and Eddy, Paul, *The Jesus Legend: A Case for the Historical Reliability of the Synoptic Jesus Tradition*, Grand Rapids: Baker Academic, 2007.

Brown, Raymond E., *The Death of the Messiah*, 2 vols., New York: Doubleday, 1994.

Buber, Martin, *On the Bible*, New York: Schocken, 1982.

——. *Tales of the Hasidim*, 2 vols., New York: Schocken, 1991.

————. *Moses*, New York: Harper & Row, 1946.

Chilton, Bruce, *Rabbi Jesus*, New York: Doubleday, 2000.

Chilton, Neusner, Green, eds., *Historical Knowledge in Biblical Antiquity*, Dorset: Deo, 2007.

Cohen, Arthur A., *The Myth of the Judeo-Christian Tradition*, (2nd ed.), New York: Schocken, 1971.

Derrida, Jacques, *The Gift of Death*, Chicago: U. Chicago, 1995.

Flusser, David, *The Sage from Galilee*, Grand Rapids: Eerdmans, 2007.

————. *Jesus*, (3rd ed.), Jerusalem: Magnes Press, 2001.

————. *Judaism of the Second Temple Period*, 2 vols., Grand Rapids: Eerdmans, 2007-2009.

Frankfort, H., *Ancient Egyptian Religion*, New York: Columbia, 1948.

Freud, Sigmund, *Character and Culture*, (Philip Rieff, ed.), New York: Basic, 1962.

————. *Civilization and Its Discontents*, New York: Norton, 1961.

————. *Moses and Monotheism*, New York: Knopf, 1939.

Frye, Northrop, *The Great Code: The Bible and Literature*, New York: Harcourt Brace Jovanovich, 1982.

George, Andrew, *The Epic of Gilgamesh*, New York: Penguin, 2003.

Goodenough, Erwin R., *Jewish Symbols in the Greco-Roman Period*, 13 vols., New York: Pantheon, 1953-1968.

Govrin, Michal, *And So Said Jerusalem*, (Hebrew), Jerusalem: Devarim/Carmel, 2009.

Greenberg, Moshe, *Studies in the Bible and Jewish Thought*, Philadelphia: Jewish Publication Society, 1995.

Halioua, Bruno, *Medicine in the Days of the Pharaohs*, Cambridge: Harvard, 2005.

Halivni, David Weiss, *Midrash, Mishnah, and Gemara*, Cambridge: Harvard, 1986.

Handelman, Susan A., *The Slayers of Moses*, Albany: State University of New York, 1982.

Herodotus, *The Persian Wars*, Cambridge: Harvard, 1920.

Hertz, Joseph H., *Sayings of the Fathers: Pirke Aboth*, New York: Behrman, 1986.

Hezser, Catherine, *Jewish Literacy in Roman Palestine*, Tubingen: Paul Mohr Verlag, 2001.

———. *The Social Structure of the Rabbinic Movement in Roman Palestine*, Tubingen: Paul Mohr Verlag, 1997.

Hilberg, Raul, *The Destruction of the European Jews*, (3rd ed.), New Haven: Yale, 2003.

Hornung, Erik, *Akhenaten and the Religion of Light*, Ithaca: Cornell, 1999.

———. *The Ancient Egyptian Books of the Afterlife*, Ithaca: Cornell, 1999.

Hugh, Arthur, and Dryden, John, *Plutarch's Lives*, New York: Modern Library, 1932.

Idel, Moshe, *Ben: Sonship and Jewish Mysticism*, New York: Continuum, 2008.

Ikram, Salima, and Dodson, Aidan, *The Mummy in Ancient Egypt*, London: Thames and Hudson, 1998.

Josephus, Flavius, *The New Complete Works of Josephus*, (rev. ed.), Grand Rapids: Kregel Academic, 1999.

Kirsch, Jonathan, *Moses: A Life*, New York: Ballantine, 1998.

Lanzmann, Claude, *Shoah*, Cambridge: Da Capo, 1995.

Lee, Bernard J., *The Galilean Jewishness of Jesus*, New York: Paulist Press, 1988.

Lichtheim, Miriam, *Ancient Egyptian Literature*, 2 vols., Berkeley: U. of California, 1976.

Meier, John P., *A Marginal Jew: Rethinking the Historical Jesus*, 4 vols., New Haven: Yale, 1991-2009.

Miles, Jack, *Christ: A Crisis in the Life of God*, New York: Knopf, 2001.

Milgrom, Jacob, *Numbers*, JPS Torah Commentary, Philadelphia: Jewish Publication Society, 1990.

Neusner, Jacob, *A Rabbi Talks with Jesus*, (rev. ed.), Montreal: McGill-Queen's U. Press, 2000.

———. *History and Torah*, New York: Schocken, 1965.

————. *From Politics to Piety: The Emergence of Pharasaic Judaism*, New York: Prentice-Hall, 1972.

————. *Judaism in Monologue and Dialogue*, New York: University Press of America, 2005.

————. *The Babylonian Talmud: A Translation and Commentary*, 22 vols., Peabody: Hendrickson, 2006.

————. *The Mishnah: A New Translation*, New Haven: Yale, 1991.

Novak, Michael, *No One Sees God*, New York: Doubleday, 2008.

Propp, William H.C., *Exodus*, 2 vols., New Haven: Yale, 2006.

Rieff, Philip, *Sacred Order/Social Order: My Life Among the Deathworks*, Charlottesville: U. Virginia, 2006.

————. *Sacred Order/Social Order: The Crisis of the Officer Class: The Decline of the Tragic Sensibility*, Charlottesville: U. Virginia, 2007.

————. (Arnold Eisen, ed.) *Sacred Order/Social Order: The Jew of Culture: Freud, Moses, and Modernity*, Charlottesville: U. Virginia, 2008.

————. *Charisma: The Gift of Grace, and How It Has Been Taken Away from Us*, New York: Pantheon, 2007.

Rosenberg, David, *A Literary Bible*, Berkeley: Counterpoint, 2009.

————. *Abraham*, New York: Basic, 2006.

Rosenberg, David, ed., *Congregation*, New York: Harcourt Brace Jovanovich, 1987.

————. *Communion*, New York: Anchor Books, 1996.

Rosenzweig, Franz, *The Star of Redemption*, New York: Holt, 1971.

Sacks, Rabbi Sir Jonathan, *The Koren Sacks Siddur*, Jerusalem: Koren, 2009.

Sarna, Nahum, *Exodus*, JPS Torah Commentary, Philadelphia: Jewish Publication Society, 1989.

————. *Exploring Exodus*, New York: Schocken, 1986.

Shakespeare, William, *The Merchant of Venice*, New York: Simon & Schuster, 2004.

Skehan, Patrick W., and Di Lella, Alexander A., *The Wisdom of Ben Sira*, New York: Anchor, 1995.

Soloveitchik, Joseph B., *The Lonely Man of Faith*, (2nd Ed.), New York: Doubleday, 2006.

Speiser, Ephraim A., *Genesis* (The Anchor Bible), New York: Doubleday, 1962.

Steinsaltz, Adin, *The Talmud: The Steinsaltz Edition*, 22 vols. (incomplete), New York: Random, 1992-1999.

Stroumsa, Guy G., *The End of Sacrifice: Religious Transformations in Late Antiquity*, Chicago: U. of Chicago, 2009.

Strudwick, Nigel C., *Texts from the Pyramid Age*, Atlanta: Society of Biblical Literature, 2005.

Taylor, John H., *Death and the Afterlife in Ancient Egypt*, Chicago: U. of Chicago, 2001.

Tigay, Jeffrey H., *Deuteronomy*, JPS Torah Commentary, Philadelphia: Jewish Publication Society, 1996.

Tolstoy, Leo, *War and Peace*, tr. Pevear, Richard, and Volokhonsky, Larissa, New York: Knopf, 2007.

Walzer, Michael, *Exodus and Revolution*, New York: Basic, 1985.

Weigall, Arthur, *Akhnaton*, London: Thorton Butterworth, 1910.

Weinfeld, Moshe, *Deuteronomy*, New Haven: Yale, 1995.

———. *The Promise of the Land*, Berkeley: U. California, 1993.

Wilson, Emily, *The Death of Socrates*, Cambridge: Harvard, 2007.

Winston, Robert P., *The Egyptian Book of the Dead*, New York: Penguin, 2008.

Yeats, W. B., *Later Essays* (Vol. V, Collected Works), New York: Scribner, 1994.

Yerushalmi, Yosef Hayim, *Freud's Moses*, New Haven: Yale, 1991.

Yonge, C. D., *The Works of Philo*, Peabody: Hendrickson, 1993.

Zornberg, Avivah Gottlieb, *Particulars of Rapture: Reflections on Exodus*, New York: Doubleday, 2001.

· A C K N O W L E D G M E N T S ·

During the period of research for this book, we visited Israel in 2007, hoping to follow up in Egypt. However, a terrorist warning for Sinai, through which we would have bused to Cairo, helped shorten our itinerary. A little later, Rhonda and I dug thoroughly into the Met Museum of New York's Egyptian collection, guided by the educated enthusiasm of David Shapiro. And thanks to newly online access to the Cairo Museum, the Louvre, and others, our global research could become extensive (including a "trip" from our home in Miami to the Fort Lauderdale Museum's hosting of "Tutankamen" and its concomitant Egyptian burial texts).

It was in Israel that we were able to dig up the ancient Jewish history of Sepphoris, where Jesus would have studied in one of its ten synagogues after his bar mitzvah, and which not long thereafter became the site of the Jewish Sanhedrin under Rabbi Judah Hanasi. Until the Arab conquest it was a center of Galilean Jewish and Christian Bible study—and later, during Crusader rule, its church was dedicated to Anne and Joachim, the Jewish parents of Miriam (Mary). The tragic history of Sepphoris had been buried in modern times beneath the Arab village of Saffuriya, and then, during the modern War of Independence, this village too became a site of battle and abandonment. The present Israeli village nearby, Tzippori, has sponsored the digs of large areas of ancient Sepphoris by teams from Duke, North Carolina, and South Florida universities, and continued since 1990 by the Hebrew University. The Center for the Study of Christianity at Hebrew University, and the Israel Museum, have also benefited our research. Thanks as well to Israel's *Kisufim* writers conference for travel assistance.

Liz Maguire, editor at Basic for the first part of this diptych in biography, *Abraham*, could not wait to see this manuscript—and it was a shock to hear of her sudden passing during its formative period. Her sense of excitement has stayed with me.

James Atlas, the eminent biographer of Delmore Schwartz and Saul Bellow, encouraged this book, hoping to publish it, and John Oakes, then at Atlas & Co., became its first editor. John's avid eye for history and sharp ear for textuality helped smooth some rough edges. In the end, the manuscript found its way to Jack Shoemaker, acquiring editor at Counterpoint, almost as if Jack possessed a literary magnet for books that might seem edgy to some publishers. In Shoemaker's hands, the integrity of the manuscript was first priority.

Howard Morhaim, my extraordinary and most level-headed literary agent, knew how to make this book possible—and keep it possible. The literary zeal and encouragement of Laura Mazer, editor, as well as Counterpoint cohorts Sharon Donovan, Kristy Bohnet, and Tiffany Lee, saw this book through with stunning expertise. And what can anyone say that would add to the status of legendary book designer David Bullen?

Sanford Rosenberg, Rochelle Broach, Walter Brown, Joyce Davidson, and Grace Schulman—their stalwart support has been critical.

Bruce Chilton read through the first draft. His erudite summary of what he found there became guide and goal.

Jed Sekoff was a model of real-time feedback. William and Bert Ramby were the model of moral support.

There is nothing I researched, wrote or thought that was not weighed in the balance of Jewish sensibility that belongs to my coauthor, Rhonda Rosenberg. Her unlimited love of Israel and Jewish history often renders me speechless, including at this very moment.

· I N D E X ·

Poet-scholar David Rosenberg is coauthor of the *New York Times*-bestseller *The Book of J* (with Harold Bloom) and the former editor-in-chief of the Jewish Publication Society. A poet of Toronto Coach House, New York School, and Jerusalem Cricket lineage, he has published several volumes of poetry.

Rosenberg is a survivor of the writing programs at The New School (with Kenneth Koch and Robert Lowell), University of Michigan (with Donald Hall), Syracuse University (with Delmore Schwartz), and University of Essex, England, where he pursued doctoral studies. He taught for several years at York University (Toronto), City University of New York, and as a Master Poet for the New York State and Connecticut Arts Councils.

At the age of thirty, Rosenberg retired from teaching. For two decades, while working as a literary editor and translator, he studied the origins of ancient Hebrew literature and the Bible, in New York and Israel (with Robert Gordis, Harry Orlinsky, and Chaim Rabin), while his work appeared prominently in *Harper's*, *The New Republic*, *Hudson Review*, *Paris Review*, and elsewhere around the globe (most recently in *Chicago Review*, *Jacket* in Australia, and *Open Letter* in Canada). *A Poet's Bible* won the PEN / Book-of-the-Month Club Prize, the first major literary award given to a biblical translation in the United States.

Rosenberg is the author and editor of more than twenty books, including volumes of contemporary writers on the Bible that first raised the question of how Judeo-Christian culture can be newly reinterpreted. During the past decade, he has studied the context for ancient biography, leading to a diptych: *Abraham: The First Historical Biography* and *An Educated Man: A Dual Biography of Moses and Jesus*. He continues to publish critical essays on poetry, as well as his long poem, *The Lost Book of Paradise*, and a literary version of Kabbalah, *Dreams of Being Eaten Alive*. His masterwork, *A Literary Bible: An Original Translation*, was recently published.